Healing through the Bones

Empowerment and the Process of Exhumations in the Context of Cyprus

Kristian T.P. Fics

Hamilton Books

An Imprint of
Rowman & Littlefield
Lanham • Boulder • New York • Toronto • Plymouth, UK

4501 Forbes Boulevard, Suite 200, Lanham, Maryland 20706
Hamilton Books Acquisitions Department (301) 459-3366

Unit A, Whitacre Mews, 26-34 Stannary Street,
London SE11 4AB, United Kingdom

Printed in the United States of America
British Library Cataloguing in Publication Information Available

Library of Congress Control Number: 2016945546
ISBN: 978-0-7618-6819-4 (pbk : alk. paper)—ISBN: 978-0-7618-6820-0 (electronic)

∞™ The paper used in this publication meets the minimum requirements of American National Standard for Information Sciences Permanence of Paper for Printed Library Materials, ANSI/NISO Z39.48-1992.

For my wife Jo, my mother Nicole
and my brothers Ryan and Morgan,
and the families of the Missing in Cyprus

Contents

Acknowledgments

First I would like to thank Dr. Sean Byrne for his patience, guidance, and encouragement throughout this process and research that could not have been done without him and his tireless efforts through the editing process and belief in me that always gives me strength. Sean in not just an advisor but a friend that challenges me and others to pursue truth and justice and this world is a better place because of people like him. I would also like to thank Dr. Jessica Senehi and Dr. Stephanie Stobbe for their support, editing, and suggestions that aided me in the direction that this work took. I would like to thank the Arthur V. Mauro Center for Peace and Justice at the University of Manitoba, Canada, for their support and the students that shared their knowledge and wisdom with me with respect to conducting field work that helped shape my direction for research. Further, I would like to thank in particular from the Mauro Center, Saad and Heba, for their friendship and insight that helped me in trying times during and after the research and the writing process.

I would also like to acknowledge the aid of Theodora in which this research would not have been done at the Committee on Missing Persons in Cyprus and everyone that conducts the arduous process of the recovery, identification, and reunification of the Missing with their loved ones. I would like to offer my appreciation and humility to the families of the Missing in Cyprus in which their courage is unparalleled in waiting and finally going through such an activity as being reunited with their loved ones after so many years and I was honored to be a part of that process and learn from it. Further, I would like to offer many thanks to all of the participants of this study in which this work would not have been possible without them and their guidance and patience with me while they were conducting such important and necessary jobs. I have the deepest respect for the participants who are leaders and peacemakers in this world and thank you with all my heart for the sharing of your stories and perspectives with me. Also, I would like to thank my Cypriot friends that I made in Cyprus, specifically, Maria, Harris, Katerina and Spyros, that discussed the conflict with me from their hearts and showed me a good time with friendship and love that helped me feel like Cyprus was a home for me and made me feel safe.

Finally, I would like to thank my families for all of their support and tireless efforts to aid in my emotional well-being, writing direction, and the constant editing and discussions of this work in which this work would not have been done. I offer my gratitude and love to my mother Nicole and my brothers Ryan Fics and Morgan Fics, including, Amanda and my cousin Nick in which I would not be the person I am today without them. Further, I would like to thank my in-laws the Vasilakis family for their support and kindness during this process. Most importantly I am indebted to my loving wife Ioanna Vasilakis. Ioanna challenged me to write clearly as possible and to be honest with my feelings all throughout the research and writing process in which I shared with her my work and my emotions on a day to day basis. She gave me all the love, support, and drive to finish. More so, Ioanna aided in the production of the diagrams in this work and creation of the Cyprus map with her talented graphic design skills that could not have been done without her. This manuscript would not have been possible without everyone mentioned and many more people and therefore I thank you all for sharing your stories with me, life with me, and time with me, and want you all to know that this work was only possible because of you. Thank you from the bottom of my heart.

Chapter One

Introduction

JOURNAL ENTRY

Date: May 23rd, 2014
On the 22nd of May, 2014, I entered Cyprus exhausted from a long trip from Canada to Heathrow Airport, London, and finally from Athens to Cyprus. Not to mention, that when I flew I had severe poison ivy on my back that was oozing pus and blood and tempting me to scratch at it but this could not stop me from my chaotic plan. The plan, in its most basic and real sense, was to fly to Cyprus, a country I have read and written about for years, in order to experience the culture, people, and conflict to find an understanding of what the Cyprus Problem is about. Moreover, my plan was to interview professionals, peacebuilders, and those who have experienced the conflict in order to gain a better understanding for my project about what does the *process of exhumations do* to reconcile people and transform relationships? The process being the recovery of Missing Persons, identification, and reunification of the Missing with loved ones.

I stayed in Athens for several days at a hostel before flying into Cyprus visiting the monuments of Classical Greece and Rome. I flew into Cyprus International Airport in Larnaca from Athens Eleftherios Venizelos International Airport. I headed to VP Hostel, a privately owned Hostel/Apartment complex for students going to or conducting research at Nicosia (Lefkosia) University among others. As I took the shuttle to VP Hostel or MYM Hall as it is called, I viewed the landscape of the tiny island. The land is dry and rocky there are few trees and vegetation is sparse compared to where I lived most of my life in Winnipeg, Manitoba, Canada. It is such a beautiful landscape filled with many hills and is very different to what I have seen in other places that I felt awed and surprised.

Population wise, South Cyprus appeared sparsely populated with houses here and there until you pass through the major city areas, Nicosia (Lefkosia), the capital city, Larnaka, Lemesos, Pafos, and Famagusta. When I arrived in Nicosia, my feeling was that it is a city coming alive, a mixture of the old with the new. Some houses were built shoddily or were very old and coming apart, and were rather small, and then across the street brand new homes and shopping centers and businesses of all sorts, etc., coexist with the old.

When I arrived at VP Hostel I saw for the first time the United Nations Buffer Zone (the Green Line) separating Northern Cyprus or rather the Turkish Republic of Northern Cyprus (TRNC) from the Republic of Cyprus. The TRNC is recognized only by Turkey in the world. The Republic of Cyprus (RoC) in the South of the island or considered politically as the whole of Cyprus by the United Nations (UN) and most of the rest of the world awaits its reunification with its other half in the north. The Green Line, which has divided Cyprus since 1974, is basically a mesh metal fence with a green stripe across it. The green stripe is missing in several places due to wear and tear on the fences that separate the north and south of the island and is headed off with barbwire on top to keep either side out. Later on I discovered that the Green Line is also constructed of various materials within the Walled City of Nicosia among other places across the island. Thus, the conflict parties used any materials available such as broken down buildings that act as a wall to keep the other side out that are readily available that make natural barriers to either side.

When I looked upon the Green Line, my heart sank so to speak. When I encountered it, I became very silent and sad, because for the first time in May of 2014 since I have written and read about Cyprus for several years now from 2011 on, seeing the Green Line in person really hit home how devastating the conflict must have been and still is in dividing the island, its peoples, ethnic groups, politics, economics, and friendships. I grew very silent and sad at the sight and some of the residents of the Hostel asked me, "Are you ok Kris?" I replied, "Yes, thank you, I am just very tired."

I met with the manager of the hostel, a Maronite Cypriot in his later years in life who previously before retirement was a mathematics professor in England. He was a very kind soul and showed me around the city for my essentials, i.e. shopping and a tour of the complexes and University in the area when I arrived by the very inexpensive Travel Express Bus set up by him. At night after the kind owner of VP Hostel took me around the Agios Dometios Municipality of the city of Nicosia, I walked along the Green Line and looked at the Army Barracks just outside my doorstep. At the back of the building in which the Green Line continues on for miles until it is out of sight, loud Turkish music rumbled from across the Line. On a small mountain (Pentadaktylos) a gigantic light show that would reveal itself slowly on the side of the hill one section at a time, electronically controlled, set to a timer, would reveal the painted Turkish Cypriot flag of the North and next to it slowly the painted Turkish flag with a famous Turkish saying, *Ne mutlu Türküm diyene* (English: *How happy is the one who says "I am Turkish"*). I think this unveiling of the Turkish flag is sent as a message to the Republic of Cyprus and its citizens as it is directed to their side of the line. When I explored what these images which can be seen clearly during the day meant to them, many Greek Cypriots stated that it is meant as a provocation to them.

As I walked closer and closer to the images during my first night in Cyprus I found a walkway, a group of very large steps that went up a hill that are cut off by the Green Line. When I saw these grand steps that went to nowhere which are divided at the top by the Green Line and United Nations Buffer Zone (UNBZ), the image fortified itself in my mind as a symbolic example of the conflict, a sort of cutting off of the path to peace, land, and connectedness that now feels very real, very discomforting, and very sad to me. At that moment all the stories, history and politics—essentially the narratives that I have read—were coming to life for me. I pondered if I was prepared, or if anyone could be, when researching a protracted conflict at ground zero.

INTRODUCTION

> The realization of peace prevents the loss of life and human capacity. Thus, peace ultimately has to be obtained by changing social structures that are responsible for death, poverty and malnutrition.
> (Ho-Won Jeong, 2000, p. 23)

The Cyprus conflict has been described as an ethnic conflict (Denktash, 1988; Ker-Linsday, 2011). The conflict is between Greek Cypriots who practice Greek Orthodox Christianity whose language is Greek and reside in the south of Cyprus and Turkish Cypriots who practice Sunni Islam whose language is Turkish and reside in the north of Cyprus (See Appendix D).

Unfortunately simply identifying the conflict as one between ethnic groups does not encompass the complexities of the escalation of violent conflict. When examining the Cyprus conflict scholarly disagreements occur about the causes of the violence that emerged like a three-headed Hydra. The causes have been attributed to international power politics and colonialism (Attilides, 1979; Kyrris, 1989;Markides, 1997); as well as, the rise in nationalist tensions and the right to self-determination for Greek Cypriots through Enosis—unification with Greece (Denktash, 1988). Moreover, some scholars claim the conflict's causes derive from identity formation in which Cypriots (Greek and Turkish) rejected, negotiated, and adapted to dominant narratives of the mother countries—Turkey and Greece (Bryant, 2006; Anastasiou, 2007). This created the emergent and distinct Turkish Cypriot and Greek Cypriot ethnicities that did not exist previously and were strengthened by co-opting politics (Navarro-Yashin, 2006). Not to mention, the role of interaction between primary and quasi mediators, the United States and Britain, including, bilateral explicit external ethno-guarantors—the coercive Greece and Turkey—and the internal co-nationals, Greek and Turkish Cypriots; who articulated, manipulated, and augmented the peace process in Cyprus toward an escalation of conflict (Byrne, 2007).

What become apparent are the complexities about the causes of the conflict in Cyprus, commonly referred to as the Cyprus Problem (Ker-Linsday, 2011). For example, ethno-nationalism became the driving force like a juggernaut for violent conflict escalation in Cyprus (Anastasiou, 2007). Understanding how ethno-nationalism can become a driving force behind the political will of a people, which can lead to inter-ethnic and intra-ethnic violence, is an aspect of what this study seeks to address by exploring the process of exhumations as an act of peacebuilding and storytelling. Ethno-territorial political conflicts such as the Cyprus conflict are highly complex and multifaceted (Byrne, 1996; 2000; Byrne and Senehi, 2012). Therefore, I now offer a brief account of some of the major events that precipitated the conflict in the formation of the Green Line in 1974 and one aspect of the devastating reality of violent conflicts universally—Missing Persons.

HISTORY OF THE CYPRUS CONFLICT

The Cypriot conflict is an Ethno-Territorial Political Conflict—via the Greek Cypriot Orthodoxy division from Turkish Cypriot Sunni Muslims. In 1878, the Ottoman Empire, which had occupied Cyprus since 1571 from the Venetians, allowed the United Kingdom to administer Cyprus under the auspices of the Cyprus convention in July of that year (Ker-Lindsay, 2011). From the start of the Great War in 1914, Cyprus was annexed by the United Kingdom making it officially a British Colony (Dodd, 2010).

In 1954, the Greek Colonel Georgios Grivas, born in Cyprus, formulated EOKA (Ethniki Organosis Kyprion Agoniston)—the National Organization of Cypriot Fighters. This organization seen as a terrorist or freedom fighting group depending upon different Greek and Turkish Cypriot view points, used violence in the insurrection aimed at military British installations and police stations in the movement for Cypriot independence from Britain (Dodd, 2010). EOKA was an ethno-nationalist movement for Greek Cypriots struggling for Enosis—unification with Greece (Anastasiou, 2007; Byrne, 2007; Ker-Lindsay, 2011). The Turkish Cypriots did not approve of unification with Greece, fearing that a new Cypriot government in which they would be in the minority would not represent their rights. Therefore, in opposition to Enosis and EOKA aims—unification with Greece—Turkish Cypriots formed a counter movement campaign to keep the island under British rule, or have it seceded to Turkey called Taksim (Ker-Lindsay, 2011). In the late 1950s the Turkish Cypriots' formulated Vulcan an organization similar to the Greek Cypriots' EOKA which came to be known as TMT (Turkish Resistance Movement) (Ker-Lindsay, 2011). The TMT countered Greek Cypriot Enosis with its political interest of Taksim or the partitioning of the island between Greece and Turkey (Ker-Lindsay, 2011). Cypriots retreated into their own separate enclaves for protection.

During the 1950s turmoil the eventual outcome was an independent nation-state—the Republic of Cyprus in 1960. From the complexity of Enosis, Taksim, and British colonial rule; Greece, Turkey and Great Britain were highly involved in the political stability of the island and formation of the 1960 constitution without any Cypriot input. However, a major contestation was the drafting of the constitution in 1960 that gave governmental consociational powersharing to Greek and Turkish Cypriots, which both sides felt was unfair. The presidents were to be elected by the Greek Cypriot community and the vice presidents by the Turkish Cypriot community. During the majority of the conflict from 1960 until 1977 Archbishop Makarios III a Greek Cypriot held office of the Presidency and Dr. Fazil Kucuk a leader of the Turkish Cypriots was Vice President. Both leaders had veto rights over bills and proposals. They presided over a Council of Ministers that according to the constitution had to be made up of at least 70 percent Greek Cypriot to a 30 percent Turkish Cypriot ratio: also, this ratio was/is to be represented by the House, Parliament, and Civil Service (Ker-Lindsay, 2011). Therefore, for the first time in Cypriot history, "the separation of the two communities was rigorously enforced under the political system" (Ker-Lindsay, 2011, p. 22); this process officially, legally, ethnically, defined and divided the Turkish Cypriot and Greek Cypriot identities.

Further, Greece, Turkey, and Great Britain, signed a Treaty of Guarantee. The treaty of 1960 stipulated the protection of the newly formed Cypriot Constitution, which encompasses guarantor powers. These powers sought to protect the sovereignty, territorial integrity, and independence of the new state. If the state's integrity was compromised then intervention by all of the treaty's three signatories or one under special circumstances was legally sanctioned (Ker-Lindsay, 2011). Moreover, a further Treaty of Alliance in 1960 as well, allowed for Greece, Turkey, and Britain to maintain military contingents that persist and accumulated over time (Ker-Lindsay, 2011). This has created huge insecurities between the ethnic groups to the present.

According to Turkish Cypriot narratives the beginnings of the exacerbation and escalation of the conflict began when Archbishop President Makarios made constitutional changes in 1963. The changes he unilaterally made seriously reduced Turkish Cypriots' rights politically and economically, in which the changes minimized their powers of veto and percentages of the Turkish Cypriots' governmental representation (Denktash, 1988). This led to the withdrawal of the Turkish Cypriots from government entirely in 1963 because their ethnoguarantor Turkey was only fifty miles away (Byrne, 2000).

As the years went on in the newly formed nation-state ethnic fighting arose between Greek and Turkish Cypriot's across the island in 1963, which led to the passing of United Nations Resolution 186. The resolution recognized the Greek Cypriots' administration and a United Nations peacekeeping force was placed in Cyprus that still exists to this day (Ker-Lindsay, 2011). From then on, tensions were high between both communities with the reformulation of EOKA-B, a terrorist group—desiring Enosis—(Unification with Greece) by General Grivas and other figures such as Nicos Sampson, which led to major attacks on Turkish Cypriot villages in 1967 (Ker-Lindsay, 2011). Eventually, EOKA-B and Greek military (during the Junta period of Greece from 1967–1974) forces led a coup against the Cypriot nation-state on July 15, 1974 (Ker-Lindsay, 2011). The coup led to the immediate invasions/liberations of Cyprus by Turkey in July and again in August of 1974 in which a mass movement of Greek and Turkish Cypriot's followed a seize fire from both sides of the island to their perspective sides of the present (Ker-Lindsay, 2011). Hence, Turkish Cypriots reside in the north and Greek Cypriots in the south now.

The invasions or liberations depending on Greek or Turkish Cypriot narratives and ethnic fighting led to the formation of the Green Line (See Appendix D). To this day, this line separates Cyprus straight down the middle through Nicosia the capital city of Cyprus. The northern region is not recognized internationally as the TRNC (Turkish Republic of Northern Cyprus) because under international law the international community perceives islands as integral political units and the partition of islands is not accepted (Guelke, 1988). The TRNC declared unilateral independence in 1983 by Turkey and Northern Cyprus led by Rauf Denktash and his National Unity Party (Right Wing Conservative) (Ker-Lindsay, 2011). The southern region which is internationally recognized as the nation-state, the Republic of Cyprus, is primarily of Greek Cypriot ethnicity and was dominated by the Democratic Party and AKEL (Progressive Party of Working People—Socialist) at the time with President Spyros Kyprianou as the leader. As a result of the devastation, large majorities of the Cyprian population were displaced and approximately one-third of the population died and over 3000 Cypriots went missing from the overall conflict (Committee on Missing Persons in Cyprus, 2015; Crisis Group Europe Report, 2006). To this day the nation-state is still divided spatially, economically, ethnically, and politically. A full resolution and reconciliation between both communities has not occurred.

Therefore, Cyprus was divided and contact between the north and south was prohibited, increasing a political, territorial, economic, and psychological fissure between both communities. Several rounds of bicommunal talks in the 1970s, 1980s, and 1990s, ended in failures for reunification and peace, led by the United Nations Secretary Generals, Javier Perez de Cuellar, Boutros Ghali, and Kofi Annan (2000s) (Cyprus ICG Report, 2006) and now Ban Ki-moon. In the midst of the talks, Greece and Turkey's hostile relations changed, and in 1998–1999 rapprochement reduced their tensions, especially with the wonton of Turkey to gain European Union (EU) membership as a candidate in 2005 (Cyprus ICG Report, 2006; Anastasiou, 2009), which didn't happen. Further, the Republic of Cyprus moved toward gaining EU membership, ascending to the EU in 2004 and the Green Line (United Nations Buffer Zone) opened in 2003 (Cyprus Profile, BBC News Europe, 2015) although the buffer zone still exists and the country is still divided. However, amidst the new developments toward a resolution of the Cyprus Problem and unification of the island, a plan proposed by the General Secretary of the United Nations Kofi Annan, the Annan Plan, for resolution of the conflict and re-unification of the island led to a political referendum for unification. The referendum in April 2004 showed promise of unification of the island via the Annan Plan based on a bicommunal, bizonal Swiss Model of government sponsored by the United Nations (Cyprus Group Euro Report, 2006). But, the Annan Plan failed its objective of unification of the island and was voted out by Greek Cypriots. Therefore the Sisyphean process of a political peace continues to reach its goal of a United Cyprus Republic to the present time.

PURPOSE STATEMENT

> Examining the record of past research from the vantage of contemporary historiography, the historian of science may be tempted to exclaim that when paradigms change, the world itself changes with them. Led by a new paradigm, scientists adopt new instruments and look in new places.
> (Thomas S. Kuhn, 1996, p. 111)

The purpose of this study is to provide a basic understanding of what the process of exhumations does in Cyprus. I define this process as the recovery, identification, and reunification of Missing Persons with loved ones. Further, it is to present the perceptions and experiences of professionals who have dealt with the Cyprus conflict and particularly one major aspect of it—Missing Persons. In the process of exhumations family members are reunited with their loved ones after a long period of absence and uncertainty of what has happened to them. In ethnopolitical conflicts that have escalated into violence it is commonplace that families have members that go missing. This study aims to understand the challenges that may arise with the recovery, identification, and reunification of the Missing with loved ones in a post-violent conflict society, and the advantages and importance of the process of exhumations in gaining a sustainable peace for Cyprus.

This study also offers a template of what needs and variables must be addressed after a post-violent conflict situation in respect to Missing Persons. As Kuhn stated in the above quote, "Led by a new paradigm, scientists adopt new instruments and look in new places" (Kuhn, 1996) which peacebuilding must approach—new methods of resolution and conflict transformation—and therefore this study is offering an understanding of an emerging paradigmatic strategy that is transforming a protracted conflict into sustainable peace through the process of exhumations.

SIGNIFICANCE OF THE STUDY

The field of Peace and Conflict Studies takes a multidisciplinary approach to understanding conflict (Sandole, Byrne, Sandole-Staroste, Senehi, 2009; Matyok, Senehi, and Byrne, 2011). This approach is important to understanding conflict in regards to achieving sustainable peace and different aspects of peace between ethnic communities in the same space. The process of exhumations is a fairly recent phenomenon in human history and peacebuilding, via DNA technology as of the late 1990s and the actual application of the process in the 21st Century (Wagner, 2011); understandably, the literature in this area is new. This research is necessary because the majority of violent conflicts are inter-ethnic and intra-state over the past several decades, in which, the instability of negotiated settlements lasted only from 3–5 years for half or two-thirds of them (Hartzell, Hoddie, and Rothchild, 2001 in Borer, Darby, and McEvoy-Levy, 2006; Licklider, 1995, in Borer, Darby, and McEvoy-Levy, 2006; Olson and Pearson, 2010).

Moreover the process of exhumations has been conducted in 83 countries by the UN Working Group on Enforced or Involuntary Disappearances among others (United Nations, 2011: 6, in Kovras 2012, p. 88). When considering the reality that violent conflict leads to Missing Persons, the need to assess the importance and relevance, including, the factors that aid in the process of exhumations is paramount for peacebuilding because so many countries are going through this process such as Sri-Lanka, Spain, Iraq, East Timor, Zimbabwe, and etcetera. Therefore, this contribution adds to the emerging and growing existing literature on Missing Persons and peacebuilding in post-violent conflict societies adding to the literature on basic human needs (Burton, 1990; 1990); in which the process of exhumations is a necessary process of peacebuilding, inter-ethnic reconciliation, and conflict transformation.

Finally, this study provides professionals and Cypriots who have dealt with the issue of Missing Persons a voice to be heard and listened to. In other words, where scientists, policymakers, journalists, and academics get to present their hands on work and experiential understanding of just what the process of exhumations do and why it is a necessary function of peacebuilding for post-violent conflict societies that may be modeled in other conflicts transitioning out of violence.

LIMITATIONS OF THE STUDY

Limitations of this study vary. First, out of the eight professionals interviewed only one was a female and the sample is not representative of all professionals who work in this area. This study does not focus on a gender analysis of the effects of Missing Persons and the process of exhumations, which could have enriched the data in relation to peacebuilding and reconciliation. A further limitation is based on the fact that all of the study participants are expert practitioners and academics in the field of peacebuilding and Missing Persons except for one professor. According to Jean Paul Lederach (2010) in *Building Peace: Sustainable Reconciliation In Divided Societies*, middle-range leadership that is represented by academics, intellectuals, and humanitarian leaders (i.e. non-governmental organizations) are people who are not controlled by "the authority or structures of the formal government or major opposition movement" (p. 41). They are also connected to the top tier elites as well as the grassroots. Therefore, these individuals offer a unique perspective in relation to Missing Persons and peacebuilding. However, this also poses a limitation on the study that the unique perspectives of Greek and Turkish Cypriots, such as the relatives of the Missing who are not professionals but have experienced the tragedy of Missing Persons as well, need to be given a voice in order to understand their unique experience of what recovery, identification, and reunification of the Missing means to them; and how it has affected them.

Further, it must be stated that I myself am half mainland Greek. My father was born in Greece and I grew up in Canada as a second generation Canadian from his side of my family. Therefore, because of my Greek heritage I was awarded some benefits and treatment during my field research that might not have occurred during my stay in Cyprus if I were from another community. The participants of the study were also aware of my Greek background because they asked me and I was open and honest about it, offering them the respect they deserve whether they were of Greek or Turkish Cypriot heritage. It is my belief that this did not affect the interviews negatively, particularly, with the three Turkish Cypriot participants of this study, but as aforementioned it must be understood that it did in some way or another affect my treatment by others while on the island.

Third, I have a basic understanding of the Modern Greek language but at a novice level and the interviews were conducted in English and the participants spoke and understood English as a second language. Moreover, I do not speak or understand Turkish, which could have benefitted the interview process and I intend to learn both languages for future research. Therefore, in regards to some of the tape-recorded interview questions I had to explain and reframe some of the questions for the purposes of understanding and expressing the questions. Yet, it is my belief as the data illustrates that all my research participants understood the questions in a fairly congruent manner.

Fourth, the ages of the participants were approximately from their late twenties to early sixties, therefore, a sample of people's perceptions of and understanding of the processes of exhumations, namely youth, were left out. Further research based on youth perspectives would have greatly benefitted this and future research in regards to peacebuilding.

Finally, it must be stated that I was fortunate enough to volunteer at the Committee on Missing Persons in Cyprus (CMP) in July and August of the summer of 2014. I was given the opportunity to observe and in some cases aid in the process of exhumations with some of the scientists that I inevitably interviewed at the end of my unpaid voluntary position with them. In other words, by participating and observing scientific and social aspects of the organization, including, the building of professional friendships may have affected some of my data and the interviewee's perceptions of me and their stories. Yet, I claim that this experience enriched my understanding of the process of exhumations and observation of the only bicommunal institutionalized non-governmental organization (NGO) on the island where Greek and Turkish Cypriot professionals work together on a day to day basis through the various phases of the process of exhumations.

CONTEXT OF THE STUDY

Missing Persons in a Global Context

> I have worked for twenty three years in five armed conflicts for the International Red Cross and I have seen first-hand that we human beings are designed to support a lot of suffering. We can go through a lot of things during a war, we can lose loved ones; we can lose limbs; we can be detained and tortured; we can be seriously wounded; we can be displaced and become refugees and lose everything we had. There is one thing however that we cannot stand—it's to live in total uncertainty with regard to our loved ones. This is the worst suffering of war. It gets worse with time. It is mental torture.
> (Paul-Henri Arni, interview and personal communication, August 8, 2014)

The systematic use of exhumation and the process of identification of Missing Persons from civil wars and state terror began in the 1980s in Latin America, specifically, in Argentina and Guatemala (Renshaw, 2011). Past cases of exhumation and identification can be accounted for in the case of the Katyn Forest massacre by the Russians of 6,000 Polish army officers and the mass killings of Jews and Slavs during World War II (Haglund, 2000; Renshaw, 2011). The foundation of the Equipo Argentino de Antropologi Forense (EAAF) has played a leading role in the investigation of Missing Persons and violation of human rights around the world aiding in the recovery, identification, and documentation of Missing Persons in Latin America from the early 1980s on during the Dirty War (Renshaw, 2011). Moreover, organizations such as the International Committee of the Red Cross (ICRC) has and continues to monitor, provide aid, and protect the lives and dignity of victims of war, in regards to International Humanitarian Law (IHL) and Human Rights Law (HRL) standards; as well as, restoring family links, providing support for the families of Missing Persons, aiding in the collection and management of personal data, and implementing mechanisms for handling cases of the Missing (ICRC, International Review of the Red Cross, 2002, No. 848 Missing Persons). The ICRC has deemed Missing Persons as the hidden tragedy of violent conflict and took measures in 2003 to organize an international conference to seek ways to help families and communities affected (ICRC, Missing Persons and international humanitarian law Overview, 2010).

Further, due to the unfortunate consequences of 20th Century interstate and intrastate wars, Missing Persons—what is commonly referred to as the *Minnesota Protocols: A Manual on the Effective Prevention and Investigation of Extra-Legal, Arbitrary and Summary Execution*—was drafted in 1989 and contains international human rights standards; a model protocol for investigating extra-legal, arbitrary, and summary executions; a model autopsy protocol; and a model protocol for disinterment and analysis of skeletal remains (University of Minnesota Human Rights Library, UN Manuel, 1991). Therefore, the *Minnesota Protocols* provides a much-needed scientific standardization of practice for legal and forensic application in regards to Missing Persons and the process of exhumations and human rights practices.

Moreover, the training of organizations such as the Committee on Missing Persons (CMP) in Cyprus on forensic analysis, logistics, and support in pursuit of finding Missing Persons has aided the process of identification (Committee on Missing Persons in Cyprus, 2015). From the 1980s onward, the process of exhumations and identification encompassed the difficult task of seeking aid from the perpetrators, and searching for the whereabouts of mass graves which still continues; and, by the interplay of information gathered from family members, friends, and historical memory, in the aid of identification processes of skeletal remains. Due to the recent advancement of science and technology in the practice of exhumations and forensic analysis, the process of exhumations can avoid some pitfalls of word of mouth markers of the Missing in the identification procedures of remains. Therefore, what I call The Modern Process of Exhumations is a fairly recent phenomenon in human history that is accomplished in its final stages via DNA technology as of the late 1990s and in the actual application of it in the 21st Century as another scholar has suggested (Wagner, 2011). Internationally, in recognizing the need to create a strategy and process regarding Missing Persons, the United Nations (UN) created the organ Working Group on Enforced or Involuntary Disappearances (UNWGEID) in 1980 (UN, 1996–2014), whose mandate is to assist the relatives of disappeared persons and identify their whereabouts and investigate whether acts of enforced disappearances may amount to crimes against humanity. The UNWGEID led to the creation of the United Nations International Convention for the Protection of All Persons from Enforced Disappearances (ICPAPED) that was adopted by the General Assembly in its resolution of 47/133 on the 18th of December 1992 (UN, 1992–2015). In December 2010 the ICPAPED entered into force and with it the Committee of Enforced Disappearances (UNCED) was established (UN, 1992–2015). There are currently 94 Signatories and 44 parties (that have ratified the Convention); Cyprus is a signatory but not a party, meaning it has not ratified the convention and is not subject to it yet (UN, 1992–2015).

Furthermore, organizations such as The International Commission on Missing Persons (ICMP) another inter-governmental organization (IGO) situated in Sarajevo, Bosnia, has accounted for over 27, 000 (70 percent) of the 40, 000 persons reported Missing in the former Yugoslavia (ICMP Origins, May 2014). This international organization was created by President Bill Clinton of the United States in 1996 at the G-7 summit in Lyon, France, and is the only international organization that deals specifically with Missing Persons. The ICMP is now the leading global international organization that deals with Missing Persons cases by aiding in developing institutional capacity, civil society organizations, assisting in the process of justice, science and technology and fieldwork by working with governments, civil society organizations, and justice institutions, to address the issue of Missing Persons (ICMP, About us, May 22, 2014).

The ICMP now has a global reach in its humanitarian mission in addressing the issue of Missing Persons, particularly, because the developed experience and expertise of this organization was called upon to aid in the recovery of the Missing during the9/11 tragedy in New York; as well as in other post disaster contexts, such as, Hurricane Katrina in Louisiana (Wagner, 2008, p.258). As Dr. Sarah Wagner (2008) points out in her work, *To Know Where He Lies: DNA Technology and the Search for Srebrenica's Missing* "Identifying the Missing thus becomes a humanitarian project, a process of delivering aid, like distributing food or providing temporary shelter" (p.262). In 2011 more than 50,000 cases of Missing Persons in 83 countries were processed by the UNWGEID (UN 2011: 6, in Kovras, 2012) for various reasons that include violent conflict; the importance of the process of exhumations cannot be underestimated in regards to its effect on peacebuilding and reconciliation globally.

Missing Persons in a Cypriot Context and Some Challenges for the Committee on Missing Persons in Cyprus

In Cyprus, the Committee on Missing Persons (CMP) has exhumed 969 and identified 601 remains of Missing Cypriots (CMP Figures and Statistics of Missing Persons, August 31st, 2015). Of the 2001 declared Missing Cypriots, 601 of were returned to their families (CMP, 2015). Both Turkish and Greek Cypriots are jointly working together in this bicommunal organization during the process of exhumations which encompasses the recovery of the Missing and their identification, for the reunification of the Missing with their loved ones which is an act of peacebuilding and inter-ethnic reconciliation. The first identified bodies in Cyprus returned to their families occurred as recently as 2007. However, historically the development of the CMP and the process of exhumations has been an arduous task that needed cooperation between the north and the south of Cyprus in order to conduct the necessary scientific/socio-political procedures for the recovery, identification, and return of Missing Persons to their loved ones.

The majority of Missing Persons who are Turkish Cypriots occurred from 1963–1964 as a result of the Turkish Cypriot actions of withdrawing from government because of the Constitutional changes that President Makarios attempted to enact unilaterally (Anastasiou, 2008; Kovras, 2012; Sant-Cassia, 2005); and attacks on Turkish villages by Greek Cypriot irregulars in EOKA. Further, in 1967 violence re-emerged in greater force, which coincided with the actions of the Greek Junta in Athens. This is what Iosif Kovras calls the first wave of violence: the inter-communal violence of 1963 to 1974 followed by the second wave he discusses as the Turkish invasions of 1974 (Kovras, 2012).

According to Turkish Cypriot narratives the majority of their Missing occurred during the first wave, particularly, in the years of 1963–1964 and in the second wave of 1974; and the Greek Cypriot narratives claim their Missing almost exclusively disappeared during the 1974 second wave of Turkish invasions (Sant-Cassia, 2005, p. 22). However, Missing Persons from both ethnic groups can also be attributed to earlier periods of the 1950s and the rise of nationalist interests, different ideologies that emerged throughout the 1950s to the early 1970s that caused inter-ethnic and intra-ethnic violence and disappearances (Sant-Cassia, 2005; Anastasiou, 2008). For example,

Greek Cypriots and Turkish Cypriots who were pronationalist and supporters of EOKA and Enosis, and/or TMT's aims of Taksim enacted violence against their own ethnic groups or individuals who were not congruent with their ideological beliefs and political objectives (Byrne, 2000; Sant-Cassia, 2005; Anastasiou, 2008).

It was during the first wave of violence that the ICRC in 1964 sent a delegate and humanitarian services to Cyprus. In regards to Missing Persons the ICRC visited detainees and traced whereabouts of the Missing Persons (Sant-Cassia, 2005); and in many cases aided in the clarification and search for the Missing whom were still alive, in hiding, or detained in hostage situations, aiding in the exchanges of both ethnic populations (Sant-Cassia, 2005, pp. 29–35).

After the 1974 invasions the governments of Cyprus and Turkey provided lists of detained and Missing Persons of Greek and Turkish Cypriot origin. Further, the ICRC also managed data and wrote to families of the Missing; as well as it was the responsibility of the family and loved one's to come forward to declare formally that a family member is/was in fact Missing. The Red Cross also provided a list of the Missing, and civil society organizations such as the Committee of Relatives of the Missing Persons provided lists of the Missing that was a contentious issue in Cyprus due to who qualifies to be on the list and perhaps this issue is still contentious to the present day (Sant-Cassia, 2005). Finally, the Government Service for Missing Persons stuck to the number of 1,619 Missing Greek Cypriot citizens until an official publication of the amount of Missing Greek Cypriots was published by the CMP, which is sponsored by the UN, so that claims of 1,508 Greek Cypriots Missing and 493 Turkish Cypriots Missing became the official formal list (CMP, Figures and Statistics of Missing Persons, August 2015). I spoke with many Greek Cypriot soldiers and Greek Cypriots during my six month stay in Cyprus who discussed the number of 1,619 Missing Greek Cypriots on several occasions which shows how powerful original figures in the stories last in the minds and memories of society in general in regards to their Missing ethnic communities.

During what Paul Sant-Cassia calls "the bureaucratization of uncertainty" in 1975 after the end of hostilities, Rauf Denktash, leader of the Turkish Cypriot's and Glavkos Clerides President of the Republic of Cyprus, set up an interim Committee on Humanitarian Issues in order to address the Missing Persons problem (Sant-Cassia, 2005). In addition, other non-governmental organizations such as the Cypriot Committee of Parents and Relatives of Unknown Prisoners and Missing Persons were also established, putting pressure on formal institutions (Sant-Cassia, 2005). The list, in effect, became for both ethnopolitical groups a cause of a community of suffering and victimization in which political objectives ensnared and manipulated the humanitarian issue that people needed to know—what happened to their loved one (Sant-Cassia, 2005).

As a result of other international conflicts, and the rise in Missing Persons in Latin America getting access to the press, the UN passed Resolution 3220 that "the desire to know the fate of loved ones lost in armed conflicts is a '*basic human need*' and 'provision should not be delayed' because of other issues pending" (UN Resolution 3220 in Sant-Cassia, 2005, pp. 63–64); which can still be seen on posters (the resolution) on one of the walls of the city of Nicosia check points that provides access to the north and south of Cyprus. Therefore, UN General Assembly resolutions that include No. 3450, 32/128, in 1977 were passed calling for a UN sponsored Committee on Missing Persons (CMP) in Cyprus which came into effect in 1981 and began investigative work in 1984 (Sant-Cassia, 2005; CMP, 2015). Again, the Committee and respective groups had to come to an understanding on the criteria to be used. The final criterion was to be, and is of a non-judicial nature in not determining culpability but in determining death and the time of death and therefore punishment for the crimes committed such as murder are not dealt with.

The tumultuous and Sisyphean task of each team (Greek and Turkish Cypriots) is to provide a list of the confirmed Missing Persons with access to their respective government documents and varieties of information from civilians, perpetrators, and the nation-states ofTurkey and Greece all took a toll on the process. It took sixteen years to come to an acceptable number of Missing Persons which has since changed the number of the Missing Turkish and Greek Cypriots that at one point were 1493 Greek and Greek Cypriots Missing and 500 Turkish Cypriots Missing (Sant-Cassia, 2005, p.66). In 1997–1998 President Clerides of the Republic of Cyprus (RoC) and President Denktash of the Turkish Republic of Northern Cyprus (TRNC) declared that the issue of Missing Persons was purely humanitarian so as to avoid political exploitation, and to provide all information for the recovery of the Missing (Sant-Cassia, 2005 p.68). As Paul-Henri Arni a Committee Member of the CMP and prior ICRC senior staff states:

> The CMP works in the absence of a political settlement. That means we also work in the absence of a commonly agreed narrative. Our mandate and our task is limited. Once the sides agreed on a common list of Missing Persons, we were tasked with locating them, exhuming them, identifying them and returning them to their families for a dignified burial. This is a long, lengthy and expensive process to address the consequences of a large number of disappearances that took place in 1963/64 and 1974. But, it is not the CMP's responsibility to tell the circumstances and who did what; this is left to others.

Thus, the CMP's primary focus is the humanitarian return of the remains of the Missing to their families that however had to go through a process of developing a commonly agreed list of Missing Cypriots, both Greek and Turkish, which proved to be a difficult task.

It was not until the opening up of the Green Line in 2003 and the finalization of the Missing Persons List with cooperation between both ethnic groups and the leaders of the CMP could a systematic scientific action in what I have called, the process of exhumations be done *en masse*. As a scientist from the CMP anthropological laboratory states in my dialogue with them below:

> Kris: In direct relation to say recovering the Missing Persons, would you say that this bicommunal aspect is necessary when recovering? Or with the CMP, must it be a bicommunal organization?
>
> CMP Turkish Cypriot Scientist 3: Practicality wise, it must be because let's say there is no contact between the Greek and Turkish Cypriots, it would not work because Missing Persons from the Turkish Cypriots are all over Cyprus. I have to cross the border and I have to go and work there to find them. Also, I have to find information for where they are so I need someone to make an investigation for me or I will make it, which is useless because families tried this before and it didn't work from what I saw. Also, Greek Cypriot Missing is all over Cyprus so they have to cross over the border and must find information. They need also from Turkish Cypriot authorities and citizens to find where possibly they are.

Therefore, the opening of the Green Line in 2003 led to the necessary territorial access for the CMP to recover the bodies and gain access to information because the process of exhumations is and must be an interethnic collaborative process in Cyprus. A feat of modern technology, the process of exhumations of Missing Persons in Cyprus represented as a humanitarian mission and mandate is a dynamic process, which intersects with aspects of interethnic reconciliation between post violent-conflict societies and ethnic groups that can serve as a model for other nation-states suffering from the effect of violent conflict—Missing Persons. With the return of the first Missing Person in 2007 the CMP effectively dug up the past and began to alter the uncertain future of Cyprus, towards a sustainable peaceful one, which I will examine throughout this work.

FRAMEWORK OF THE STUDY

The manuscript is divided into seven chapters: Introduction, Literature Review, Methodology, and Results presented in three distinct chapters, and a Conclusion. Each chapter starts with a journal entry that is relevant to the content of the chapter to offer a personal emotive and experiential effect, which I as the principle investigator went through in order to ease into the discussion.

Chapter one introduces the study by offering a brief account of the Cypriot conflict in general with a purpose statement and presents the importance of the study on Missing Persons in this day and age. Moreover, this introductory chapter hones in on the context of the study from a global holistic perspective on relevant historical developments on Missing Persons to the more specific focus of this study, Missing Persons in Cyprus and the recovery, identification, and reunification of the Missing with loved ones and its effects. The chapter discusses some other issues such as, political collaboration, list formation and territorial access in order to unite the Missing with their loved ones. Finally, the chapter outlines the overall framework of this study.

Chapter two presents a literature review based on current and related studies. It also presents concepts and theories from a multitude of disciplines that include, peace and conflict studies, psychology, and anthropology in order to offer a multidisciplinary or transdisciplinary approach in understanding the process of exhumations with respect to peacebuilding, reconciliation, and restorative justice. This is the overall goal of the field of Peace and Conflict Studies—to offer a multidisciplinary approach to understanding conflict and peace (Byrne and Senehi, 2011). The literature review is divided into three main areas that correspond to the three findings chapters. The first section discusses aspects of chapter four on Uncertainty and Psychology with an emphasis on basic human needs, empowerment, trauma studies and justice. The second section centers on theories surrounding the Bicommunal Relations chapter five with an emphasis on inter-ethnic reconciliation and restorative justice frameworks, bicommunal contact and inter-ethnic relationship development. The third section presents the role of storytelling and historical non-reoccurrence and its role in inter-ethnic reconciliation in post-violent conflict societies and Missing Persons in Cyprus.

Chapter three presents the methodology used to conduct this study. I, myself being the principle investigator discuss/outline how I used a qualitative semi-structured interview approach. I discuss who my participants were, in some cases presenting their identities and in others just their vocation according to the consent of those interviewed. I also outline how I gathered data, through journal entries, photography, interviews, and direct participant observation during my volunteering with the CMP in July and August of 2014 during my stay in Cyprus. Further, chapter three also offers the limitations of the study on a subject of this magnitude highlighting other avenues to be pursued and not covered in this work regarding the subject matter. It also discusses gaps and difficulties encountered in conducting this research. Finally, I discuss how I analyzed the data gathered inductively in order to get at the understanding of just what does the process of exhumations do in relation to peacebuilding in Cyprus and perhaps beyond.

The fourth chapter presents the first core concepts and their themes on the analysis of the research findings on Uncertainty and Psychology. In particular, it outlines and discusses the effects of the uncertainty of what happened to loved ones that are Missing for the relatives of the Missing with respect to aspects of closure and psycho-social aspects of it that are a part of basic human needs; which essentially encompass empowerment through reunification of the Missing with loved ones. Further, it outlines a brief account of the truth versus justice debate in regards to how amnesty instead of retribution affects the return of Missing Persons, reconciliation, and peacebuilding in Cyprus. As well it discusses the relevance of the transgenerational transmission of trauma to next generation Cypriots with respect to the issue of Missing Persons.

Chapter five is on the core concept of Bicommunal Relations as an aspect of interethnic reconciliation and its themes are based on the analysis of the results of the research findings. Its focus is on expanding the concepts of the formation of relationships between Cypriots because of the bicommunal nature of the CMP. It presents the challenges of having a high percentage of Missing in a post-violent conflict society that within the gambit of time affects the nature of inter-ethnic relations between Greek and Turkish Cypriot's and reconciliation. Further, it provides evidence of the formation of loci for the development of friendships and the importance of leadership in matters of interethnic reconciliation and restorative justice.

The sixth chapter presents the third core concept of Storytelling and its emergent themes through the analysis of the results of the research findings. It argues for the importance of constructive storytelling and just what storytelling represents as a necessary intervention in the context of Cyprus and through the process of exhumations. It presents the importance of information effect in a constructive manner that is necessary for inter-ethnic psycho-social rehabilitation to occur and the need for reducing the chances of the historical reoccurrence of the violent conflict through a shared narrative of Missing Persons and victimization for all Cypriots whether Greek or Turkish.

Finally, chapter seven is the concluding chapter that summarizes the manuscript. The chapter argues that the process of exhumations is a process of empowerment. It further provides an overall account of the findings reflecting that an intervention model must be aware of the advantages of the process of exhumations and the pitfalls that should be avoided. Further, it includes recommendations for future research on the process of exhumations and Missing Persons as an aspect of peacebuilding, inter-ethnic reconciliation and restorative justice.

CONCLUSION

This chapter offers an introduction and outline of the study and how it is to proceed. It presents the significance and overall objective of the study and a brief context of the Cyprus conflict and Missing Persons. Following this chapter is the literature review that frames the study.

Chapter Two

Literature Review

JOURNAL ENTRY

Date: June 1st, 2014

The last several days I have slept a fair amount considering that I unfortunately contracted poison ivy before starting this trip. It seems to subside in some areas and spread in others. Fortunately, it appears that the worst of it is over. Besides my wonderful sleeps on the beautiful island of Cyprus, I have walked the area in the Agios Dometios Municipality. There is the University of Nicosia which is very well put together and pleasant looking. I have been told that the University has a very high international student volume. It also holds the office of the United Nations Educational Scientific and Cultural Organization (UNESCO). I will look for a volunteer position at UNESCO if I can't volunteer for the Committee on Missing Persons.

Today, while biking through the city of Lefkosia (Nicosia), I began to feel the vibe of the island life of Cyprus, which is very relaxed and easy going. There are Orthodox churches every couple of streets. Some of the churches are very old by several hundred years. I walked through one and it was beautiful and ostentatious, filled from wall to wall with gold ornaments. I had the good fortune to witness a marriage taking place in the church in the traditional Greek custom. Greek Cypriots seem to be highly religious in Cyprus. I also came across an old Anglican Church near the city center.

Anyone traveling to Cyprus will realize how easy it is to bike around. It gave me such a sense of pleasure to see the city from the bike while it was over thirty five degrees Celsius with a very dry heat. One day, at the end of my biking around and sightseeing, I came across a cemetery that was attached to the Green Line several blocks east of VP Hostel in the Agios

Dometios Municipality. There was a gate and a very small building in which a Greek Cypriot soldier stood at guard.

I biked up to the gate and asked him about the cemetery. I asked, "Katalavenete agglika (English Phonetics)" meaning, do you understand English in Greek. He said, "Yes." I asked him if the road that was blocked by one of those moving army red and white striped poles that lets cars go through was the start of the Green Line that he was guarding. He said, "Yes, three miles up you would run into Turkish soldiers."

I mentioned that I was doing research here on the conflict and if I could ask him some questions that would not offend him. He responded, "Sure." I asked him if the graveyard to his left was filled with fallen Greek Cypriots from the 1974 war. He said, "Yes, the graves are filled with people who lost their lives from 1974." It was a memorial center and collective burial site for those who lost their lives and for the family members who attended it. I asked him if I could go in. He replied, "No." I asked him "How could I get access to the gravesite?" He said, "You have to go to the police station and get special permission, and you are only allowed to visit on Sundays." He also said, "You know people still come and visit the graves of their families here," a bit more sternly. I asked him, "Can I take a picture from here of the Green Line and the gravesite." He said, "No pictures are allowed, sorry."

I bothered this young Greek Cypriot soldier one more time and asked him, "Hey, can I ask you one more question you might find personal." He said, "Okay." I asked, "Why did the Greek Cypriots vote no for the Annan Plan in 2004? What do you think would have happened if they voted yes?" And, "What is the main reason why the Greek Cypriots voted no?" A couple of seconds went by and he put his hands together as a gesture of unification and said, "You mean become one?" I said, "Yes." He said "*No, they would have killed each other if this had happened and that's why.*" I thanked him and was on my way.

After that response I realized how much more complicated getting my research done was going to be. In some way, I get a strange feeling that certain aspects of the conflict are purposefully hidden as much as they can be from tourists for obvious economic reasons. But they are very real in the minds and hearts of Greek and Turkish Cypriots.

INTRODUCTION

> [A]t its core, this book is about why people seek out the remains of their loved ones—what it means to them—and how the advent of a DNA-based system of post mortem identification has helped transform this process of recovery, remembering, and reckoning. It is a reminder that among the various registers of meaning, the individual is our entry point into the social.
> (Sarah Wagner, 2008, p. 266)

A literature review is used to aid in understanding the findings. For example the literature on grounded theory shows gaps or bias in existing knowledge and is not supposed to provide the main hypotheses and concepts for the findings (May, 1986 cited in Creswell, 2007). Further, a literature review provides a framework of theory that can unpack and aid in understanding the findings. Moreover, this framework assists in understanding the participants' perceptions with an emphasis on understanding—what the process of exhumations do and why they are conducted.

The literature review is organized into three main areas that correspond to the three findings chapters. The first section discusses chapter four's Uncertainty and Psychology with an emphasis on basic human needs, empowerment, trauma studies, and justice. The second section centers on theories surrounding the Bicommunal Relations chapter five with an emphasis on inter-ethnic reconciliation and restorative justice frameworks, bicommunal contact and inter-ethnic relationship development. The third section presents theories that aid in understanding chapter six, Storytelling, and the role of storytelling constructively with a brief mention of historical non-recurrence and its role in inter-ethnic reconciliation in post-violent conflict societies and Missing Persons in Cyprus.

BASIC HUMAN NEEDS

John Burton (1990) set out defining human needs theory in his work *Conflict Resolution and Provention* that can aid in understanding the significance of the exhumation process for peacebuilding and why the process of exhumations must be conducted and what it does. Human needs can be hard to distinguish and are universal in nature. They must be dealt with in the assessment of structures and address their systems. Human needs can be defined by cultural and contextual mores; although, people need a certain caloric intake and water to survive. Needs are further defined in relation to values and interests that ultimately intersect. Where basic needs (food, water, shelter, psycho-social necessities) and values (culture and identity) are closer in relation then interests which are more structurally created, politically oriented and ideological (pp. 37–43).

Thus, human needs are universal and non-negotiable. They represent more than just basic needs of survival that include sustenance, water, and shelter; they encompass a certain amount of autonomy and empowerment that include psycho-social necessities such as psychological security as research suggests in Bosnia post Camp David Accord (Redekop, 2002). Among many needs scholars Manfreed Max-Neef (1992) identifies basic human needs such as subsistence which would be universal in every culture that are made up of satisfiers such as water, food, and shelter that are non-negotiable to avoid conflict. His main point is that human needs are context-dependent and it is the satisfiers such as the type of food or shelter that defines the cultures being addressed that meet the universal need of subsistence (pp. 199–200). Thus, there are many ways to define basic human needs and many scholars suggest different basic human needs for different contexts and offer different ways of defining human needs and their fulfillment strategies (Galtung, 1979; Burton, 1990; Max-Neef, 1992; Nussbaum, 1996; Cavanaugh, 2000; Sen, 2001; Redekop, 2002). The non-negotiable needs fulfillment are meant to avoid the escalation of conflict which gives food for thought in how to identify them in different contexts going through the process of exhumations across the world. Hence, the specific context and people will reveal how to fulfill those needs and arguably the best manner to get at how to fulfill those needs is to ask those in need just what does the process of exhumations do in their context as this research has done; in order to reduce any form of violence that is happening and can happen again in the future (Galtung, 1979).

Burton (1990) acknowledges that human needs are context-dependent. Human needs may vary according to the group's specific needs fulfillment, particularly, when a group feels a lack of distributed justice due to the societal failure to fulfill their human needs, which are not up for bargaining, can explain the rise of social conflicts that may end up in violence if they are not met and denied. If basic human needs are not unearthed and met they are arguably a major reason why protracted ethno-political conflicts are not resolved as in the case of Cyprus (Cavanaugh, 2000). Hence, conflict repression and coercive settlements without the fulfillment of non-negotiable needs—basic human needs—leads to the exponential increase of conflicts (Kriesberg, 1991). However, if the context-dependent needs are acknowledged and met then conflict provention will occur that address the systematic and structural issues that are repressing the fulfillment of people's basic human needs (Burton, 1990).

When looking at the specific effect of violent conflict that is—Missing Persons—and within the specific context of Cyprus the core concept of Uncertainty emerged. In November 1974 the UN passed Resolution 3220 that states "the desire to know the fate of loved ones lost in armed conflicts is a '*basic human need*' and 'provision' should not be delayed because of other issues pending" (Sant-Cassia, 2005, pp.63–64). Thus, the desire to know the fate of loved ones from violent conflict which creates a context of uncertainty has a long history. Among this history is the 1949 Geneva Convention with rule 112—Search for and Collection of the Dead—within the gambit of Customary International Humanitarian Law that states, "Whenever circumstances permit, and particularly after an engagement, each party to the conflict must, without delay, take all possible measures to search for, collect and evacuate the dead without adverse distinction" (ICRC Customary IHL, https://www.icrc.org/customary-ihl/eng /docs/v1_cha_chapter35_rule112). Thus, a *conditio sine qua non* of respect and for the return of remains, decent burial, and identification is the duty of each party that was in conflict as well as the duty of international bodies such as the UN. Further, the ICRC states that people who go missing in war causes "anguish and uncertainty for their families and friends . . . Such families often face the pain of ongoing uncertainty and are unable to grieve" (ICRC, https://www.icrc.org/eng/war-and-law/protected-persons/Missing-persons/overview-Missing-persons.htm). Thus, uncertainty as a core concept is highly important with respect to Missing Persons and the basic human need for relatives to know what has happened to loved ones after violent conflict is a non-negotiable need.

In addition, within Burton's (1990) theory of basic human needs an intersection emerges which incorporates: 1) psycho-social needs; 2) values, meaning cultural practices, rituals, and aspects of identity; and 3) interests, that of political objectives so that each aspect must be understood as not existing within a vacuum. Thus, when examining the core concept of Uncertainty an intersection of these aspects was unpacked. For example, psychological needs revealed themselves in which the participants expressed the need for a relative to know whether their loved one was dead or alive. This need when fulfilled by the process of exhumations and identification of the survivor's basic human needs that encompass the values of Cypriots to culturally perform social and religious rituals of death through the burial of material remains and a process of mourning for both Greek and Turkish Cypriots. The importance of such rituals is intertwined with the right to know and the basic human need to dispel the uncertainty of death for Greek and Turkish Cypriots in order for them to heal. Access to the bodies or remains of the Missing Person is a basic human need for survivor's to perform ritualistic burials and remembering.

Thus, through the identification of remains comes the empowerment of relatives to provide the cultural and religious rites of passage for the dead, allowing for processes of closure to come to life. Understanding the psychosocial aspects of basic human needs within the Cypriot context can be aided by comparison to the work of Dr. Sarah Wagner's (2008) *To Know Where He Lies: DNA Technology and the Search for Srebrenica's Missing*. Her work discusses the nature of absence and "technologies of repair" (p. xiii). For each victim the "Term Missing signals the absence of a story, a personal history yet untold, for each victim. For families of the Missing, the label reflects the state of emotional limbo in which they must live until they receive the news that the mortal remains of their Missing relative have been identified" (p. 7). Therefore, through recovery, re-association, and recognition of the Missing individually and collectively identity is articulated by technologies DNA testing power, as well as, family's recognition of identity and death, and politics that affect the basic human needs of relatives to fulfill psycho-social factors that aid in bringing about closure that were absent before.

Thus, closure is absent when the survivor's unable to move through and gain access to psycho-social basic human needs that were denied due to the uncertainty of what happened to their loved one that is missing. Shari Eppel's work (2006), "“Healing the Dead:” Exhumation and Reburial as Truth-Telling and Peace-Building Activities in Rural Zimbabwe," argues that it was/is the "corruption of community values and ways of being is what most offends and disturbs our survivors, and it is this loss that is still being mourned years later" (p.263) due to the massacres and violence in rural Zimbabwe in the 1980s and enforced disappearances; in which the fulfillment of basic human needs of a proper burial and respect for the dead has been denied. She explains the specific context of the Amani in the Matabeleland region of Zimbabwe with respect to Missing Persons, cultural values and rituals that impact the ability of the community to mourn the dead and find closure. As Eppel (2006) states:

> The Significance of ancestral spirits in Ndebele belief systems is of central importance: it is the spirits of the dead that play essential roles in the lives of every family, guiding and nurturing them. In order for an ancestral spirit to its true task in protecting the family, it needs an honorable funeral . . . A spirit that has not been honored becomes an angry and restless spirit, bringing bad luck to the family and the community at large (p. 264).

Hence, the basic human needs requirement in the Amani context would be for the strategic fulfillment of necessary psycho-social practices so the dead can continue their duties of protection and be given the respect they deserve from the living.

Consequently, through the process of exhumations and facilitating community healing with Amani involvement Shari Eppel (2006) argues that to "heal individuals very often has a ripple effect that leads to healing simultaneously at the level of a larger community and its value system" (p. 266). Further, she claims that to confirm their deaths is to confirm that they (the Missing) in fact lived and failure to go through the social and communal event is to deny their lives and achievements in any culture (p. 268). And so it goes in Cyprus that in order for the community to heal and go through aspects of closure and healing the identification of the Missing and their return must occur for relatives of the Missing to move through psycho-social rituals to heal.

Therefore, in comparison to the Cyprus context Paul Sant-Cassia (2005) contends in, *Bodies of Evidence: Burial, Memory and the Recovery of Missing Persons in Cyprus,* that in Modern Greek culture "it is one of the worst fates possible for an individual's body not to be buried without proper religious rites" (p. 97). Further, the Missing Greek Cypriots are deemed revenants—which are considered symbols of liminality—which is a type of limbo in which their bodies are separated from their souls "and are not laid to rest by the living and therefore torment the living as ghosts" (p. 100).

Sant-Cassia (2005) avers that Turkish Cypriot relatives also want and need the body of loved ones in order to mourn. However, the TRNC government in the north tried to script that all their Missing were dead (Turkish Cypriots) and to move on with life and the Greek Cypriot RoC government scripted that their Missing were perhaps alive. This powerfully argued politicization of the Missing led to what Sant-Cassia (2005) calls the Bureaucratization of Uncertainty, which maintains inter-communal tensions and effects memory and closure for all Cypriots (p. 60). Thus, the respective government policies of silencing the right to know what happened to the Missing and maintaining narratives of loss has also aided in maintaining the conflict.

Therefore, it is arguably that relatives and their Missing in Cyprus are stuck in liminality (moving from one stage to the next) or what my research participants revealed as paralysis of their basic human need to move beyond aspects of uncertainty. They need to know whether their loved one is dead and they need access to their remains to move through psycho-social aspects of closure such as burial that has been effectively paralyzed by a political past for an extended period of time. Therefore, relatives of the Missing become empowered through the process of exhumations with access to the remains so that they can move beyond liminality or what my participants expressed as the paralysis of closure via uncertainty, and to start the processes of psychological mourning that addresses the absence and loss of loved ones.

PSYCHOLOGICAL IDEAS AND TRAUMA

Intersecting with Burton's (1990) Basic Human Needs theory are the psychological theories on absence, loss, and mourning, in which post violent conflict societies with a large percentage of Missing Persons have as remnants that must be addressed. Thus, Paul Sant-Cassia (2005) argues that both Greek and Turkish Cypriots were faced with absence and loss and that in normal mourning processes absence is worked through as loss. When absence is acknowledged as loss this leads to the survivor's fuller acceptance of the absence of the survivor's loved one (p. 165). However, on a societal level Sant-Cassia (2005) claims that Greek Cypriots have never fully worked through the relationship of absence and loss (p. 165).

Scholars such as Vamik Volkan emphasize that, "Humans cannot accept change without mourning what has been lost" (Volkan, 1997, p. 36). Therefore, a significant way to reduce the uncertainty of death is through the process of exhumations that allows relatives of the Missing to go through the psychological processes of mourning and loss which aids in closure. The stages of mourning the death of a loved one include: 1) Crisis Grief, which includes shock, denial, bargaining, sadness, and feeling anger; 2) next, follows the stage of mourning, which helps the mourner assimilate and adapt to reality (Volkan, 1997). The mourning stage accepts the loss of the person, a component of closure and the survivor can move on.

Unfortunately, things can go terribly wrong, such as the formation of *perennial mourners*, where the "perennial mourner unconsciously remains in a state of limbo" (Volkan, 1997, p. 38). However, Paul Sant-Cassia (2005) in particular disagrees with Volkan and argues that *perennial mourning* is really the notion of unforgettable grief and can be seen as a cultural resource or strategy to cope with loss. The loss is articulated and manipulated by politics that is apparent for the relatives of the Missing who were denied private mourning rights, but not for the whole society who has used the issue of Missing Persons to socially construct and manipulate chosen traumas as a projection onto land loss and other issues derived from the conflict (Sant-Cassia, 2005, pp. 170–73). Perhaps, there is some truth to this argument. Yet with respect to my findings and the participants perceptions, the argument of uncertainty and lack of basic psycho-social human needs which is felt by relatives of the Missing, their friends, and communities, and Greek and Turkish Cypriot societies coupled with the possibility of the transgenerational transmission of the trauma (to be discussed below) to youth is definitely an argument for the former.

Consequently, the individual process is very similar to large groups who also mourn moving from absence to loss. Uncertainty on a societal level or the need to know what has happened to loved ones can prevent psychological closure, paralyzing inter-ethnic reconciliation in the promotion of social perennial mourning and leading to the persistence of the conflict (Volkan, 1997). Further, Volkan claims that an event that damages the tissue of a community that is caused by another group of people, the enemy, formulates feelings of helplessness, trauma, and humiliation, which can cause post-traumatic stress disorder (PTSD) (Volkan, 1997). Therefore, an internalized version of trauma stays with the victims who relive the trauma in an imaginary but very real form. An internal theatre of victim, victimizer, and rescuer encapsulates a play of the mind. Thus, Volkan (1997) writes "One of the ways to deal with this shared dilemma is for individuals to 'envelop' their traumatized (imprisoned) self-representations (images) and externalize and control them outside of themselves" (p. 42). Thus, the data revealed that Cypriots held sway to the view of victim and victimizer, *us and them* in-group mentality, that revealed that Turkish and Greek Cypriots feel that they are the victims and the *other* is the victimizer/perpetrator.

Further, Judith Herman's (1997) monumental work *Trauma and Recovery: The aftermath of violence from domestic abuse to political terror* expands on PTSD stressing that "psychological trauma is an affliction of the powerless" (p. 33). The feelings of intense fear, helplessness, and threat of annihilation may be sustained by persons who have experienced such psychological trauma and violence from the Cypriot conflict because of the loss of a loved one. Thus, the symptoms A) Hyperarousal, B) Intrusion, and C) Constriction, of PTSD are explained as follows with examples of what they can cause psycho-physiologically: A) Hyperarousal, in which psychosomatic complaints occur in which the person or group exists in permanent alert with generalized anxiety symptoms, and specific fears; and B) Intrusion, in which people relive the event as though it is recurring in the present and it is as if time stopped at the moment of the trauma. Further, the trauma becomes encoded abnormally as a form of memory which brings flashbacks spontaneously cued by almost anything living in the emotional force of the original event consciously or unconsciously by emotional feelings of duress. Finally, symptom C) Constriction, in which the person goes into a state of numbness in which terror, rage, and pain dissolve and most importantly, "Because these altered states keep the traumatic experience walled off from ordinary consciousness, they prevent the integration necessary for healing" (p.45). Most people who go through severe trauma are in a flux of all three states. Thus, as Herman (1997) states:

> Finally, the survivor needs help from others to mourn her losses. All of the classic writings ultimately recognize the necessity of mourning and reconstruction in the resolution of traumatic life events. Failure to complete the normal processes of grieving perpetuates the traumatic reaction (p. 69).

In which it is arguable that in the context of Cyprus and beyond people who have dealt with violence and in our case dealing with the issue of Missing Persons, have symptoms of PTSD mentioned and need resolution of such traumas of absence and loss that the process of exhumations is ultimately empowering them with tools of recovery and healing.

Therefore, feelings of captivity and the perpetrator's control over their lives may exist in the form of the victimization narrative espoused by my participants that both Greek and Turkish Cypriots maintain in general. However, perhaps sharing a victim narrative together can add to what Herman (1997) outlines as a healing relationship in which, "Recovery, therefore, is based upon the empowerment of the survivor and the creation of new connections" (p. 133). Consequently, through the survivor's basic human need to dispel of uncertainty through the process of exhumations; relatives, loved ones, and society by and large are empowered and new connections in some cases inter-ethnically are formed at the interpersonal level and within the CMP, and relatives of the Missing.

Next, Pauline Boss (1999) in her monumental work *Ambiguous loss: Learning to live with unresolved grief* discusses her major theory of ambiguous loss defined as a loss of a loved one that is incomprehensible in which the loved one is physically lost or psychologically lost. The two types of ambiguous loss with respect to Missing Persons are first when people are physically absent yet remain psychologically present. Therefore, even if the person is presumeddead and his/her remains are not found, the families are still preoccupied with the loss psychologically. The next type of ambiguous loss is when a physical presence exists but a psychological absence occurs, in which the survivors are emotionally and cognitively unavailable to those around them (2002). As Boss (2002) states:

> Both types of ambiguous loss can occur in the same family. For example, families affected by the attack on the World Trade Center may have included a Missing parent whose remaining partner is so depressed and preoccupied with the Missing mate that children are ignored and feel as if they have lost both parents—one physically, the other psychologically (p. 39).

Therefore, questions arise about how to cope, grieve and move on without a body and with hope that the Missing Person may still be alive (Boss, 2002). The consequences can be devastating to family members and relatives of the Missing. Many go through long term effects of depression, anxiety, helplessness, and relationship conflict and somatization effects that are suggestive of trauma and PTSD. These effects occur because it is difficult for individuals to make sense and deal with what has happened; not knowing what has happened to the person "prevents reconstruction of family and marital roles, rules, and rituals" (p. 39). It is a physically and mentally exhausting process and most importantly with respect to protracted conflicts "ambiguity causes even the strongest of people to question their view of the world as a fair, safe, and understandable place" (p. 40).

In addition, Boss (2002) states that those who live reasonably well with respect to having a loved one Missing hold two opposing ideas in their mind: 1) they may believe their dead loved one is still with them in some sense; and 2) they may move on with their lives while still holding out hope that the body will be found (p .40). This dialectical nature of thought can begin a healing process even while confusion persists while needing the retrieval of a body is usually a cultural necessity for many to begin grieving processes and rituals of death that breaks down denial for closure (Boss, 2002). However, when there is no body to bury closure should not be expected or required, whereas having the body of a loved one empowers letting go of it (Boss, 2002). Without a body many experience physical ambiguity about the loss of a person's life that is filled with uncertainty about what happened to them such as are they really dead; so that they are stuck in a frozen grief and cannot move through normal stages of mourning and grief. When the death of a loved one is ambiguous and uncertain because there is no proof of death, and it is combined with the actual loss of a loved one the results can be "agonizing and immobilizing" even across generations (Boss, 2002, p. 40).

My findings indicate that psychological healing and catharsis were the beginning of a release from ambiguous loss for relatives of the Missing thus aiding in the expunging of uncertainty and death so that they were able to access mourning and grieving processes. This led to the major finding of psychological relief in which relatives of the Missing can perhaps be relieved of the chains of this uncertainty and ambiguous loss, and move through aspects of closure melting away Boss's (1999) theory of "frozen grief" in which the paralysis of Cypriots with Missing loved ones and concomitantly the communities at large can move on and heal.

Furthermore, Vamik Volkan's theory of "transgenerational transmission of trauma" is useful. It is defined as "when an older person unconsciously externalizes his traumatized self onto a developing child's personality" (Volkan, 1998, p. 43). A transmission of trauma due to the need to mourn through rituals and psycho-social aspects of closure from the adult to the child is passed on generationally via relatives of Missing Persons. So that in order for healing to occur communally the next generations must mourn and reverse the humiliation and "feelings of helplessness pertaining to the trauma of his forebears" (Volkan, 1998, p. 43). If the group's circumstances cannot allow the past generation to deal with these prior aforementioned feelings, it still bonds the group together because victimhood arises, and *Othering* may emerge in which the survivors all feel that they are victims. Thus, the process of exhumations aids in the reduction of the transgenerational transmission of trauma providing an avenue to psycho-socially heal from the individual level, trickling out to the community at large in which this traumatic transmission generationally is not fixated on frozen grief and ambiguity that aids in the maintenance of the conflict generationally.

PEACEBUILDING AS SUSTAINABLE RECONCILIATION AND RESTORATIVE JUSTICE

The concept of peacebuilding was introduced in light of the development of interstate and intrastate conflicts by the UN General Secretary Boutros Boutros-Ghali (1992) in his work "An Agenda For Peace: Preventative Diplomacy, Peace-making and Peacekeeping" that provided a mandate for the future of the United Nations to be a cooperative body to enforce and aid in maintaining peaceful relations between sovereign states, including, peacebuilding efforts. Thus, one peacebuilding effort supported by the United Nations that came to fruition is aiding and supporting the issue of Missing Persons in

Cyprus. Section 59 of Ghali's (1992) work states that peacebuilding incorporates strengthening democratic structures, institutions, and development so that *social peace* is as important as political peace. Therefore, arguably social peace is dependent upon the process of exhumations in the context of Cyprus. Social justice that seeks to reduce social stratification and all forms of discrimination, including a satisfaction of basic needs is linked to democratic structures and economic satisfaction (Galtung, 1996). Not to mention, social justice emphasizes the need to include marginalized children and women in Truth and Reconciliation Commissions to promote restorative justice and reintegration issues (Ghali, 1992) as well as in this case including the needs of relatives of Missing Persons to be heard and dealt with. Further, with respect to this work one can add that social justice issues tied to peacebuilding are as well dependent upon the return of Missing Persons to relatives to address their psycho-social basic human needs; such as the need to disperse with uncertainty of just what happened to the Missing to bring about closure for the relatives.

In addressing Ghali's work, Ho-Won Jeong (2005) in *Peacebuilding in Postconflict Societies: Strategy and Process*, emphasizes that an important part of peacebuilding deals with reconciliation that supplements Ghali's work. He states that "reconciliation can be generally defined as a process of mutual accommodation comprised of acknowledgement of past wrongdoing and contrition from the perpetrators in exchange for forgiveness offered by victims" (p. 156). This act of peacebuilding through reconciliation needs offers a much needed space for people to mourn and share traumatic experiences through individual, family, and communalization process of *grieving* that was not accommodated prior to the process of exhumations that allows for ritualistic burials and psychological closure that represent the nature of restorative justice.

John Paul Lederach's (2010) work, *Building Peace: Sustainable Reconciliation in Divided Societies* provides a means to understand the importance of the development of relationships between the conflicting groups for a lasting and sustainable peace to emerge. Lederach (2010) emphasizes that "peacebuilding must be rooted in and responsive to the experiential and subjective realities shaping people's perspectives and needs [and therefore] toward a frame of reference that focuses on the restoration and rebuilding of relationships" (p. 24).

His framework of reconciliation addresses the systemic issues of divided societies through the forming of relationships and specifically in this context of Greek and Turkish Cypriots, my data revealed how the process of exhumations provided an avenue for inter-ethnic relationships to come to life. For instance, Lederach states that the engagement of the conflicting groups represents an encounter. As Lederach (2010) argues "People need opportunity and space to express to and with one another the trauma of loss and their grief at that loss, and the anger that accompanies and the memory of injustices experienced" (p. 26).

Thus, the process of exhumations provides space for an intra-ethnic and inter-ethnic encounter via the reunification of the Missing with loved ones because the CMP is a bicommunal organization. Hence, encounters happen during the exhumation process during the recovery of the remains as well as both communities. That leads to a form of what Lederach (2010) calls acknowledgement that allows for the hearing of "one another's stories [that] validate experiences and feelings and represents the first step toward restoration of the person and the relationship" (p. 26).

Therefore, an interdependence forms and a vision of a shared future becomes possible through the four cornerstones of Lederach's (2010) theory of reconciliation as follows: 1) Truth, which is acknowledgment of the past through transparency of the conflict that leads to clarity; 2) Mercy, which is the need for acceptance, forgiveness, compassion and support; 3) Justice, which represents individual and group rights and restitution; and 4) Peace which represents interdependence, harmony, well-being, and security (pp. 28–31). All of the aforementioned cornerstones of reconciliation lead to the focus of the restoration of relationships and harmony in Cyprus with a locus of intra-ethnic and inter-ethnic encounters where the conflicting parties—Turkish and Greek Cypriot—can heal.

Henceforth, the process of exhumations through the CMP bicommunal organization provides an avenue for the locus to change the relationships of Cypriots to one of necessary interdependence for the recovery, identification, and return of remains, the development of relationships—friendships—through available encounters that offers empowerment because the family has knowledge of the loved one's death that leads to—acknowledgement—of loss. The encounters happening through CMP inter-ethnic work in the field recovering bodies in public spaces with Cypriot on-lookers, as well as, at work because the CMP is bicommunal and through the aid of witnesses communicating stories for the whereabouts of Missing Cypriots. Thus, this complex process allows for mercy via acceptance and forges opportunities for forgiveness to occur that provides access to justice in the form of righting and restoring relations and therefore well-being, security, and mutual respect between Turkish and Greek Cypriots.

RESTORATIVE JUSTICE

With respect to the nature of justice and relatives of the Missing an impossible and unanswerable question arises that the data revealed—what about retribution for the relatives of the Missing and punishment of the perpetrators? In regards to peacebuilding and inter-ethnic reconciliation Iosif Kovras and Sarah Wagner aided in my understanding of my data in terms of the—*advantageous uncertainty* of retributive justice and the advantages of the bicommunal CMP in chapters four and five.

Sarah Wagner's (2007, 2010) works on retributive justice discusses the publicizing of the process of exhumations in Bosnia for evidential reasons that is co-opted by high politics in the form of extreme nationalism that has historicized mono-ethnic memorial centers, that aid in the formation of competing narratives of victimization and conflict. Further, she discusses the emergence of internationally based interventions via international concepts of rights such as the right to know and right to justice. The right to know what happened to a loved one and the right to retribution are codified in national legislation law on Missing Persons in Bosnia and its effects on inter-ethnic reconciliation creates tensions in/between the ethnic communities (Wagner, 2010).

The International Commission on Missing Persons (ICMP) in Sarajevo focuses on the right to know what happened in the former Yugoslavia and where a Missing Person is located for family and community members and how s/he died which intersects with a right to justice and punishment through a collaboration of the International Criminal Tribunal for the Former Yugoslavia. The ICMP provides evidence for prosecutions, calling upon staff members that find the remains of the Missing for expert testimony that are used to strengthen or refute claims of culpability (Wagner, 2010). However, rather than creating a common ground for inter-ethnic communicative and collective history and healing, victims narratives have exacerbated conflict while the ICMP's neutrality is delegitimized. Thus, it can be argued that focusing on the humanitarian issue of finding the Missing in Cyprus without assigning culpability for the return and restorative nature of relations between Greek and Turkish Cypriots might be the best possible solution for Cyprus with respect to creating a sustainable peace.

Iosif Kovras (2012) points out that "Enforced disappearances and reconciliation has a negative correlation in post conflict settings in the dominant academic discourse" (p. 95). However, he argues that when it is done through *de-linking* humanitarian processes from politics and transitional justice formulations that deal with solving impunity and criminal law, community building and healing emerges as a result (2012). The retrieval and return of Missing Persons increases the prospect for political settlement because there is no moral, political, or legal responsibility attached to it. For example, anyone coming forward with information on Missing Persons is given amnesty in Cyprus, and the mandate on finding remains is amnesty oriented promoting its much needed resolution (p. 95).

Missing Persons can cause unresolved trauma which prevents closure because the family is not able to bury relatives which affects culturally embedded rituals and mourning (funerals; tombstones to visit the dead) that can hijack empathy and suffering for others (Kovras, 2012). Unfortunately, when exhumations are linked to transitional justice issues of impunity, they can be highly politicized and used by political elites and extreme forms of nationalism in blaming and de-humanizing the other. Yet, when the process is bicommunal, de-linked from impunity and law, it can aid in healing. An example of this point is the development of grassroots movements in Cyprus that Kovras (2012) argues is happening because of the de-linkage from retribution; and my data also supports his suggestion as well that community healing that is bicommunal in public spaces that emerged for Greek and Turkish Cypriots works toward peacebuilding. This aids in transforming victimhood and blaming into a shared experience of mourning and truth recovery that I discuss in chapter six on Storytelling. Thus, nationalism when used in its extreme forms can be destructive in Cyprus (Volkan, 1998; Byrne, 2000; Anastasiou, 2008), particularly when it is linked to the process of exhumations. My participants revealed that in general, nationalism is not destructive with regard to the process of exhumations; it is so only if it is used for justification of dominant narratives of victimization and hatred of the other—expressed in its extreme forms in chapter six on Storytelling.

The process of exhumations is also promoting restorative justice. Zehr (2002) claims that restorative justice is not in direct confrontation with retributive justice (punishment of offenders), rather it focuses on restoring relationships and emphasizing restorative justice metaphorically as a river which incorporates a fluid nature between victims, perpetrators, and communities that have experienced violence (2002). A primary focus of restorative justice is its emphasis on the needs of crime victims that aren't adequately met (p. 14) such as the return of Missing Persons in Cyprus. The needs of victims that aren't met by traditional forms of retribution and Western legal punishment for offences are offered by Zehr (2002) namely: 1) Information on why the offense has happened and what has happened since; 2) Truth telling of the crime offers healing through storytelling to audiences and to the perpetrator; 3) Empowerment, is a component of control that may be implemented by aiding in the agency of the victim through case process; 4) Restitution, whereby the offender takes some sort of responsibility for the crime committed offers vindication—that is a basic need (2002).

Therefore, the survivors basic needs of righting relationships which is a consequential outcome in the development of interethnic relationships through encounters of recovering and reunifying the Missing in Cyprus, are necessary for restorative justice in a supplementation of traditional forms of justice that focus on culpability and retribution by legal punishment. Information can be understood in the form of knowledge of dispelling uncertainty about the Missing that aids in psycho-social aspects of closure and relief via burial and commemoration.

Next, truth-telling by recovering the remains of the Missing proves and provides a narrative of loss and that violent conflict did occur which allots for the inclusion of a space for healing inter-ethnic relationships and remembering loved ones. Empowerment of relatives of the Missing occurs through the knowledge of what happened to their loved one and their involvement during and after the process of exhumations with respect to describing who the Missing Person is. Also, their rights to the body and mourning practices on return of the Missing are made available with respect to opening up a space for dialogue and storytelling.

Finally, restitution where the offender takes responsibility for the crime can be argued to come from storytelling all along that reveals the location of the bodies, the respective governments of the TRNC and RoC in legally allowing for the process of exhumations to occur in the north and south geographically. Perhaps a facet of restitution is in the form of an apology via the work of the CMP itself, national and international financial aid, and the sharing of the possible whereabouts of the dead remains. As stated by the need for an apology from high politics by the participants in a bicommnal manner by the Presidents may aid in the support of the issue of the Missing in Cyprus that would be a necessary ingredient for restitution on behalf of all Cypriots. Thus, if both more formally apologizing publicly in the future together for the past the data revealed aspects of restoration that will aid in retribution without punishment for the future, such as the possible formation of a Truth and Reconciliation Commission to be determined by Cypriots.

STORYTELLING

Storytelling is paramount in the process of exhumations. Without storytelling from the extent to which the perpetrators, historical evidence, hearsay, gossip, remains and artifacts, and the relatives memory and remembrance of their loved ones, the process of recovery, identification, reunification and psycho-social healing would be next to impossible. Jessica Senehi's (2011) "Building peace: Storytelling to transform conflicts constructively," claims that storytelling is telling someone else what has happened and "Through these processes of storytelling and story reception, how we view the world is always being formed, reproduced, negotiated, resisted, or changed" (p. 202). In other words, during the process of exhumations stories are being told that may not be inherently good or peaceful, which may intensify social cleavages, privilege some cultures and silence others as in the case of memorials that are entirely of one ethnic group and through ethno-national discourse publicized by rival groups (Smith, 1986).

Therefore, Senehi's (2011) distinction between *destructive storytelling* and *constructive storytelling* is relevant to the Cyprus context and for the process of exhumations. As Senehi (2011) states, "narratives may enhance peace when they involve a dialogue characterized by shared power" (p.203) such as a sharing in the recovery, identification, and reunification of the Missing with loved ones via the CMP; telling stories of loss and burial through the media and online as in the case of Sevgül Uludağ and inter-ethnic storytelling at schools through organizations such as Together We Can. Hence, when storytelling engenders mutual recognition of suffering and victimization, and when it promotes consciousness raising and serves to resist domination, or teaches conflict resolution strategies it is constructive and can build peace (p. 203).

Further, Senehi (2011) expresses her codification of storytelling regarding knowledge in this context of identity and death; identity in the form of members of a community of Missing Persons (negatively/positively as national identity); socialization (glorification or justification of violence/peace) via the Missing; emotions (unacknowledged collective trauma or healing) by acknowledging the basic human needs that incorporate the fulfillment of the process of exhumations in Cyprus; morality, time and memory, and geography. All of these aspects of story aid in understanding themes of storytelling that are affecting the process of exhumations in Cyprus that formulate a non-negotiable effect of psycho-social rehabilitation in post violent conflict societies that are going through the process of exhumations (Senehi, 2011).

Consequently, Senehi's framing of constructive storytelling can be seen as a tool for organizations such as the CMP in Cyprus for enhancing policy during the process of exhumations that fosters inter-ethnic empowerment through inclusion and flexibility, which can aid in the healing of community trauma and collective mourning through bringing about closure via storytelling in all its forms.

Henceforth, if storytelling is constructively done in the manner of a shared past of victimization with respect to Missing Persons via the families of the Missing, perhaps historical non-reoccurrence of violence can occur. If a collective narrative can be organized and written by historians and storytellers based on their experiences on the history of the Missing Persons of Cyprus as a collective loss of Cypriots' both Greek and Turkish, then it can be taught in schools in the TRNC and RoC. In order to be able to share a common victimization of loss, grieving, pain, suffering, mourning, and healing then inter-ethnic reconciliation can occur generationally.

For example, Michalinos Zembylas's (2011) "Personal narratives of loss and the exhumation of Missing persons in the aftermath of war: in search of public and school pedagogies of mourning" analyzes two groups reactions to exhumations in which the mothers of victims share in the experience of mourning, which creates a bridge of relatedness through shared vulnerability and suffering (p. 771). In effect storytelling and the sharing of people's experiences can be seen as a form of psycho-social rehabilitation in the exchange of stories of mourning and how they felt about the exhumations of their Missing in Cyprus. As Senehi (2011) notes storytelling can aid in the psycho-social rehabilitation of groups through its power of socialization and reproduction of narratives that effect emotion and change toward peace if it is constructive.

Further, Vamik Volkan's (1998) theory of Chosen Trauma through which nation-states express past injustices by choosing historical traumatic moments to teach to children, such as, the 1974 invasion and occupation of the northern Cyprus by Turkey as a dominant Greek Cypriot narrative. Compared to the liberation and freedom story of Turkish Cypriots in 1974 by Turkey's involvement for Turkish Cypriots in their educational history can promote transference and transmission of trauma generationally (Volkan, 1998, 2012).

In effect, in order to ensure historical non-reoccurrence of violence Michalinos Zembylas (2008) states that education that reduces dualistic thinking of we are good and they are bad and we are victims and they are victimizers is necessary to change the politicization of trauma and revenge via a critical emotional praxis in education that provides space for people's awareness of inhabitation or the reproduction of the same world view (2008). Thus, the process of exhumations embedded in storytelling and affirmation of its critical existence by historians and presented with a view of shared suffering; of Missing Persons for Greek and Turkish Cypriots; can create a shared narrative of relatives of the Missing that provides space for a shared past and a shared future for generations to come on the island of Cyprus.

CONCLUSION

As evidenced by the literature review, the process of exhumations in the context of Cyprus is highly complex and multifaceted addressing many factors such as the individual, relatives, and societal with respect to inter-ethnic relations and reconciliation. The review is not exhaustive yet addresses large arrays of issues such as the basic human need to dispel uncertainty and provide avenues of closure and empowerment for the survivors. This approach will offer a sustainable future. Thus, storytelling and psycho-social basic human needs fulfillment offers a possibility of psycho-social rehabilitation for the survivors because the process of exhumations in the Cyprus context is a model of inter-ethnic reconciliation and restitution of relationships that empowers the survivors and relatives of the Missing. Thus, the research methodology used in this study is outlined in chapter three.

Chapter Three

Methodology

JOURNAL ENTRY

Date: July 29th, 2014

My first interview was with Dr. Marios A. Cariolou. I had no idea what to expect nor did I expect him to be my first interviewee. What an honor! Dr. Cariolou is the department head and Lab Director of the Cyprus Institute of Neurology and Genetics. When I got to Cyprus I wasn't sure how to go about finding people from the CMP to interview but I had a game plan. My goal was to use a snowball sampling technique; find one person who was willing to be interviewed and hope others would follow suit. But due to the nature of the subject matter—Missing Persons—I knew it would be difficult to get people to meet with me, and share their thoughts and feelings on such sensitive matters.

Moreover, I had never done research like this. Personally, I had never interviewed a person active in the field before. I was going to use my phone to record every interview, but then I realized it was not an adequate device for recording so I bought a proper Sony recorder. I practiced starting and stopping the tape recorder so that during the actual interviews, I would not be impeded by technical interruptions. I did not want to be fiddling with my device while the interviewees were in the throes of sharing sensitive information.

During my interview with Dr. Cariolou, I felt anxious and constantly looked at the recorder to make sure it was on. I remember trying to stay on task with my questionnaire. I was trying to control the conversation at times to influence the direction it would take. After about twenty minutes I felt a connection with him and began to relax. I noticed how our bodies moved closer together as we got deeper into the discussion and all my reservations dropped away. I felt the walls breaking down between us and soon it was like two old friends meeting over coffee to discuss a really serious subject matter. Sometimes I heard myself gasp for breath at some of the information he shared with me and at other times I became jovial. At one point near the end of our interview, he became really candid about the process of exhumations and I felt overwhelmed and teary-eyed. In fact, it seemed as if we both did.

I remember wondering if it was the job of the researcher to remain objective at all times during an interview? Does being objective mean that the principal investigator should be emotionless? How should one dress when going to an interview? How should one behave? What does it mean to really listen and what does it mean to guide the conversation without corrupting the data or the responses given? After the interview I realized I had a lot to learn. Yet it was also an invigorating experience and one I will never forget.

INTRODUCTION

> Basic research was primarily done at universities; applied research in public or private "think tanks" or consulting firms. Today, the distinction is blurred. Most social scientists construe their work in both basic and applied terms. A discernible trend toward a merging of theory, research, and practice is evident, particularly in the field of CA & R.
> (Druckman, 2005, p. 312)

This study used a qualitative research method to explore my respondents' perceptions, challenges, and professional experiences as they have dealt with the process of exhumations and how they have been touched by it. Further, it explores and expresses how my respondents' perceive the process of exhumations effects on inter-ethnic reconciliation and healing in the context of Cyprus from the individual, organizational, relational, familial, societal, and nation-state perspectives. I used a semi-structured interview schedule when interviewing the participants to get at the process of exhumations and what it accomplishes, and how it is best done with respect to the challenges that arise when conducting these activities.

RESEARCH LOCATION

The research took place in the nation-state of Cyprus. However, it must be stated that Cyprus is a divided island with two nation-states. I conducted research on both sides of the divided island in the Turkish Republic of Northern Cyprus (TRNC) and in southern Cyprus (recognized internationally as the Republic of Cyprus (RoC)). Moreover, the majority of my research took place in the capital city of Nicosia, which again is divided by the UN

Green Line that goes right through the center of the city and the ancient Venetian Walls of downtown Nicosia.

In downtown Nicosia, my interviews occasionally led me to various locations such as cafes and offices on either side of the island. In some cases, discussions and interviews took place in the Dead Zone or the United Nations Protected Areas of the island. Due to the sensitive nature of the topic and for reasons of confidentiality, I am not able to disclose all of the details with respect to some of my interview locations to protect the anonymity of my interviewees. However, I performed a fair amount of research through participant observation and was able in some cases to assist in the process of exhumations within the Anthropological Laboratory in the United Nations Protected Zone near the University of Nicosia, as a result of my volunteer position at the Committee on Missing Persons in Cyprus (CMP).

As the weeks passed, a fair amount of my time was taken up reading and reviewing notes recorded on my experiences in Cyprus. Most of these activities were completed at the University of Nicosia library and in the United Nations Protected Zone in downtown Nicosia at the Home 4 Corporation and Cafe. The Home 4 Corporation and Cafe is located in the United Nations Protected Zone, an area considered to be no man's land, which exists to maintain peaceful relations between the two sides. This particular Zone in downtown Nicosia houses the majority of the International Non-governmental Organizations working on the Cyprus conflict.

The UN Protected Zone is a safe place for Turkish and Greek Cypriots to meet over coffee—particularly at the Home 4 Corporation—to discuss issues surrounding peacebuilding and inter-ethnic reconciliation. It is a marvelous place with a library on the second floor and a conference room on the first floor where meetings are regularly held on peacebuilding and reconciliation initiatives. The café part of the Home 4 Corporation also has great food and a friendly atmosphere. I highly recommend visiting Home 4 Corporation and this area of downtown Nicosia to anyone conducting research on Cyprus. They will receive unexpected guidance and leads regarding peace initiatives and research on the Cyprus conflict. I was fortunate enough to stumble upon it by accident one day when I was lost downtown after already residing in Nicosia for several weeks.

Some of my research also led me to museums in Southern and Northern Cyprus that includes the National Struggle Museum in northern Nicosia and the Nicosia Police Museum in the south. The museums, among other monuments, dedicated to the conflict gave me insight on what, and how the governments/communities of both respective ethnic groups represent the conflict and the issue of Missing Persons.

I also visited mass grave memorials in the capital city of Nicosia in the South called the Tomb of Makedonitissa that houses the graves of Greek Cypriots who lost their lives in the Turkish invasions of 1974. This memorial also has empty graves with tombstones that await the return of Missing Persons from the process of exhumations. Following up on this visit, I went to a Turkish Cypriot mass gravesite memorial in the north of Nicosia that houses Turkish Cypriots who lost their lives from the violence of the 1960s to 1974.

All of these experiences were eye opening and edifying with respect to the tragedy of the conflict and how powerful memorials to the dead and Missing can be. I was particularly impressed with how each memorial was organized—the use of space and color, how statues were presented, the writings and tombstones—all of which contributed to a story with a powerful message not only to each respective ethnic community but to foreign visitors as well.

QUALITATIVE RESEARCH STRATEGY

Conducting research in politically charged and conflict-ridden settings can be challenging with respect to trust issues when people are sensitive to certain topics. This is particularly true when there are strong barriers and opinions as to who is an insider and who is considered an outsider who should not be trusted (Bogdan and Biklen, 2003, p. 100).

When conducting my research, I was open and honest about my genealogical identity that I am half Mainland Greek. Fulfilling my research with those I interviewed was not dependent upon this fact, however, when researching particular groups it is considered potentially beneficial to be identified (in one way or another) with a particular group you are studying (Bogdan and Biklen, 2003). Due to the nature of the Cypriot conflict and the fact that I volunteered with the CMP, which is run by Turkish and Greek Cypriots, the question of my national identity and ethnic origins came up. In such cases I was open about my national origins (Canadian) and the ethnic heritage of being half Mainland Greek. It was best to reveal certain aspects of my identity in order to build trust when conducting interviews and with respect to those interviewed (perhaps because they were middle-tiered Greek and Turkish Cypriots as well as elites and professionals within their respective communities). And even though the majority of those I interviewed were conducting bicommunal work, the threat of data corruption was not prevalent whatsoever.

Choosing to do a qualitative study over a quantitative study is not to say that a quantitative study would not aid in our understanding of what the process of exhumations does. Due to the fact that there is little literature on the process of exhumations as an act of peacebuilding and reconciliation, my research aims to provide a theoretical template to give direction to future scholars that are interested in understanding and pursuing such a normative concept. It is also breaking new ground in the Peace and Conflict Studies (PACS) field. Thus, when researching topics that are fairly normative and untouched the advantages of using qualitative research and in particular grounded theory is that it is a good design to use when a theory is not available to describe a process (Creswell, 2007, p. 66.). A theory is needed to explain how people are experiencing the phenomenon (meaning the process of exhumations).

The research questions posed in grounded theory are put together in such a manner as to understand how the research group experiences the process and what the steps in the process are. The questions posed to the respondents are to get at the process to reveal the core phenomenon, causal conditional strategies, and their consequences with regard to the effects of the process of exhumations on CMP workers, relatives of the Missing, and the nation-state in the context of Cyprus with respect to inter-ethnic reconciliation (Creswell, 2007). Also, when it comes to conducting qualitative research the researcher is not put in such a position of rigidity with respect to the questions asked, leaving room for an open dialogue that aids in gathering rich data and descriptive data that might have been lost in a quantitative design approach (Bogdan and Biklin, 2003, p. 5).

Finally, qualitative research is used to get at understanding a process and not the outcome (Bogdan and Biklen, 2003). With respect to the process of exhumations and the Cyprus conflict, the methodology of qualitative design best suits the constant growth and change associated with finding Missing Persons and its effects on both respective ethnic societies, (in this case, Greek and Turkish Cypriots) in terms of peacebuilding and reconciliation. Qualitative methods assume that everyone has a story to tell, and a perspective that warrants a voice—even the Missing (Bogdan and Biklin, 2003).

SEMI-STRUCTURED INTERVIEWING

Generally qualitative research interviewing is used in two ways. First, it is considered a dominant strategy for data collection (Bogdan and Biklin, 2003). In this method of data collection the researcher is a stranger to the participants in the study and meets them for the first time and poses semi-structured questions from a questionnaire that focuses on particular topics to be discussed. The second form of research interviews is when the researcher is familiar with the participants of the study because his/her research has been conducted in conjunction with participant observation—participating in and observing the everyday processes that the participants live and perform in. Near the end of the study, the researcher sets up formalized interviews with the participants s/he is familiar with to answer a questionnaire or discuss topics of concern (Bogdan and Biklin, 2003, p. 103). Therefore, as Bogdan and Biklin (2003) state, "The best-known representatives of qualitative research studies . . . are those that employ the techniques of participant observation and in-depth interviewing (p. 2)." I conducted both forms of interviewing because I had the good fortune of volunteering with the CMP in Cyprus in July and August of 2014. Consequently, half of the interviews at the beginning of my study were blind—meaning I met the interviewees for the first time—and the rest of the interviewees, particularly with the CMP scientists, were conducted near the end of my volunteer time with them in which case I had gotten to know them quite well.

I used a semi-structured interviewing technique in which the same general questions and/or topics are brought up to each of the participants involved in the study (Bogdan and Biklen, 2003, p. 275). However, the researcher has the liberty to include sub-questions as part of the research that probe at basic themes that emerge throughout the data collection process. In doing so, certain coherent patterns may reveal themselves that the interviewer then incorporates into his/her questionnaire throughout the process of data collection in order to get at important topics that s/he was not aware of prior to the interviews. A rigid and structured interviewing technique in which the participants are asked questions in their exact order wouldn't expand the field of knowledge and data collection (Bogdan and Biklen, 2003, pp.103–104). Further, unlike un-structured interviewing (also called open-ended interviewing where the interviewer encourages the participant to talk in their area of interest and probes deeply into topics the respondent initiates) semi-structured interviewing holds the middle ground position of following selected questions, in this case with probing sub-questions that aid in deeper meaning and understanding of the area of the interviewer's interest (Bogdan and Biklen, 2003, p. 104).

This was my procedure and I followed my set of interview questions and added sub-questions that probed particular statements of interest to the participant to get a richer understanding of the process of exhumations. I also incorporated the sub-questions that continuously arose due to my prying—such as the nature of the CMP organization as a bicommunal organization—because it frequently came up in the interviews with respect to matters of inter-ethnic reconciliation.

ROLE OF THE RESEARCHER

What is the role of a researcher? Scholars and researchers have debated this topic with respect to the participant/observer continuum *ad nauseum* (Bogdan and Biklen, 2003). At one extreme, the researcher observes without interference (as much as possible) and at the other end of the spectrum, the researcher fully immerses him or herself with the participant's behaviors, work, and life in general. As the principal investigator living in Cyprus for six months and volunteering with the CMP in July and August of 2014, I became immersed in the culture of Cypriots, along with everyday activities such as shopping, eating, going out, watching football games, and CMP work. The point was to experience Cyprus and the conflict in all of its elements. But it was also to experience Cyprus from the scope of Missing Persons and how that affected the everyday interactions of Cypriots, their social organization and the symbolic representations of its effect.

This is not to say that in every encounter, the topic of conversation revolved around the conflict and the Missing Persons. However, the nature of my role as a researcher in Cyprus would come up regularly. I would reveal that I was there to study the conflict without being fully explicit on the topic of Missing Persons and the process of exhumations. Interestingly, the topic of Missing Persons was brought up by Cypriots of their own accord from time to time, which gave me some insight into its significance in Cyprus.

I would also like to clarify that although I volunteered at the CMP with Greek and Turkish Cypriots and other international workers, I did not hang out with them outside of work. While volunteering and conducting my interviews (which were all completed in August 2014), I did not spend time in a less formal atmosphere with any of them because that may have corrupted the integrity of the interviews. Yet, I do believe that spending time in a less formal atmosphere would not have corrupted the data. My reasoning is that when conducting research within the context of a conflict or another highly sensitive area, there might be a high level of inclusivity within particular groups that the researcher is studying. If the interviewees feel marginalized or are under any pressure to act in a certain way then the data and the interviews may be corrupted (Bogdan and Biklen, 2003, pp. 92–93). Yet, I feel that due to the nature of those interviewed and their positions as middle tier professionals, this was not the case.

Furthermore, when conducting research that touches upon sensitive areas (or areas of intense and highly charged emotions), sharing feelings of discomfort or excitement, etc. can aid in developing rapport, trust, opening up further dialogue and sharing (Bogdan and Biklen, 2003, p. 101). I was honest with my own feelings with respect to the process of exhumations and in observing and working around highly sensitive material such as the remains of humans and their reunification with relatives often placed me into highly emotional states. It was inevitable that I would share my feelings right from the start. The intentional decision I made to remain vulnerable and authentic helped me to develop closer relationships with the CMP workers because I genuinely felt compassion and empathy for the challenges they faced every day.

DATA GATHERING TECHNIQUES

The primary data gathering technique was based on semi-structured interviews. The interview questions (See Appendix A) were broad but designed to direct the conversation towards several topics that might affect the process of exhumations. When discussing the questions with each respondent (usually posed in the same order), I added probing questions when significant statements and similar patterns of statements throughout the interviews repeated themselves. The point was to get at their experiences, perceptions, and challenges about what the process of exhumations is, and what is it that it actually accomplishes.

I started the project with the intention of completing three interviews in Cyprus and three interviews in Bosnia. However, because the data gathered in Cyprus was so rich and because of my opportunity to volunteer with the CMP, I decided that conducting eight interviews in Cyprus and writing on the Cyprus context alone was more than enough field research for my manuscript. Further, time constraints and financial realities also led me to the decision to focus solely on Cyprus.

Each interview was conducted for about an hour. Some interviews went over an hour and some just under an hour. All of the interviews were recorded on an audio recorder. An audio or tape recorder is good when conducting long and extensive interviews to maintain accurate information (Bogdan and Biklen, pp.112, 129). After the interviews, I transcribed the data onto a computer and used acronyms and pseudonyms to protect each participant's privacy and anonymity.

Next, I took pictures, video recordings, wrote journal entries and collected popular culture documents (Bogdan and Biklen, 2003, pp. 133, 138) that aided me in understanding the conflict. However, they were not analyzed with respect to the manuscript but they will be used for later research and publication.

On a completely different note, I always respected the privacy and laws of Cyprus with regard to the conflict, as well as the CMP. I did not violate any laws or confidentiality or the privacy of these agencies by taking illegal photographs/video, or by taking questionable material illegally.

Finally, I took notes on my observations during my volunteer hours with the CMP and while spending time with the scientists (during particular phases of their work such as the Archaeological and Anthropological Phases). The notes are based on the questions I asked them regarding what they were doing as well as any ideas that would come to mind. I wrote my notes on three small notepads. However, I never used specifics with respect to the CMP and/or the families, and those missing. I sometimes wrote my field notes after my experiences due to the delicate nature of the experience. It was important to take into consideration the respect and dignity of those working, the bereaved, and also the Missing Person. I gathered field notes from my participant observation and they were written as descriptive notes only in order to objectively capture the details of what occurred (Bogdan and Biklen, 2003, p. 120). I wrote about private conversations by reconstructing some dialogue; described physical settings; took accounts of particular events; observed activities; and, wrote on the observer's behavior (my behavior). I wrote journal entries when I felt it necessary to express how I felt and what I had learned (which was at times was destabilizing). I treated myself as an object of scrutiny in order to check any biases or assumptions, and to re-evaluate my emotions in order to reduce data corruption and faulty analysis (Bogdan and Biklen 2003, p. 122).

DATA ANALYSIS AND GROUNDED THEORY

The data used in this work was analyzed and organized through a grounded theory approach. Grounded theory is a "qualitative research design in which the inquirer generates a general explanation (a theory) of a process, action, or interaction shaped by the views of a large number of participants" (Strauss and Corbin, 1998 in Creswell, 2007, p. 63). After transcribing the estimated eight hours of interviews, I read over the entire series of interviews and through inductive analysis, codified and chunked the data into emerging themes and categories. A category "represents a unit of information composed of events, happenings, and instances" (Strauss and Corbin, 1990, cited in Creswell, 2007, p. 64).

The participants interviewed were theoretically chosen through *theoretical sampling* to help the researcher form the best theory (Creswell, 2007). In choosing participants the practice of snowball sampling was also used to get "referrals from subjects to get other people who might be included in the study" (Bogdan and Biklen, 2003, p. 275).

The process of taking information from the data collection and comparing it to the emerging categories is the *constant comparative* method of data analysis. Thus, the process of data analysis went as follows:

1. The researcher begins with open coding of the major categories of information.
2. From open coding a form of axial coding emerged in which I identified one open coding category to focus on called the core phenomenon.
3. Then the researcher goes back to the data and creates categories around this core phenomenon that consist of casual conditions meaning what factors caused the core phenomenon; strategies meaning actions taken in response to the core phenomenon; contextual and inter-

vening conditions meaning broad and specific situational factors that influence the strategies; and consequences meaning outcomes from using the strategies (Creswell, 2007, pp. 64–65).

4. The final step is selective coding in which the researcher takes the model and develops hypotheses that inter-relate the categories in the model or s/he assembles a story that describes the interrelationship of categories in the model (Creswell, 2007, p. 65).
5. The final theory can then be presented in the form of a narrative statement, a visual picture, or a series of hypotheses or propositions (Creswell, 2007, p. 65).

Grounded theory is a good design to use when a theory is not available to describe a process (Creswell, 2007, p. 66.). Further, a theory is needed to explain how people are experiencing the phenomenon within the context of Cyprus, the process of exhumations and its effects on the Cyprus conflict. The research questions posed in grounded theory are put together in such a manner as to understand how the test group experiences the process and what the steps in the process are. The questions posed are to get at the process to reveal the core phenomenon/s, causal conditions, strategies and the consequences (Creswell, 2007).

Next, analysis occurs in which the researcher creates the categories in a form of open coding. In doing so the researcher segments significant statements and information and words that have an impact and which frequently come up. I chunked the interviews around significant statements that had a high frequency related to core concepts that emerged such as, for example, Uncertainty, Psychology, Bicommunal Relations, and Storytelling.

In selective coding the researcher may write a story line that connects the categories as well as specifying the hypotheses or propositions that have emerged from the data. The data that emerged is presented in a manner to provide a template of the challenges and benefits to avoid the pitfalls of the process of exhumations in a post-violent conflict society.

The final result of this process is the development of a substantive level theory close to a specific problem or population of people. The emergent theory could later be tested by quantitative data to determine if it could be generalized to a larger sample or populations. My research goal was to generate a theoretical template on the process of exhumations and to see what it does (Creswell, 2007).

The literature review in grounded theory shows gaps or biases in existing knowledge and is not supposed to provide the main hypotheses and concepts (May, 1986 cited in Creswell, 2007). The findings sections present the theoretical schema, which used references from the literature review to show evidential support for the model. However, when analyzing the data in order to avoid bias on theorizing I wrote the findings chapters first through the emergent themes derived from the core concepts and then implemented theory after it was written. Also, I wrote the literature review chapter to support the findings after the findings section was written. The persons I interviewed deal directly with the process of exhumations. They were most strongly affected because their ideas and stories were considered the most important when examining challenges, and exactly what the process of exhumations accomplishes.

Finally, I included my own stories through some of my journal entries because I volunteered with the CMP and had spent a significant amount of time in Cyprus, to tie the findings together. I wanted to provide the reader with my own subjective feelings and experiences while I also conducted the research objectively. This process was invaluable in checking myself through emergent biases, and feelings, etc. that might corrupt data gathering and analysis.

STUDY PARTICIPANTS

In choosing participants for this study, the practice of *snowball sampling* was used, that is, "getting referrals from subjects to get other people who might be included in the study" (Bogdan and Biklen, 2003, p. 275). The participants I interviewed were also theoretically chosen—*theoretical sampling*—to help the researcher best form the theory (Creswell, 2007). Theoretical sampling refers to choosing subjects and situations based on emergent themes and models and experiences (Bogdan and Biklen, 2003, p.275).

Of the eight participants I interviewed in the study, all were male with the exception of one female. This was not intentional. The results were based on those who agreed to be interviewed in a comfortable manner. The participants were also ethnically divided with threeTurkish Cypriots, two Greek Cypriots, one Greek Mainlander and finally two international CMP workers. The participants ranged in age from their late 20s to their early 60s.

Several of the participants specifically asked to be named in the study, and they are Paul-Henri Arni who is a Committee Member of the CMP and former Head of Delegation of the International Committee of the Red Cross; Dr. Marios Cariolou who is a Professor and Department Head of the Laboratory of Forensic Genetics of the Cyprus Institute of Neurology and Genetics; and Sevgül Uludağ who is an Investigative Journalist in Cyprus for Yeniduzen Newspaper in Turkish published in the northern part and for POLITIS Newspaper in Greek published in the southern part of the island, as well as a blogger on the Cyprus Conflict and Missing Persons issue (http://sevgululudag.blogspot.com/). These participants gave me explicit permission to use their names and asked to be identified in the research. Then, there are the participants who were given pseudonyms to protect their identities. The designations were as follows: *Professor*, at one of the major universities in Nicosia, Cyprus; the *CMP scientists* designated as CMP Turkish Cypriot Scientist 1, CMP Greek Cypriot Scientist 2, and CMP Turkish Cypriot Scientist 3; and CMP Staff Member.

The reason why the interviewee's ethnicities are mentioned in the study is because in several of the interviews, my participants deliberately revealed their ethnicities through their discussion and stories. Some ethnicities were also revealed through names that were easily distinguishable as either Greek or Turkish Cypriot. And finally, they revealed their ethnicities because the Cyprus conflict and the issue of Missing Persons in Cyprus (as revealed through the data) is a bicommunal problem and is being resolved in a bicommunal manner. Therefore, my respondents empower this study by revealing their ethnicities, and by offering how similar their perceptions and understanding of the conflict and the process of exhumations are with respect to both ethnic communities. Also, in mentioning their ethnic backgrounds, readers are able to compare and better understand their experiences and perceptions of what the process of exhumations achieves with regard to both conflict groups, be they Turkish or Greek Cypriot.

Finally, it also gives credibility to this work because there are roughly an equal number of people from both ethnicities with respect to conflict groups as well as the international persons involved with the conflict. This reflects how the return of the Missing is dealt with through the CMP in Cyprus where both Greek and Turkish Cypriots are aided by international figures put in place by the United Nations in terms of logistics and capacity building measures. Thus, in some respects, this study also reflects the nature of how the process of exhumations is being conducted by the local CMP organization in a process of everyday localized peacemaking.

It should be stated that prior to conducting my interviews, I applied for and received human ethics approval from the University of Manitoba, Canada. All the participants were provided with a consent form just before the interview, which explained the study, including the questionnaire. At the time of the interview the participants were given a questionnaire sheet. If they did not approve or wanted to discuss any of the questions, they had the opportunity to do so.

Throughout the duration of the study all of the transcripts, recordable devices, and sensitive materials were safely locked away and hidden from plain sight in the apartment I was renting in Cyprus. Further, at every point of the research the participants were codified through pseudonyms and protected safely on a password protected computer with encoded files that do not reveal the nature of their data. All of the material with respect to the participants' information will be destroyed after two years of the completed work as stated in the consent form provided to the participants, which they all approved.

During the completion of the manuscript all of my participants were given the opportunity to review and object to the use of any material that related to their interview transcription. All specific locations and designations with respect to material that was too sensitive to mention were changed to more general locations such as the North or South of Cyprus. No specific names or Missing Persons were identified in this material out of respect to the bereaved families and the circumstances of their deaths. Upon completion of the work all of the research participants will be given a copy of it.

PROBLEMS/CHALLENGES ENCOUNTERED CONDUCTING RESEARCH

Many problems/challenges are encountered when conducting research of this nature and magnitude, such as when people do not want to meet with the researcher. Due to the sensitive nature of Missing Persons and the process of exhumations itself some people either forfeited the interview or did not want to be bothered to do it. My motto became try not to take no for an answer, with respect of course, and not to take things too seriously if my plans and goals did not work out. Through the course of this study, I learned to be as flexible as possible and to have patience with respect to conducting the research in a fluid manner as well as maintaining my integrity and desire to get the data I needed. Finally, I learned to be malleable with respect to gathering data. Acquiring a variety of experiences about the conflict opened up avenues I would not have encountered had I been rigid with my structure and data gathering techniques.

One can never underestimate culture shock or differences in customs and communication that may affect the research process when one is conducting research in a different culture (Bogdan and Biklen, 2003, pp. 93–94). For example, the fact that I was not on time or managing time was not as important as it would be in an ultra-capitalist society like Canada or the United States. Also, everyday interactions and humor are a major factor in conducting research in Cyprus. People can be very blunt and open regarding their feelings, emotions, and affection, which is something I found comforting because thankfully I have that same type of personality. This may not be true for some Westerners who could become uncomfortable faced with such different social norms and behaviors.

The weather can also play a major part in the physical and emotional well-being of researchers particularly with regard to Cyprus and the intense humidity and heat in the summer months, where we experienced temperatures of 40 to 45 degrees Celsius and higher. The heat is so different in Cyprus than in Canada that it took several weeks for me to get used to it. In fact as I write this work I recall sleeping a fair amount during the day—

sometimes sixteen hours during the intense heat—until I became accustomed to it. Thus, weather and climate can be a challenge biologically when one is trying to conduct research in a different country. It can also affect the customs of the society. In my situation, this affected how and when I was able to conduct research and schedule interviews. I learned very quickly when to expect the availability of persons to sit down to talk with me around work, break times, the coffee culture, and leisure times, which are greatly influenced by the Mediterranean climate.

My next challenge was that I often felt isolated and lonely. I often felt feelings of suspicion and isolation among both ethnic groups that I was working with (Bogdan and Biklen, 2003, pp. 96–97) because the social networks that aid in maintaining one's identity and purpose of research can become confounded because these networks are not proximally available. Fortunately, due to modern technology and Skype I maintained contact with family, friends, and other academics in the field who have/were conducting research of a similar nature so I was able to share my feelings with them, which was very important. I went through a lot of introspection on what it means to be Greek while conducting research in Cyprus. Thus, one issue that affected my research that benefitted me in Cyprus was the fact that I am half Greek and look Greek. Therefore, blending in and sharing in some cultural understandings aided my research and helped me to gain acceptance from the Greek Cypriot society.

However, I am at an elementary level when it comes to speaking, reading, writing and understanding Greek (and I am not yet familiar with the Turkish language) so I felt isolated much of the time. Luckily for me, Greek Cypriots are familiar with enough English so that I was able to conduct research in Cyprus in English and get by. Yet it is still difficult to rely solely on English. Moreover, in the TRNC, Turkish Cypriots are not as familiar with English as they are in the South (RoC) so it was much more difficult in the North to get by on English from my experience. However, Turkish Cypriots are also very welcoming, kind, and helpful so that my travels in the North of Cyprus were positive and beneficial.

Finally, I recall having emotional experiences that were at times debilitating and exhausting due to the nature of this research on the process of exhumations. Some of the emotions I went through fluctuated from panic attacks, emotionally heightened states of angst, suffering, remorse, anger, sadness and despair. Actually one of the greatest challenges for me was when I saw the aftermath of violent conflicts—Missing Persons skeletal remains—as well as witnessing family reactions during the Viewing process of their relative's remains.

My best method of coping was to share my feelings (and to be honest about how I felt) with the CMP scientists and those closest to me without jeopardizing any confidentiality. I was authentic with my emotions and feelings so that bonds of respect and friendship opened up with the scientists that positively aided in my mental health, research and rapport (Bogdan and Biklen,pp. 101–102). I believe that sharing one's vulnerability can be a bonding experience regarding one's emotional states when studying Missing Persons.

One of the challenges I had while writing this manuscript was to work through my own personal memories of the experiences I had which were emotionally intense. When these feelings arise I channel these emotions onto paper and remember that giving those Missing people a voice when their voices were taken from them is why I am doing this research and why the process of exhumations is so important.

CONCLUSION

The PACS field is multi-disciplinary and is reflexive in nature, in which research and theorizing is coupled with real world experience and practice (Byrne and Senehi, 2011). The point of conducting this research is to aid in our understanding of what the process of exhumations accomplishes, and to provide a theoretical template of the challenges, factors, and outcomes of why such a process should be done in the context of Cyprus as well as in other post-violent conflict societies. In doing so, my hope is to offer new information about why this process is happening, who it is affecting and how it is influencing inter-ethnic reconciliation and healing as well as in promoting a sustainable peace on the island.

In this chapter I provided the methodology I used to conduct the research and completion of this work. I explained where, how, why, when, who and what in order to gather data, analyze it, and express some of the important challenges faced when researching, experiencing, and writing on such a politically charged topic as the return of Missing Persons in a post-violent conflict society.

The work I accomplished could not have been made possible without experiencing Cyprus first hand and volunteering at the CMP. I and my research have benefitted immensely from this opportunity. This work aims to accurately portray what my study participants expressed in their perceptions, image and experiences. Their stories about what the process of exhumations does and can do with regard to peacebuilding and reconciliation are presented next in the findings chapters. These chapters explore uncertainty and psychological factors of the return of the Missing; bicommunal relations and inter-ethnic reconciliation and friendship building; and the creation of a space for healing and expressing storytelling that would otherwise go unheard and undone if the delicate process of exhumations is not conducted in Cyprus. Thus, I now turn to chapter four, the first findings chapter Psychology and Uncertainty which unearth the great importance of the reunification of the Missing with their loved ones.

Chapter Four

Uncertainty and Psychology

JOURNAL ENTRY

Date: July 15th, 2014
I was just sent an email that the Committee on Missing Persons in Cyprus (CMP) finally accepted my application to do volunteer work with them. I couldn't believe it! Months earlier I had sent them an online application and never heard back. Now it felt like destiny. Just when I was shifting my attention to leave Cyprus and continue my research in Bosnia, CMP responded favorably and granted me an interview. My foot was in the door.

The interview was to take place inside the designated United Nations (UN) protected area (near the University of Nicosia) close to where I was staying in Cyprus. I was familiar with this area because I had once walked up the road leading to the protected zone and asked the UN guards whether I could enter in order to speak with someone from the CMP. The guards told me I had to be officially invited and I was summarily turned away. That was until now.

The day came for my interview to take place. I had to be driven inside in order to get into the UN area because one needs a pass to even enter the gate. As we drove into the UN zone I felt anxious about how the interview would go and tried to imagine what I would encounter when I arrived. I imagined being led into an office for a formal interview and then sat down and questioned about what I was doing in Cyprus. I was not ready for what actually transpired.

As we drove several miles into the protected zone and reached the CMP's Anthropological Laboratory, I calmed down readying myself for the questions I might have to answer. I was led up to the main entrance to meet one of the lead scientists of the committee. Once introductions were made, I was led right into the lab analysis area where bodies, fragments of bones, and artifacts were laid out on tables covered in white. I gasped for air and my anxiety levels rose dramatically. I felt faint and dizzy. Right then and there, in front of those dismembered bones I was introduced again and questioned about what it was I wanted from the experience. I told both scientists that I wanted to understand the whole process and just to observe and learn what it was like from the field to the lab, etcetera. Truthfully, I wasn't quite sure what I wanted from the experience anymore.

I thought I wanted knowledge about CMP's procedures, or to understand the everyday interactions of the members, or what really went on in this demanding process. But what I realized in that moment was entirely different. Reading and writing about Missing Persons was one thing, but actively engaging with them and seeing firsthand the aftermath and horrifying outcome of violent conflict—death and the *uncertainty* of bringing back the Missing and the complex nature of this process—felt like a brick had been thrown into my face.

INTRODUCTION

> If someone is Missing, then they are neither dead nor alive. They live in the twilight zone. And for the relatives of the Missing, their lives are completely paralyzed and they sit and wait because they have not seen any proof of death—which is necessary in our cultures. Because if somebody dies, you bury them in a grave and you mourn. But for the relatives of the Missing, because this process has been suspended, there is an endless waiting. And no matter what you would tell them and even if logically after fifty years they should know that their seventy-year-old father could simply not be alive, still their heart refuses to believe.
>
> (Sevgül Uludağ, interview and personal communication, July 1, 2014)

After reviewing the interviews and analyzing the data, I became aware that all of my participants expressed several concerns about the importance of the process of exhumations and what it does—which leads to four important core concepts that intersect with one another and that are the titles of this chapter and the next two findings chapters. This chapter focuses on the interrelated core concepts of *Uncertainty* and *Psychology*. Within these intersecting components of the process of exhumations, several themes emerge that aid in our understanding and which highlights important factors that must be addressed and understood. I define these as recovery, identification, and the reunification of the Missing with their loved ones.

The emergent themes derived from the core concept of *Uncertainty* include Uncertainty and Knowledge of Death, Uncertainty and Closure, Uncertainty and Burial, and Uncertainty and Time. The emergent themes in the second core concept of *Psychology* are as follows: Psychology and Time,

Psychological Healing and Catharsis, Psychological Relief, Psychologically Shared Suffering, Victimization, and the Transgenerational Transmission of Trauma.

This chapter discusses each of the core concepts of *Uncertainty* and *Psychology* through the emergent themes that are significant factors in addressing post-violent conflict in the Cypriot context and one of the key effects of it—Missing Persons.

UNCERTAINTY AND KNOWLEDGE OF DEATH

> I have worked for twenty three years in five armed conflicts for the International Red Cross and I have seen first-hand that we human beings are designed to support a lot of suffering. We can go through a lot of things during a war, we can lose loved ones; we can lose limbs; we can be detained and tortured; we can be seriously wounded; we can be displaced and become refugees and lose everything we had. There is one thing however that we cannot stand—it's to live in total uncertainty with regard to our loved ones. This is the worst suffering of war. It gets worse with time. It is mental torture.
> (Paul-Henri Arni, interview and personal communication, August 8, 2014)

Within the particular context of Cyprus, my participants were asked about the process of exhumations and what it did for them. They expressed the relatives need to know whether their loved one was dead and where the remains lay. The majority of my participants expressed the need to rectify that uncertainty or not knowing, which is arguably a basic human psychosocial need that affects social and cultural values of mourning (Burton, 1997). For example, Turkish Cypriot CMP Scientist opines about why the CMP reunites the Missing with loved ones—"At least they know what happened to their Missing loved ones. Either he's alive or not. If he is dead, then they get to make a proper funeral for the Missing Person."

The uncertainty of the Missing Person's death brings to a halt the processes of burial and mourning. For example, Eppel (2006) and Sant-Cassia (2005) express the importance of rituals of burial and mourning within specific societies and cultures, in this case Greek and Turkish Cypriot that are part of their non-negotiable needs. The relatives and loved ones of the Missing become paralyzed because in order to fulfill the religious and cultural practices and rituals of death, the knowledge of where the dead are located is necessary. As Sevgül Uludağ, a Turkish Cypriot journalist states:

> If someone is Missing then they are neither dead nor alive. They live in the twilight zone and for the relatives of the Missing, their lives are completely paralyzed and they sit and wait, because they have not seen any proof of death, which is necessary in our cultures. Because if somebody dies, you bury them in a grave and you mourn. But for the relatives of the Missing because this

> process has been suspended, there is an endless waiting. And no matter what you would tell them, and even if logically after fifty years they would know that their seventy-year-old father could not simply be alive, still their heart refuses to believe.

The knowledge of death empowers the relatives and loved ones of the Missing in Cyprus. It gives them an opportunity to put to rest the uncertainty of whether the Missing Person is dead or alive—which is what causes the paralysis. This appears evident to CMP Staff Member. When discussing the delicate nature of the problem of recovery and identification of the Missing when bodies aren't fully articulated, (meaning they aren't complete—only fragments and a smaller number of bones are found and identified which are then reunited with relatives) he states, "I mean with these small bones and with our analysis usually come the certainty that people died, right? So that still helps people get closure. So even there, the impact isn't entirely negative."

This facet of closure is highly problematic but must be unraveled in relation to the—Missing Persons issue. Therefore, when I analyzed the data, closure came to represent a key factor in the core concepts of Uncertainty and Psychology. Next I discuss what participants stated about it—which connects to the core concept of Uncertainty.

UNCERTAINTY AND CLOSURE

Closure is a very complex and complicated concept. It is particularly complicated in relation to Missing Persons and their effect on loved ones. In reviewing the data, my study participants unpacked what they perceived and understood as the process of exhumations for relatives and loved ones in relation to closure. When there is uncertainty over a loved one's death then closure (or the processes that aid in respect to closure) can become paralyzed for the relatives.

Reunification of the Missing with their loved ones occurs during stage IV—the final stage of the process of exhumations—which includes the return of the remains of the Missing Person (CMP, *What We Do*, http://www.cmp-cyprus.org/what-we-do/phase-iv-identification-and-return-of-re/). This is what CMP Scientists call the Viewing, where relatives and family members are reunited with the remains of their loved ones.

During the Viewing the relatives are informed of all the stages involved when gathering information and evidence about their loved ones via a video presentation. A projector displays the evidence and the phases of recovery, identification, and reunification are presented in a successive order as follows: Archaeological Phase I, Anthropological Phase II, Genetic Phase III, and the Identification and Return of Remains (Phase IV) and the CMP scientists are involved in each phase.

Numerous relatives of the Missing—when they review each phase are present—so they are informed, gain knowledge and perhaps get some closure with respect to acknowledging the death of their loved ones. When the person acknowledges that their loved one is dead then the reconciliation process can begin (Jeong, 2006; Lederach, 2010; Senehi, 2011). Of particular importance to the family is whether the skeletons had any artifacts with them when they are found. An artifact is roughly defined as a specific object that aids in the identification of the person. It can be a personal belonging such as a ring, specific clothing, glasses, or memorabilia that family members and relatives and loved ones of the Missing recognize as belonging to the person. As Greek Cypriot CMP Scientist 2 states:

> It's funny the fact that they don't really care about the scientific aspect. I mean they listen. Most of them try to listen. Most of them try to follow all the facts about the exhumation; the anthropological analysis, the DNA. You see them. They are looking but they're still not a hundred percent convinced. We give them numbers, statistics, ok. I mean when they walk in—it has happened to me—families have seen a skull and they say this is him, it looks like him. It has not happened only once it has happened many times. Or they see something on the skeleton or on the clothing and that's when they are convinced. That's when they know that this person is their loved one; a cross, a ring, even shoes. Anything that they remember, anything that is tangible to them is what convinces them, not the science. This is a fact that I have seen. But this is not to say that the science is not necessary. The science brings them to the eighty to ninety percent level and the rest of the ten percent—which is the most important percentage of them being accepting and understanding and realizing that this is their person—. . . are those things that I mentioned before.

The Viewing is a very difficult process for the relatives and loved ones of the Missing when entering the second condition of the Viewing—*reunification*. This happens when all the CMP presentations are done and the relatives and loved ones are informed that the remains are indeed those of their brother, mother or father, etcetera. They then encounter the skeleton of their loved one in a second room provided by the CMP. The skeleton is laid out on a table with the utmost respect and care. This can also be seen as the beginning of the restorative process in which the acknowledgement of death and identity through restorative justice needs are met via information empowerment that the offence happened, and what has happened since is disseminated to the family (Zehr, 2002).

In this phase, after forty or more years of uncertainty, relatives and loved ones are reunited with the remains of their friend, brother, sister, mother, father or son, etcetera. The *reunification* is very intense and emotional. I observed the Viewing—*reunification* of the Missing with their loved ones—

several times and experienced heightened emotions; sadness, confusion, curiosity, pain, suffering, happiness, relief, and in some viewings emotional release and crying. One cannot claim that all uncertainty of death (linked to the skeleton's identity as that of the Missing Person) brings about full closure and final recognition that the person is truly dead, but it is a start. However, in some documented rare cases in other contexts it has taken years for relatives of the Missing to sign off that they legally recognize that the remains are their relative (Wagner, 2008). This is an overall complex process, empowered through science, knowledge, and reunification of the material reality of the skeletal remains and artifacts (when available) to loved ones. As CMP Greek Cypriot Scientist 2 notes:

> But the aspect of closure that you know what happened is of very high importance and that's what we give. In general if the whole of everyone is identified and we put this past behind us, and if we are mature enough of a society to move on from it I hope so. I really wish it can happen and I hope it will. At the end we will see.

However, closure in relation to uncertainty also brings about several issues, which often come up during the viewing process that are addressed next.

During the Viewing, the part of closure when the family deals with knowing what happened to their family member brings about questions that result in trauma. The CMP is mandated to recover, identify and return the Missing Persons to their relatives and families but is not responsible to determine culpability. In other words, who did it and/or what was the actual cause of death is not determined. As Paul-Henri Arni, Committee Member of the CMP acknowledges:

> The CMP works in the absence of a political settlement. That means we also work in the absence of a commonly agreed narrative. Our mandate and our task is limited. Once the sides agreed on a common list of Missing Persons, we were tasked with locating them, exhuming them, identifying them and returning them to their families for a dignified burial. This is a long, lengthy and expensive process to address the consequences of a large number of disappearances that took place in 1963/64 and 1974. But, it is not the CMP's responsibility to tell the circumstances and who did what; this is left to others.

Therefore, culpability is left out of the CMP's work of this long and lengthy process which is unique to the Cypriot context because of the absence of a political settlement. However, when the family goes through this process of recovery and identification trauma analysis is available to them (meaning the bodies show signs of harm) and it is recorded by the CMP. Thus, during the Viewing and reunification of relatives with their loved ones, evidence of physical trauma to the bodies (which may have led to the death) is provided by the CMP.

During the Viewings, I witnessed first-hand the explanation provided to relatives with respect to the trauma analysis of each loved one's body. This can be a very difficult task for the CMP scientist, as well as psychologically traumatic and emotional for the relatives of the Missing. Moreover, I watched relatives ask and/or receive explanations as to where the physical trauma had taken place on the body be it a gunshot wound or other means of killing the person. During the reunification of the family with the skeletal remains, the CMP scientist physically points out, and in some cases holds the skeletal remains, and explains the trauma to the relatives and loved ones. It is a very intimate moment; a grey area in which the science of identification merges with the humanization of loss and suffering.

However, trauma analysis and the transparency of knowledge, which the CMP provides and shares with relatives of the Missing, always seem to lead to the question of culpability. Who did it and why? The uncertainty of who committed the atrocity and why, and the circumstances surrounding the death are not known by CMP scientists.

CMP Scientists related to me that these questions of who and why often come up during the Viewing process. I too remained silent during the viewings, focusing only on the reunification process. As Dr. Marios Kariolou Department Head of the Laboratory of Forensic Genetics for the Cyprus Institute of Neurology and Genetics in Cyprus states, "But, ok. There are individuals on both sides that view things a little bit differently. The question is: why my relative? And that question as I said before, remains constantly on their minds."

This facet of uncertainty remains unanswered. In one way or another, it may confound the return of the remains to relatives of the Missing with closure because people are left without the knowledge of who committed the crime. For example, this leads to a responsibility and justice issue in regards to closure in which CMP Greek Cypriot Scientist 2 opines:

> But, the fact that we just do it to identify and not to place any blame is like a double edged sword. And this is my personal opinion. It is different in Bosnia: they find who did it and why, including, the aspects of prosecutions and judges and the whole process. Here it is not like that for various and many, many reasons. It is not like that. One aspect of it is that it is better because it doesn't dig up everything again and to forgive and to forget and maybe this is a better way for some people. For some people it is not, some people want justice—not some people but most people. I don't know though if justice will bring peace or if it will just prolong the problem that most families have. If you lost your father would you be ok with it? I mean, that's the question you have to ask yourself. Would you be ok with just, "yeah it's him"? But the question still remains inside of you—who did it? I think it would still remain in all of them.

Thus, questions of culpability may remain for relatives of the Missing and that might have an effect on uncertainty and closure for them.

However, Cyprus does not have a political settlement as of yet. Consequently, the advantages of uncertainty and seeking justice as part of the family's closure is briefly mentioned in the findings chapters in relation to the core concepts. The context of Cyprus is unique. In addition, when exploring closure and uncertainty Cyprus does not have a political settlement—which causes several conflicts surrounding recovery, identification, and reunification of the Missing. The CMP's focus is on the humanitarian issue of finding and returning the Missing to relatives of the Missing. For example, CMP Staff Member reflects on the relevance of uncertainty and justice; justifying the mandate as strictly humanitarian for the following reasons:

> Well here it takes place in a de-facto divided island. So the only way to work on the entire island is to do it in cooperation between both communities. It wouldn't work the other way. And we also are very peculiar in the sense that unlike in Bosnia, Cyprus hasn't seen a political settlement. And as a result of this, many things happen. But as a result of this, we have a very limited mandate. It is a strictly humanitarian mandate. We don't have a judicial mandate as Bosnian's do, who don't only exhume, they also try to establish judicially relevant information about how did people die and who might have done it. We are not interested in these questions.

With these points in mind, the uncertainty of the culpability issue (which may affect closure) in Cyprus and perhaps in other similar situations may be necessary for the strict purpose of solely reuniting the relatives of the Missing with their loved ones. This leads to certain necessities. For instance, the need for cooperation from the north (considered a de-facto state according to the international community The Turkish Republic of Northern Cyprus) and the South, in order to exhume bodies of Greek or Turkish Cypriots in the South (or North), should mean that both governments allow this process to occur because of community pressure.

As CMP Staff Member avers, "[A]t the individual family level, it addresses absolutely critical needs . . . There's enough . . . very considerable interests groups on both sides mainly made up by the families to sustain the process politically." The gathering of information—such as people identifying sites that have Missing Persons/skeletal remains—would arguably become nonexistent, stunting this humanitarian process if the information was used to punish perpetrators. For example, CMP Turkish Cypriot Scientist 3 discusses the importance of providing information and finding the Missing:

> Actually it starts before because you know without information it is not possible to recover any Missing persons. I don't know how this stuff is being organized but there are some responsible people for information. They collect

> information data and then the authority does decide. I mean the authority of the CMP decides about the sites. You know about where to go and where to excavate. So the process starts with witness information and then goes to the field.

All of my study participants discussed information gathering as a challenge as well as a necessary function of CMP work—from recognizing witnesses to key events, and hearsay (or stories)—and the necessity of finding Missing Persons. However, Greek Cypriot Scientist 2 avows in regards to the uncertainty of justice and punishment that might impact closure for the relatives that:

> Oh, no one would come forward I think because it is a much smaller community and everyone knows, even though there is no problem. But this is hearsay. I have no evidence of this, but yeah people are still scared to come forward even though nothing would happen to them. It's the social ah . . . if you say it you are not a true patriot or stuff like that happens.

Thus, in consideration of difficulties that can hamper information gathering and, therefore, the reunification of the Missing with loved ones—which complicates the family's uncertainty with regard to closure—one may argue that in certain countries like Cyprus that lack a political settlement (countries that have a large percentage of Missing Persons and a small population) may provide room for what I call *advantageous uncertainty* with regards to justice as part of the closure process. Consequently, a restorative model of justice is taking shape through the process of exhumations where relatives of the Missing are empowered by acknowledgement, truth telling, and restitution of the return of the bodies without access to retribution (Zehr, 2002).

Yet as Dr. Marios Cariolou suggests, punishment may aid in sending a message of deterrence to perpetrators and future Cypriot generations, which might be necessary for a lasting peace and so that this sort of travesty will never happen again:

> If I distance myself from the process . . . and looking at the entire program . . . I am not sure whether the people that have done and they committed these crimes . . . it's good that they will go unpunished. Again this is a personal opinion. I believe that in some way —and I'm talking for the individuals who have killed people, innocent people, from both communities—that these people should have been punished. Because this again would have given another strong message—don't do it again. But this is not the case. I think the way the CMP operates right now is that they want to find the Missing Persons and more or less inform the relatives and return the skeletal remains to their loved ones rather than punishing or concentrating on punishing. And maybe that is a good approach. But in my opinion if a crime remains unpunished then it is more likely that it will be repeated. But ok . . . this is a personal opinion.

Therefore, the truth versus justice debate as it has been called in the right to know what happened and the return of a loved one to relatives of the Missing and the right to justice through punishment most necessarily complicates the closure issue in relation to uncertainty.

However, Sarah Wagner's (2008) *To Know Where He Lies: DNA Technology And The Search For Srebrenica's Missing* discusses issues of justice versus reconciliation. The international community is punishing perpetrator's as evidenced by the emergence of internationally based interventions via international concepts of rights, such as, the rights to know and the right to justice for relatives of the Missing that were codified in national legislation law on Missing Persons in Bosnia as well as the International Criminal Tribunal for the Former Yugoslavia's (ICTY) punishment of offenders. Their effects on inter-ethnic reconciliation in Bosnia created tensions in the ethnic communities with competing victimization narratives and memorials (Wagner, 2010). In stark comparison, as Iosif Kovras suggests (2012) in the context of Cyprus community building and healing emerges as a result when the return of the Missing is done through *de-linking* humanitarian processes from politics and transitional justice formulations that deal with solving impunity from criminal law.

Further, to complicate this debate between closure and *advantageous uncertainty* as I am describing it, the question arises of whether one can have both—a sustainable and lasting peace in post-violent conflict societies that have a political settlement. Paul-Henri Arni states:

> Shall justice be delivered or shall the priority be to provide peace to the families? Because it is hard to see both done simultaneously. In countries of the former Yugoslavia it's one of the only examples where you have both. You have the humanitarian effort, which is finding the human remains, identifying and returning them to the families. That is the humanitarian aspect of the question to have families lay their pain to rest. Then there is the judicial process, which aims at punishing the culprits. In the Western Balkans they have the two. But, because of the judicial process that is going on in the Hague and in national courts, information leading to more recoveries is trickling down and almost drying up. Mainly because there is a sort of unwritten rule that if a person was a witness and he talks he will be dead the next day. In Italian it's called *omerta*—collective silence in a village for instance. No one speaks in a village and no one has heard about the massacred; of course everybody knows but no one speaks because if you start speaking you're dead. Sometimes one has to choose between helping families to turn the page and heal their pain or serving justice. In Cyprus it was clearly decided between the two sides, the two leaders, that they would privilege the humanitarian approach and not the judicial approach. So, in 1990, judicial authorities in the north and in the south wrote down a text that is still valid today whereby they provide judicial immunity from prosecutions to witnesses talking to CMP. This is why after forty or fifty years people still give us information.

Perhaps there is another way of dealing with *advantageous uncertainty*. Sevgül Uludağ mentions that Cyprus could perhaps form a Truth and Reconciliation Commission like in South Africa when dealing with culpability and punishment and in bringing about closure for families (later on or during the process of exhumations). She states the following on the issue of justice and the recovery of the Missing:

> For the moment because we need to find where they are buried we do not go after who did what. But, during the investigation all of this information comes to us but we do not publish names or point out fingers like you did this, you did that, etc. But, I'm not sure whether . . . you see we need a process like in South Africa—a Truth and Reconciliation Commission perhaps. Or, whatever the two communities decide, the two main communities of the island decide. Shall we pardon these perpetrators like in South Africa if they come and admit the crime? Shall we pardon them? Shall we put them in prison? The two communities have to decide what to do with them, but together and not separately.

The problem surrounding uncertainty in relation to closure and justice is very complex and there may be various ways to deal with it in specific contexts. But in the Cyprus context, in order to fulfill the humanitarian mandate perhaps *advantageous uncertainty* is the best solution for reunification of the relatives with their loved ones. I now examine how the process of exhumations specifically affects Cyprus. Next, we turn to burial as a core component of uncertainty.

UNCERTAINTY AND BURIAL

Burial rights, religious rights, and the cultural practices of Sunni Islamic Turkish Cypriots and Greek Cypriot Orthodox Christians are very important to both communities. My goal here is not to explain the rituals or practices of either community in relation to death—which could (and should) constitute another manuscript in itself with regards to the process of exhumations. My aim is to offer what the participants discussed as a need for the burial process to occur in relation to uncertainty and Missing Persons. Burial and rituals of religious mourning are by all accounts a non-negotiable basic human need for Greek and Turkish Cypriots because they fulfill psycho-social necessities for the relatives and consequently the communities affected by Missing Persons. These basic human needs are based upon the value system that individuals identify with culturally so that the empowerment of the bereaved is a strong argument for healing and proventing the escalation of future conflict exists (Burton, 1997). Thus, Shari Eppel's work (2006) "“Healing the Dead:” Exhumation and Reburial as Truth-Telling and Peace-Building Activities in Rural Zimbabwe," argues that it was/is the "corruption of community values and ways of being is what most offends and disturbs our survivors, and it is this loss that is still being mourned years later," (p. 263). Eppel is referring to the loss of fulfilling social and cultural practices specific to the Amani issue of Missing Persons in Zimbabwe. Hence, she contends that to "heal individuals very often has a ripple effect that leads to healing simultaneously at the level of a larger community and its value system" (p. 266).

What becomes apparent from the data is when the paralysis of the uncertainty of death comes into question, reunification of the Missing with loved ones leads to the recognition of identity that is of the utmost importance to eventually fulfill the bereaved, psycho-social basic human needs of mourning and religious burial. For example, CMP Turkish Cypriot Scientist 3calls this the *ceremony of identification*. A *release* happens when the material reality of skeletal remains reunifies with the relatives of the remains. The release of the remains/person brings about closure of the case for the CMP scientists. As CMP Turkish Cypriot Scientist 3 states:

> So at this point we arrange viewings at our anthropological laboratory coordinated together with psychologists. We set up the viewings here and participate in the viewings. Both archaeologists and anthropologists join in the viewings and we make presentations to the family and we make them understand what's going on. Every single step we show pictures, power point presentations, and we meet them and speak with them. Then after the viewing we release the bodies and that is the last thing we do. After the release the case is closed for us.

Moreover, the release of the bodies coupled with case closure for the CMP's scientists may be seen as the beginning of another metaphysical, psychological and existential dilemma release for the relatives. The relatives and loved ones of the Missing Person are empowered for the first time to physically perform the rights, rituals, and customs of death and mourning through the performance of religious burial, which some anthropologists suggest are part of a liminal stage of moving from Missing to death and burial (Sant-Cassia, 2005; Wagner, 2008) in which relatives of Missing Persons could not move through the limbo of uncertainty. As CMP Turkish Cypriot Scientist 3 observes:

> Well I believe that the families will never get peace if they have a Missing Person, relative, or a family member. There are still old people that are Missing or don't know where their son is who went Missing. It's been more than forty years sometimes. People still, I think. It is a very, very big problem for them. They want to say in a way goodbye. This ceremony of identification is like saying goodbye. They realize what happened and it is bad but at least their question mark will be no more. I think after the release the families feel much, much better.

The ceremony of identification and release of the person's remains, along with the scientific closure of the person's status from Missing to returned, offers up and challenges the physical/material paralysis with regard to now performing the rights and rituals of death and mourning. But what does that mean?

According to my participants the process of exhumations provides "proof of death, which is necessary in our cultures because if somebody dies, you bury them in a grave and you mourn," as Sevgül Uludağ says. Therefore, as Dr. Marios Cariolou emphasizes, "Now the individual has been buried according to the customs of the ethnic communities," which is very important to both communities in Cyprus as a rite of passage for Cypriots to the next life. Moreover, empowerment is associated with the release of the remains and reunification with the relatives who "they get to make a proper funeral for the Missing Person," as CMP Turkish Cypriot Scientist 1 states. Paul-Henri Arni also claims that in Cyprus it is very important to have a body and a tomb in order to perform the necessary religious rituals and that is why the CMP's work of recovering the bodies is important for the healing process:

> It does constitute in certain cultures like Cyprus a very important element. In Cyprus it is definitely one of the reasons that explain why we are still working so hard forty to fifty years after, which is a very long time after the events to recover human remains. Because for both Turkish and Greek Cypriots, Muslim and Orthodox believers it is of paramount importance to have a tomb, a body, in order to perform the rituals and restore the dignity of the person who went missing.

The remains are very important for both communities because it provides the families access to a proper funeral as well as a burial site—a place for prayer and visitation—of their loved one as CMP Turkish Cypriot Scientist 3 claims: "I think after the release the families feel much, much better. There will be a graveyard and they can go and pray and they can visit from time to time and it is very important and I think it is a very big part of the problem in Cyprus."

The release of the remains to the relatives of the Missing offers loci of mourning and prayer through funerary rites and burial; it offers them a connection to the person. Perhaps one can say that it is a psycho-material connection that aids in the closure of uncertainty—and it is a challenge to the paralysis that family members go through when their loved ones are Missing. Therefore, as CMP Greek Cypriot Scientist 2 states, "at least they know and at least they find out what happened; where they were and now they are in a better place like buried in their cultural and religious beliefs and that's the start of a process [of healing]."

Finally, family and loved ones of the Missing Person/s are further empowered with their right to decide what to do with the remains and how they will be buried. In some situations if the Missing Person was a soldier for example, he is buried in a collective memorial site and memorialized with other soldiers. Moreover, in some cases Cypriots are collectively memorialized in a mass burial site as I have seen in the North in Nicosia (in the Turkish Republic of Northern Cyprus) and in the South (in the Republic of Cyprus in Nicosia). However, as Paul Arthur suggests (2011), memorialization in the form of constructed sites can serve many purposes, in which its utilization for remembering the past as victims or triumphalism at the expense of another group is counterproductive to reconciliation (pp. 377–78).

In the final findings chapter on Storytelling, I discuss some of the facets of burial and memory. However, it is important to understand that the relatives of the Missing are empowered because the process of exhumations gives them the ability to decide what to do with the body of their loved one. This can be seen as part of the process of the beginning of mercy and justice,which represent the empowerment of individual and groups rights of restitution which are acts of reconciliation (Lederach, 2010). Particularly interesting is the fact that most relatives choose to bury their friend, sister, brother, father, mother, son, daughter, in non-communal graves. As Dr. Marios Cariolou states with regard to burial practices:

> I think in Cyprus the general rule, if I may call this a rule, is that the families would choose a grave where their loved one will be buried. They are given the choice of deciding if the person was military personnel that person can be buried in a military graveyard. If not, then the relatives can decide where that person will be buried. So I don't think we have a lot of communal graves at this point. There may be a need at the end, because . . . during the exhumation process as you probably know there are a lot of small skeletal fragments that are recovered that cannot be attributed to any individual. So these accumulate with time and at some point these would have to be buried. Although even in these cases what the authorities in Cyprus do when a mass grave is discovered and there are such skeletal elements that cannot be attributed to any single individual and the relatives are given more or less a choice to decide this by themselves. If there are seventeen in this so they will be given some of the skeletal elements or they decide where these skeletal elements will be buried together. But these in most cases will be away from the major skeletal body of their loved one. So usually we have a single grave for a single Missing Person.

Therefore, burial and funerary rights including the religious rituals of death are highly important for relatives of the Missing in Cyprus. Yet in order to properly perform those rituals of death and mourning for Cypriot relatives, the process of exhumations must be fulfilled, challenging the paralysis of knowledge of death. This leads to the ceremony of identification and therefore recognition of the Missing Person's identity, which incorporates the release of remains to families that further leads to rites of burial and the performance of religious/cultural practices that empowers them for the first time in forty years in fulfilling their non-negotiable basic human psycho-social needs. However, in some cases in the process of exhumations, the Missing Persons bodies are not fully articulated meaning—as Dr. Marios Cariolou stated they are incomplete and hard to identify. Therefore, this proves to be challenging to the process of exhumations and reunification of the Missing with loved ones. Unfortunately, commingled bones (several skeletal bones that belong to several Missing Persons) can make identification more difficult. The issue of commingled remains is further complicated by what is called secondary and tertiary mass graves, where a second crime of relocation of the Missing Persons remains is done to cover up the crime, which complicates the process of exhumations in relation to ridding the family's uncertainty of recovery, identification, and reunification of remains with relatives in the aid of closure.

Thus, it is important to take into consideration how time affects the process of exhumations that runs through the three chapters and the core concepts derived from the data. I now turn to the final component of uncertainty—time—and its effect on the process of exhumations.

UNCERTAINTY AND TIME

When I posed the study participants question three of my questionnaire: What problems arise when the processes of exhumations are done? Several concerns arose. However, I prefer to use less striking language and will instead refer to problems as challenges when discussing the process of exhumations and its effects. As Sarah Wagner has pointed out the reality of disarticulated bodies (not complete) and commingled and secondary mass graves create challenges of recovery, identification, and reunification of the Missing with loved ones (2008). The challenge that arises in post violent conflict societies can be particularly devastating to families and loved ones. For example, CMP Staff Member claims:

> CMP Staff Member: Then there's a problem of relocated graves where we only find minuscule remains of, remains that have been otherwise relocated to another place, which adds also trauma to the family that won't have a full skeleton returned but only a finger bone. It's a big psychological problem, a literal problem.

In addition, Paul-Henri Arni had the following to say on the issue:

> Paul-Henri Arni: We discover sometimes only very few remains. There was a case recently from a village where dozens of bodies were recovered—only a few of them were complete. For most of the individuals there were only a few bones. The site had been reopened years later to cover the initial crime and the

> remains, with a caterpillar had been collected and put elsewhere and they forgot the few remains that we found. This is a very serious problem.

The CMP does its best to challenge the uncertainty of identity from disarticulated bodies (incomplete remains) by providing as much completion of the Missing Person as possible to the families. As CMP Turkish Cypriot Scientist 3 states:

> You know, realizing a person is not just realizing the bones; we try to complete the body as much as we can. We don't want to give some pieces of bones. We try to make the families in a way not happy but we try to give them as much as we can, so this is another thing.

Moreover, Greek Cypriot Scientist 2 claims that in such cases, at least there is scientific evidence of why the loved ones are receiving partial remains of the Missing Person:

> Ok, there are some cases where certain things have happened, such as, that we either don't find complete skeletons. Those are problems that happen during identification when they come to the Viewing and they have problems in the sense that where is the skull and where is his leg and why is he not complete and all of these questions. I don't see it as a major problem. Usually and most of the time we have all the explanations that we scientifically can gather to explain why certain elements are Missing.

Thus, the CMP does its best to return complete bodies to loved ones to close the gap between uncertainty and the identity of their loved ones. However, as Dr. Marios Cariolou claims, in such cases distrust may arise between the communities because of questions as to why the skeletons are incomplete and how did relocation occur in the first place. Dr. Cariolou goes on to say the following:

> Ah well . . . I am not quite sure whether this question refers to the scientific or the political, or the society . . . cause I can start saying that . . . it is very, very difficult when some of the remains or parts of the remains are found of an individual. The relatives wish to have the entire skeletal remains. And . . . if that is not the case of course they ask a lot of questions again. This creates a un-trust. They do not trust the other side because they believe that their loved ones have been moved to another place and that other place is not relieved. So that doesn't help bringing the two communities together. So . . . one of the problems is partial remains will lead to questions and they will increase questions from either side and of course this does not help the reconciliation process. Now, if we do not have partial remains and we assume we have the recovery of whole skeletal remains then initially I believe that . . . again, it raises questions why my loved one had to die in this way but eventually it does bring reconciliation in the long run. We have examples of Greek Cypriots' and

> Turkish Cypriots' relatives getting together after the identification of loved ones. Now other problems, I cannot think of any other problems right now.

Therefore, it is important to notice that the return of fully articulated bodies is important so the question arises why are Missing Persons remains only partial? There are many factors and reasons that can be conveyed here but I will only mention a few. These include the relocation of remains to cover up the crime as well as environmental factors and change such as river systems that carry remains away and the building of roads etcetera, and the effect of time as a key significance that creates challenges for the process of exhumations. Time in itself is a major factor in reducing uncertainty in the recovery of remains, artifacts, and reunification and recognition of a loved one for relatives of the Missing. Further, in examining time and its relationship to uncertainty the longer that the process of exhumations takes, it can be argued that the harder it is to fully recover articulated remains and artifacts. As Sevgül Uludağ points out the topography changes—meaning that the land changes over time making it harder to find burial sites:

> The second big problem is that physically the geography has changed dramatically and I bring witnesses to possible burial sites and sometimes they cannot recognize the area because things have changed; a new road has been built, trees have been cut, there is an apartment there.

Another factor that further complicates the recovery and identification of remains when finding the burial sites is the displacement of artifacts or personal memorabilia belonging to the Missing. The passage of time affects corroborating evidence of memorabilia and the deliberate hiding of identities in some cases reduces the chances of Missing Persons recovery and recognition. As stated by CMP Greek Cypriot Scientist 2:

> Artifacts are very important but due to the fact that it has been so long it is rarer to get solid evidence or corroborating evidence from artifacts because it is always a fact that people were changing their clothes; people were trying to escape; people were trying to hide; people were trying to not to have identities on them so as to avoid problems and this is another issue concerning artifacts.

Henceforth, time can be critical in the recovery, identification and reunification of the Missing with loved ones. For example, Sevgül Uludağ points out several effects of time on the process of exhumations which relates to the uncertainty of reunification of the Missing with their loved ones. She states that not actively searching and cooperating to find the Missing constitutes a second crime in itself:

> The relatives of victims . . . you see what's different about Cyprus from Bosnia is that there is a second crime. The first crime is making the people Missing.

> The second crime is that both sides in Cyprus, Turkish Cypriots and Greek Cypriots, they did not start actively searching and cooperating to find them; they waited forty years at least and in the meantime witnesses died, perpetrator's died, geography changed completely, roads were built and houses were built over the burial sites so it became more difficult to find them. The relatives in pain waiting for forty years or fifty years. When the digging began in 2005 and 2006 they got excited and they expected. They are still waiting, most of them.

Thus, the lapse of time can be understood as critical in the process of exhumations for the recovery of remains, artifact recovery and corroborating evidence for identification, which is critical with respect to peacebuilding via reconciliation. However, it must be stated that the point of discussing time in this work is not to make moral judgments because several debates may arise about the right time strategically and politically to mandate the process of exhumations for reasons of peacebuilding after violent conflict. For example, Ho-Won Jeong's (2005) *Peacebuilding in Post Conflict Societies: Strategy and Process* discusses the evaluation of peacebuilding processes and outcomes with respect to time:

> While peacebuilding continues to be directed mainly at conflict management, its ultimate success will be judged in terms of the effectiveness of policy instruments designed for addressing the root causes of violent conflict . . . There are different interpretations of what should be considered success because of a lack of clear agreement on criteria and a time frame . . . Peace is not likely to be achieved in a linear time frame and with a single area of focus . . . As progress varies in diverse sectors, some peacebuilding components may be considered more important than others in determining success (pp. 35–36).

The point here is to bring about the question of how *time* affects the process of exhumations and its power to heal and reconcile that includes relatives memories of loved ones of the Missing, iterated through stories that also affect the remembering of geographical locations of the whereabouts of the Missing (Senehi, 2012). Consequently, it is clear that time affects the science of recovery, identification, and perhaps reunification through recognition of the Missing with loved ones. With this in mind, I now turn to the second core concept of this chapter—Psychology—and begin with examining how time affects the relatives and loved ones of the Missing psychologically, from the perspective of the study participants.

PSYCHOLOGY AND TIME

It has been said that time heals all wounds. Yet according to the study participants no it does not and cannot in the case of Missing Persons. Therefore, my goal here is to present what the participants have to say about what the process of exhumations does in relation to the psychology of the relatives of the Missing. Further, the psychological realities of absence, loss, grief and mourning intersect with Burton's (1990) Basic Human Needs in that it impacts the relatives of the Missing in post-violent conflict societies that arguably affects the Greek and Turkish Cypriot societies at large.

What Sevgül Uludağ stated at the beginning of this chapter is very powerful in relating time and psychology so I will repeat it again here:

> If someone is Missing then they are neither dead nor alive. They live in the twilight zone and for the relatives of the Missing their lives are completely paralyzed and they sit and wait because they have not seen any proof of death which is necessary in our cultures because if somebody dies you bury them in a grave and you mourn. But for the relatives of the Missing, because this process has been suspended, there is an endless waiting and no matter what you would tell them and even if logically after fifty years they would know that their seventy-year-old father could not simply be alive, still their heart refuses to believe.

As Sevgül Uludağ notes a paralysis psychologically stops processes of time and in many cases healing because relatives are always waiting for the return of their loved ones. A prominent psychologist and scholar on the Cyprus conflict Dr. Vamik Volkan claims, "Humans cannot accept change without mourning what has been lost" (Volkan, 1997, p. 36). The stages of mourning the death of a loved one include: 1) Crisis Grief, which includes shock, denial, bargaining, sadness, and feeling anger; and 2) next, follows the stage of mourning, which helps the mourner assimilate and adapt to reality (Volkan, 1997). The mourning stage accepts the loss of the person that brings about closure so that the survivor can move on. Unfortunately, things can go terribly wrong, such as the formation of *perennial mourners*, where the "perennial mourner unconsciously remains in a state of limbo" (Volkan, 1997, p. 38) particularly with respect to not knowing what has happened to a loved one. This individual process is very similar to large groups who also mourn moving from absence to loss. Sevgül Uludağ offered an example of how psychologically traumatizing waiting can be especially for the wives of the Missing men:

> So last year, I brought together a group of painters for the first time in our history. And we do everything without funding and this is our principle; we don't apply for projects because it's not about money, it's about the humanitarian issue and everybody should volunteer, we think. And what we did was first, we had the artists sit together with relatives from the Missing from both sides and we told them, "What does it mean to have a Missing Person in the family"? They listened to them. Then we visited homes of relatives of Missing [Persons] from both sides and they saw what it means to wait. They saw how a

> woman polishes her husband's shoes still, after forty years . . . and all of his clothes are hanging and ready because she thinks if he comes back, they should be ready. If you go anywhere on earth to the house of the relative of the Missing—especially the wives—it is the cleanest house on earth because they wait . . . any moment the husband will come, so everything should be ready.

From the example above, it is apparent that the traumatic effects of time (waiting for reunification of the Missing with loved ones) dramatically stunt the psychological processes of loss and healing even after forty years or more. Sevgül Uludağ further states that people who have gone through major traumatic experiences become psychologically paralyzed at that specific age, if they do not receive psychological help:

> I realized through my research—that of investigation and through sitting together with relatives, through storytelling—that whatever age you were traumatized at; if you were five and you witnessed something or you saw something, something dramatic happened to your family; or if you were twelve, or if you were seventeen emotionally . . . if you are not getting any psychological help, you stay at that age. You never grow up.

As some trauma scholars suggest the unfortunate consequences of sustained trauma (the psycho-social needs of death and mourning) and not dealing with a traumatic event can lead to Post-Traumatic Stress Disorder (PTSD) (Herman, 1997; Volkan, 1997) in which "psychological trauma is an affliction of the powerless" (Herman, 1997, p.33). This statement becomes particularly damning when the traumatic effects of waiting for a loved one to come home (or waiting for news about what happened to them) are not realized. Hence, the effects of PTSD may be realized. The following story by Greek Cypriot Scientist 2 is an example of what happens in the reunification phase of the process of exhumations during the Viewing.

> Yeah, most of them feel very happy, very relieved after everything, after all the crying and all the pain that they feel. They still feel the pain. But, they do express admiration for what we do and what we see. Most of them don't even know what to expect when they come here. I mean it's not something within normal life. Life and death has always been, but missing someone and not knowing if they are dead and not knowing what you are going to come and see after forty years [is different]. One family brought a suit with them to dress their Missing, their loved one, but it was all bones. How can you? I mean I am trying to tell you . . . they don't know what they are going to see. It is a much unexpected thing, unexpected process and no one really talks about it.

Thus, one can ponder how the memory of a loved one and the traumatic fact that s/he is still Missing has paralyzed the person from the initial violent conflict during the 1960s and in 1974. I now turn to what the study participants had to say about the psychological dimension of healing and the process of exhumations that challenges the paralysis of time and change.

PSYCHOLOGICAL HEALING AND CATHARSIS

When the study participants were asked their opinion about what the process of exhumations accomplishes they all said that *it aids in the process of healing*. In particular, these conclusions came in response to two questions in my questionnaire (See Appendix A); question five: *Does the process of exhumation facilitate the process of healing for individuals and society? Or does it increase communal trauma?* And question eight: *Does the process of exhumations only provide the identification of victims or does it also provide community healing, reconciliation, and bring about closure as an aspect of peacebuilding?* Paul-Henri Arni had this to say:

> Every identification diminishes, digit by digit, the antagonism between communities. Basically, when people have not been given human remains of their loved ones who went missing they shout publicly. They are very harsh on the authorities and harsh on the other side. You saw that in the Balkans a lot. But, when people receive the remains they go from public anger to private mourning. They talk to their loved ones on their new tomb after all these years—for them to catch up for what they missed—and this becomes another process, which is more intimate and more painful. But it's part of the healing process, therefore it contributes digit by digit to diminish the tensions between the communities. You can't measure that. There is no Geiger counter to measure this sort of toxic feeling in a community but we see it and it does contribute Missing Person by Missing Person to diminish the antagonism and the hatred.

I now turn to how the participants of the study unpack and express the healing process.

PSYCHOLOGICAL RELIEF

What does it mean to be relieved? Moreover, what does it mean when someone has been waiting over forty years to be reunited with their Missing Person? Their loved one? And what happens when they finally are reunited? It has been suggested that moving from trauma to healing is based on "Recovery, therefore, [it] is based upon the empowerment of the survivor and the creation of new connections" (Herman, 1997, p.133). Thus, during the process of exhumations old connections are reformed and new ones emerge as expressed by the reunification process of the Missing with loved ones that empowers the survivor.

During the reunification of relatives with their loved ones in the Viewing process, I remember experiencing many reactions, as well as seeing, hearing, and feeling many emotions such as angst, sadness, crying, sorrow and even quiet deafness, among others. As I write this, I recall walking into the second room in which two sisters saw their older brother for the first time in over forty years. He was lying on a white tablecloth. He had gone Missing and they waited to know what had happened to him for over forty years; and now they knew.

As I leaned against the wall on the inside of the room near the door, I watched in sorrow as the sisters sat in two chairs next to his skull. My knees buckled and I felt the density of the air thicken with emotion. They reached out with their hands ever so delicately and held his skull. They were positioned on either side of him. Slowly but surely both sisters pressed their heads against his skull, kissed him, and wept. All the while they wept as they held their heads close to his, holding firm. They were finally reunited with their older brother, with their past, present and future unfolding before them. I too began to shed tears and I told myself, "Be strong Kristian," but I realized in that moment that sharing in this powerful experience was being strong, so I too, cried. In fact, this powerful emotion led everyone in the room to cry. It was a gigantic release of what I am still not quite sure. Perhaps, our crying and release of emotions was related to a *relief experience*.

In reviewing the data, the word relief continuously comes up. For instance, Greek Cypriot Scientist 2 expresses his perception of the Viewing process as a relief of finding and being reunited with their loved one for families of the Missing:

> Yeah, of course there is shock. In the one-hour, one and a half hour, maximum two hour viewing experience, you see people going through shock or amazement—not speaking, crying. And towards the end, thinking, and feeling. You see the relief in people's eyes. The relief is the best for us, for me personally when I feel that they have been informed adequately, scientifically, and responsibly by us and they are satisfied, you see the satisfaction in their eyes, the relief. That's the best we can do and the best we can give. And that's all we can do.

This relief and release of emotion (that one could claim has been bottled up for decades) may come as a shock and feel initially traumatic. However, as Dr. Marios Cariolou claims, reconciliation with the reality of the person's death from the finding of remains, and access to burial customs ultimately brings relief to the family:

> . . . Well, definitely at the very beginning I think it's extremely traumatic. But again, it's exactly as any other individual who dies . . . initially there is a

trauma. But then after that, I think people more or less reconcile with the idea and I believe there is a relief from the fact that the skeletal remains have been found, they have been identified and now the individual has been buried according to the customs of the ethnic communities. So, initially there may be a trauma but at the end there will be reconciliation.

In addition, the participant Professor from one of the Universities in Cyprus stated that the cornerstone of the issue in Cyprus is the trauma that people feel, but that the process of exhumations can bring about relief for some in relation to the trauma of finding loved ones:

The point, the bottom line is that people still live with their trauma. Trauma is let's say, is the cornerstone of this issue . . . I really don't know if there is a healing process for individuals and even society. Even if they exist—the Missing Persons you know—some of them have been recognized but through excavations, cemeteries, in different areas through occupied territories and free territories. The point is that maybe some people feel relief because of this; because they found their people and graved them and so on but generally speaking it's a huge trauma. I cannot find another word, you know that, and this maybe says a lot.

He goes on further to say that he does not think that the process of exhumations directly relates to peacebuilding because the major issue for the Cyprus conflict and the peacebuilding process has to do with security issues and the standing foreign armies in the north and south. Nevertheless, the Professor also claims "But at the same time the process of exhumations when it gives the identification of the victim, it brings with it a relief. And psychologically it contributes in certain ways."

Perhaps this process is not directly related to peacebuilding in a top down approach where politicians or other major figures are influencing a peace process between the north and south toward creating a final political settlement. However, maybe the process of exhumations effects peacebuilding in a horizontal or bottom up process through the transformation of relationships (Lederach, 1995) between both ethnic communities—Turkish and Greek Cypriot in which reconciliation as a cornerstone of peacebuilding is about the building of relationships between the conflicting groups for forging a sustainable peace (Lederach, 2010), within and between the Missing and relatives, CMP workers, and conflicting groups.

For example, Greek and Turkish Cypriots work bicommunally (the Viewing phase being the only exception) through all the phases of the process of exhumations. In the next chapter, I discuss the nature of the bicommunal expression of the CMP's work, but the reason I mention it here is because even though CMP Turkish Cypriot Scientist 1 was not at any of the Greek Cypriot relatives' Viewing process, he still claims that families and loved ones are very grateful to both Turkish and Greek Cypriot scientists who bicommunally aid in the return of their relatives. This has been his experience about all Cypriots working to find their Missing:

> I am a Turkish Cypriot and I don't know what's happening at the Greek Cypriot viewings. More or less it is the same procedure but we don't know what the families reactions are if they don't send a thank you to us and only tell the scientists that were at the viewing. From my experience they are saying thank you for this issue and it doesn't matter whether you're a Turkish Cypriot or Greek Cypriot. One or two times a Turkish Cypriot family came with flowers and they said to us, "This is not only for the Turkish Cypriot scientists—it is for both scientists: Turkish Cypriot and Greek Cypriot scientists. Can you tell that we are saying thank you to you? And can you tell them thank you."

This does not happen in all cases but it is a very powerful representation of how important the return of remains can be and perhaps also in regards to repairing relations between the two communities. However, the question arises about whether this process allows for psychological closure and healing for relatives of the Missing? It seems apparent that a cathartic release of emotion occurs in reunification during the "ceremony of identification" (as one of the CMP scientists called it). Therefore, relief can emerge as a powerful psychological effect, yet the question remains . . . does closure surely follow?

PSYCHOLOGICAL CLOSURE

Discussing closure psychologically, particularly in relation to the reunification of the Missing with loved ones is such a difficult task because the concept seems loaded and superficial. Yet the very nature of this grandiose closure concept serves us well. Rather than disregard it, we must unravel it in order to get to how participants view it with their expertise in regards to the reunification of the Missing with loved ones. Therefore I now briefly review several words that came up in the interviews with regards to closure: *relief* was repeatedly mentioned; *healing* as mourning and burial; *grieving*; and finally *pain*. One scholar who articulates well the notion of loss with respect to the context of relatives and the issue of Missing Persons is the prominent therapist Dr. Pauline Boss. In opening up the discussion of mourning the loss of a loved one and grieving, in which the death of a loved one is unexpected or unknowable she created the category of *ambiguous loss* (Boss, 1999). The two types of ambiguous loss with respect to Missing Persons are: 1) People are physically absent but remain psychologically present. Therefore, even if the person is presumed dead and her/his remains are not found and the family are left pre-occupied with the loss psychologically; and, 2) Physical presence of the relative in mourning but psychological absence, in which relatives of the Missing are emotionally and cognitively unavailable to those around them (Boss, 2002). As Boss states (2002):

> Both types of ambiguous loss can occur in the same family. For example, families affected by the attack on the World Trade Center may have included a Missing parent whose remaining partner is so depressed and preoccupied with the Missing mate that children are ignored and feel as if they have lost both parents—one physically, the other psychologically (p. 39).

This loss can lead to *frozen grief* due to the physical or psychological unexpected loss of a loved one that paralyzes healing thus freezing the psychological state of grief and process of grieving for the family members (Boss, 1999). However, when there is no body to bury closure should not be expected or required but having the body of a loved one empowers the family to let go of it (Boss, 2002). Therefore, I elaborate on what the study participants said with regard to how these words/concepts came up that aid in our understanding of how powerful the process of exhumations is with respect to healing and relief from ambiguous loss and frozen grief.

Turkish Cypriot Scientist 3 states in relation to closure that, "People still, I think . . . it is a very, very big problem for them. They want to say in a way, goodbye." The relatives of the Missing want and need to mourn through their religious rituals and cultural practices. As Sevgül Uludağ states (which can be related to closure) "for the relatives of the Missing their lives are completely paralyzed and they sit and wait because they have not seen any proof of death which is necessary in our cultures because if somebody dies you bury them in a grave and you mourn."

The process of ritualized mourning has been suspended for loved ones of the Missing and therefore so has its psychological effects on facets of closure. For instance, one major feature that relates to mourning and death is the ability to go through the psychological processes of grieving as suggested by many theories on normal grieving processes such as Freud on mourning and melancholia (Freud in Strachy J. (Ed), 1961); Lindeman's normal and pathological grief (Lindemann, 1944); Kubler-Ross five stages of grief via denial, anger, bargaining, depression, acceptance (Kubler Ross, 1969); Bowlby's phases of attachment theory and grief (Bowlby, 1973); Parkes grief as process and phases(Parkes, 1996); and Warden's passive to active tasks of mourning (Warden, 1991). That are all described succinctly in Buglass's article "Grief and Bereavement Theories" (Buglass, 2010). However, because it is so important in Cypriot religious and cultural practices for families to have a body (or for that matter to know what has happened to a loved one), the grieving processes become paralyzed or frozen so that grieving and healing is uniquely tied to Boss's theory of *ambiguous loss* (Boss, 1999, 2002). As CMP Staff Member avows about the process of exhumations, "In most general terms . . . it puts an end to a good extent to the uncertainty that families have . . . and it allows them to start grieving to bring that to some kind of closure you know. That's at the family level." Therefore, the reunification of the Missing with relatives empowers the survivor's psychological processes of grieving which is arguably, a necessary facet of mourning and closure in which *relief* from uncertainty and frozen grief is an important concept of psychological healing adding to the literature of grieving.

Moreover, the question arises whether complete closure is even possible in circumstances where a relative or loved one has gone Missing and their right to life has been violated in the midst of horrible circumstances. Thus, as CMP Greek Cypriot Scientist 2 claims, the pain may always be there even after reunification: "Yeah, most of them feel very happy, very relieved, after everything, after all the crying and all the pain that they feel. They still feel the pain. But, they do express admiration for what we do and what we see." Further, as CMP Turkish Cypriot Scientist 3 states, "Well I think complete closure is not possible because the social memory is not very easy to have complete closure."

Closure becomes even more confounding in relation to the psychological processes of healing and pain. But this begs important questions such as should complete closure even exist or matter in the context of post-violent conflicts regarding Missing Persons? Does complete closure compel a presupposed notion of moving on and the extinction of pain for relatives and loved ones? I am not quite sure. Yet, when reviewing the interview data, a very interesting concept emerged in terms of shared suffering, or the sharing of pain. What could this mean, if anything, for closure and the potential for lasting peace between Greek and Turkish Cypriots?

PSYCHOLOGICALLY SHARED SUFFERING

Pain and trauma can be debilitating and stunt a person's process of change. Yet perhaps when the pain of uncertainty changes into the pain of loss, death, and mourning, it becomes beneficial to go through the co-creative rise of a *shared suffering*. In other words, there may be advantageous parts of pain and loss in creating a common space of suffering for relatives of the Missing for both Turkish and Greek Cypriots. In this process they would no longer see one another as antagonistic forces but as human beings (for e.g., a mother, father, brother, son, daughter, etcetera) Missing their loved ones in the exact same way—both literally and emotionally—and who feel the same pain. Volkan (1997) claims that an event that damages the tissue of a community caused by another group of people, the enemy, formulates feelings of helplessness, trauma, and humiliation, which can cause post-traumatic stress disorder (PTSD). Therefore, an internalized version of trauma stays with the victims who relive the trauma in an imaginary but very real way. An internal theatre of victim, victimizer, and rescuer encapsulates a play of the mind. Thus, Volkan (1997) claims "One of the ways to deal with this shared dilemma is for individuals to 'envelop' their traumatized (imprisoned) self-representations (images) and externalize and control them outside of themselves" (p. 42). A slippery slope can emerge in which people view themselves as victims and others as victimizers or in which through the empowerment of the process of exhumations people can actively engage with the process becoming agents of change and sharing in a narrative of a common suffering inter-ethnically. For example, as CMP Turkish Cypriot Scientist 1 states from his experience:

> I see some Greek Cypriots or Turkish Cypriots turning around in Cyprus and trying to find [their] loved ones. While he is doing this he is helping the other side. To find his Missing relative he is also . . . [trying] to find other people's Missing relatives. I know some people; let's say . . . Turkish Cypriots who are not only looking for themselves, (some of them), they are also looking for the Greek Cypriot's Missing people—trying to find them—because some people can see that he is suffering and he can understand the other one is also suffering. So he tries to help . . .

This example of the survivor's acknowledgement of common suffering—through compassion and understanding of another human being's pain—has evidently led to mutual aid and cooperation between the relatives of both Turkish and Greek Cypriots when it comes to finding their loved ones. This driving force and humanization of the conflict can be seen as a very powerful catalyst in terms of reconciliation between the two communities and in the transformation of their relationships in which acknowledgment, compassion, and making things right are components of reconciliation (Lederach, 2010). As CMP Staff Member claims, it demonstrates to both sides that they face the same hardships, pain, and suffering and their need to reduce hatred:

> First of all the people that we work with that we hire don't have this hatred because otherwise they wouldn't want to work on a project like ours. Well it certainly—if at all—helps to remove it (hatred) because usually one of the things it does is to show both sides that you know they face exactly the same hardships, emotional pain, and suffering families. So that's a healthy effect to make people recognize that there are victims on both sides and they have exactly the same problems. It certainly doesn't exacerbate hatred in the country.

Thus in the act of recovery, identification, and reunification, a common ground is revealed that allows room for the recognition of a shared victimization through the pain of Missing Persons and the ensuing shared problems. Also, culpability and retribution is left out of the political context in regards to the process of exhumations as a humanitarian mandate, which might provide *advantageous uncertainty* in the formation of a common suffering (and therefore, a common victimization narrative from a third party) takes shape on Cyprus. This third party remains unidentified as being of Greek or Turkish ethnicity, and as a culprit of violent acts or as a collective community entity. This third party is rather, simply an unnamed perpetrator of a crime—an unidentifiable *uncertain* third party. This process creates room for a common victimization narrative to emerge. Dr. Marios Cariolou expresses this notion of an unidentifiable victimizer that aids in forming bonds between families of the Missing below:

> . . . The majority of the people will understand that even the relatives on the other side, and of course, since they don't know who has actually pulled the trigger to kill the individuals, they more or less sympathize. It brings families together—both Greek Cypriots and Turkish Cypriots—because they know that their loved ones more or less have suffered in the hands of the third individual, the same things. So it does bring them together.

Moreover, when it comes to post-violent conflict societies, the narrative of victimization for a particular group can be detrimental in terms of forging reconciliation and inter-communal relationships between ethnic groups creating an us and them relation with us as the victim and them as the victimizer. This can become very dangerous when moralized into us as good/virtuous, righteous and innocent victims and them as bad/unvirtuous, wrongdoers who are victimizers and therefore enemies. When such Manichean binary formations of good versus evil are instilled in a group, a slippery slope exists that may escalate groups into violence—or lead to the reoccurrence or repetition of tragic circumstances from the history of their past. Therefore, I now briefly turn to what the participants related to me about how Turkish and Greek Cypriots feel in relation to victimization, which arguably effects future generations.

VICTIMIZATION AND PSYCHOLOGICAL TRANSGENERATIONAL TRANSMISSION OF TRAUMA

Sevgül Uludağ claims that a realization of a common pain can create a common future in the wake of the next generations. She states, "If we realize we have a common pain we can use it to create a common future because we don't want this pain to continue for other generations." Therefore, an emergent understanding of a common pain caused by violent conflict (Missing Persons) when addressed through the process of exhumations may bridge people's horizons and create a space of recognition in which Greek and Turkish Cypriots are both victims of a third party and tragic circumstances.

When answering question seven from my questionnaire (See Appendix A): *Does the process of exhumations relieve community guilt, or does it allow for the victim narrative to be dominant for victim or perpetrator*, the responses were very common. The study participants related to me that the victim narrative is already entrenched on both sides and the process of exhumations does not exacerbate victimization narratives. As CMP Staff Member states, "Well . . . the victim narrative is entrenched on both sides. There is nothing you have to do to bring that about. It's already there." Further, Dr. Marios Cariolou claims that he has not seen an exacerbation of victimhood from burials of the Missing. However, he states that it can create patriotic feelings when symbols of nationalism are used during the burial process:

> To be honest, I have seldom seen this. Surely, it creates patriotic feelings and that's why we always have the national anthem and flags and symbols like that during the burials of the skeletal remains of Missing Persons . . . however I don't think that I have seen "ok, we have become victims and let's go and get them" in most cases.

Further and congruent with Dr. Marios Cariolou's statement is Greek Cypriot Scientist 2's who argues that the feeling of victimization is up to the individual after reunification with the Missing but if it continues to exist, then forgiveness of the perpetrator(s) will be difficult. Yet he also expresses that there are people who are willing to forgive and that's a start. Moreover, it also depends on how the politicians portray victimization and the process of exhumations in maintaining a victim narrative. This is what Greek Cypriot Scientist 2 had to say on the issue:

> It is down to the individual. If you are going to feel victimized then your ideas will not change. The fact that someone killed your father probably won't change it if you still feel victimized. Everything that is happening to you is the result of this conflict or that you lost your father in your life is bad. The thing is, it is down to the individuals. We cannot change peoples' perceptions. We can only give them this answer—"here is your relative." What you do with the answer is down to the person individually and generally what the politicians do with these things and what they do with these answers. If they propagate the fact that everyone is victimized and that we have been under the rule and this and that it doesn't help. But there are people who understand and who are ready to forgive. At least if these people exist it's a beginning and it's a start.

It has been claimed by scholars that nationalism (Byrne, 2000; Anastasiou, 2008) and extreme forms of nationalism (Volkan, 1998) can increase the likelihood of violence between ethnic groups. Further, high political agendas definitely manipulated the process of exhumations in Cyprus for their own gain affecting people's healing and grieving processes of mourning and efforts to bring about closure (Sant-Cassia, 2005). Therefore, I examine nationalism and the process of exhumations in the storytelling chapter of this work and continue here with the observations of other study participants about victimization and trauma.

As a University Professor from Cyprus states (a point similarly made by Greek Cypriot Scientist 1) victimization is an individual and family dependent reality and that people feel they are victims of history in Cyprus as a result of several factors but that trauma still remains as the dominant factor in Cypriot society:

> It's a question that goes to each individually, to the family. It depends on the family, it depends on the individual. But definitely when you talk with them and when you interact with them you will see that they carry with them the trauma and therefore they feel victims of history. They feel the atrocities of history. They are victims in their own country by a history that is/was created by Turkey, Britain, the Junta of Athens; all of these factors play an important role in a way when we talk about the Cyprus issue today. Again the bottom line is that definitely the exhumation process is a process that does not give an answer to everything because people still feel angry. It is something that still dominates everyday narratives. If you scratch the body of language I would say of each person you would find lots of things. If you go deeper and deeper you will see there is something . . . a trauma still remains as a dominant factor in our society.

Keeping in mind that it has been over forty years since the violence of the 1960s and 1974 campaigns in Cyprus the question arises, how is this trauma maintained? It is important to comprehend this point to appreciate what the University Professor stated about "trauma as a dominant factor in our society." Perhaps, this is a loaded question and there are many answers and more questions. However, in appreciating what my study participants have stated about victimization as a dominant force on both sides of the island and for both ethnic groups, it should be noted that both Greek and Turkish Cypriots see themselves as innocent and do not feel guilt for the calamities and tragedies of loss from the conflict of the past. For example, Turkish Cypriot CMP Scientist 1 states, "Because both sides believe they are innocent," and the trauma may be transmitted transgenerationally—meaning to Cypriot children and their children and so on. Vamik Volkan (1998) defines the *transgenerational transmission of trauma* as "when an older person unconsciously externalizes his traumatized self onto a developing child's personality" (p. 43) with "feelings of helplessness pertaining to the trauma of his forebears" (p. 43) and by adding the ambiguity to the loss of a loved one the results can be "agonizing and immobilizing" even across generations (Boss, 2002, p.40). Therefore, there is arguably a chance that the transmission of trauma in a real sense and its paralysis is aiding in the maintenance of the Cyprus conflict in which the process of exhumations is attempting to dispel the factors that aid in the transmission of trauma such as uncertainty of death.

Further, Vamik Volkan's theory of *chosen trauma* in which nation-states and politicians popularize and sustain past events by choosing historical moments of trauma or triumph against a perceived enemy or group influences the next generations world view as well (Volkan, 1997). As Paul-Henri Arni has experienced (working on Missing Persons with the International Red Cross in many countries) when history is not confronted up front it can repeat its tragedies, time and again. Here he recalls what happened in the Former Yugoslavia in the early 1990s—historical reoccurrence of violence:

> History is made of grey areas and not of black and white. But in the Balkans it was black and white for several consecutive conflicts since 1877 that effected six generations. So in every family you had a clear vision of who were your great grandfather's enemy, your grandfather's enemy, your father's enemy, and your own enemy as a result. In the absence of history written by independent historians, people were left, generation after generation, with the deadly mix of family trauma, including missing loved ones, and nationalistic views on history.

Thus, many of the study participants discussed the importance of the process of exhumations in changing the transgenerational transmission of a victimization narrative and trauma to the next generations. And for that matter, the repercussions of tragedy and history stayed buried and Missing. For instance as Turkish Cypriot CMP Scientist 1 claims:

> But if you have these kinds of problems (Missing Persons), they are important individually for the families and very important for the social groups. It is always a problem that you killed the people and you don't tell them and you keep it. Or you took them as a prisoner and you don't know where they are. And both sides said/say this. So when we solve this problem (Missing Persons) the formal negotiation will be open and people will not have any excuse to continue to hate each other maybe after a generation; because if I tell my son that your grand uncle, grandmother or grandfather is Missing and we never found him and at least we see that no one is doing anything for them; he will tell it to his son that Greeks are bad they did this to my grand grandfather. At least some years later I think people will stop saying "other people, others did this to my family."

As stated earlier because families, relatives, and extended families are affected by having a Missing Person in their family, their stories and their feelings of trauma and conflict are transmitted to future generations *vertically* to direct descendants and *horizontally* to extended family members and relatives. Therefore, one can argue so is the possibility of their trauma, pain, and anger because of the uncertainty of what has happened. The processes of burial, mourning, and healing have been stunted and paralyzed. However, because of the process of exhumations and the reunification policy of the Missing Person with family members and relatives, at least something was/is done about finding their Missing one's by a bicommunal organization in which a lot of family members are present including extended family members (new generations/grandchildren). I witnessed this personally. This holds the potential to affect the transgenerational transmission of trauma and even the healing process itself. Dr. Marios Cariolou reflected on this issue in the following way:

> Yes. Actually, in the Cyprus project when the relatives will be shown the remains—and of course this is done at a special facility and in most cases during that time there will be a lot of relatives coming in—close and distant relatives. Distant relatives often provide support for the closest relatives because it is more likely they will be the ones most affected by this process, because when they go into this room and they see this skeletal body lying on a table it's not the easiest thing and surely it is very traumatic. Yes, we see this quite often that you will have a lot of family members, relatives, coming in together to provide support to each other. And of course, there are also provisions from the community to the families via psychologists, etc. It's part of the process. And I think it's an essential part of the process.

Many people including the nuclear family, close and distant relatives and new generations are affected by the process of exhumations directly during the Viewing process and otherwise, where understanding and knowledge is transmitted regarding the mistakes of the past in hopefully a new direction, which empowers the next generations. As Dr. Marios Cariolou states:

> Well one of the things emerging from this process, (of the identification process), is that younger people understand the mistakes that their fathers or their parents have done. And this definitely gives them an example not to follow because they realize that . . . killing somebody creates a lot of pain and this pain sometimes really takes . . . sometimes would take a lot of years to disappear. If it ever disappears. I don't know if it ever does. This is something that you need to ask a relative. I assume it probably doesn't. It's probably . . . it's somewhere buried. But it's an example for the new generation not to do these horrible things that some people have done. Killing innocent individuals of course . . . making them Missing, putting them into this Missing Person's catalogue. We hope that younger people will learn from our mistakes. Again, this brings (I believe) some reconciliation and brings the communities together.

In addition, Sevgül Uludağ avows that it is the acknowledgement of what was done and its tragic outcome of Missing Persons that challenges the in-group and out-group mentality, where one group perceives the other community as an *Other*. As she states, this perception will continue generationally unless there is an acknowledgment of common suffering and loss from both sides. "If we don't acknowledge what we did to each other then there is no future for Cyprus, because that healing of being a victim and making the other community the other will always remain, and will pass from generation to generation—the stories and everything."

As most of the study participants of the study state, if a political settlement is reached without reconciling or attempting to reconcile the Missing with their loved ones, problems will emerge later on. As Turkish Cypriot Scientist 1 states below, future generations must know the truth of what happened, and this is linked to both sides admitting fault and apologizing which are necessary for reconciliation and building a sustainable peace (Lederach, 2010):

> And . . . if you don't say sorry to each other and I don't let my son know about the truth about Cyprus and a Greek Cypriot doesn't let his son, (or if he doesn't learn the truth about Cyprus) even with a contract we will say we made peace, but later on we will have problems. Because I didn't say sorry. And what it means saying sorry is that I see and I know what we did and I will not do it again. Same for the Greek Cypriots. I know. I see. And I will not do it again.

In conclusion, the process of exhumations becomes a way for new generations to see and know what happened and exactly what was done. In this way, it may positively alter the transgenerational transmission of trauma and the victimization narrative. Perhaps it is an indirect way of apologizing, thus relieving some deeply buried community guilt. CMP Turkish Cypriot Scientist 3 noted this point in the following way:

> Yeah, well the blaming is always there—since the day of the incident. The blaming is always there and will always be there, I think. That's my personal idea. What about relieving community guilt? Well maybe . . . my personal idea and maybe I am wrong . . . maybe, it will relieve community guilt a bit. I mean maybe it is like . . . apologizing in a way. I think yeah, a bit, but not completely of course. The guilt will always be there. Nobody can change the reality but it's a good start.

As all of my study participants mentioned in many ways the process of exhumations affects the transgenerational transmission of trauma through the knowledge of pain by affecting victimization narratives and perhaps by exposing a *shared suffering* in order to have a shared future.

CONCLUSION AND SUMMARY OF KEY FINDINGS

In conclusion, chapter four is comprised of two core concepts—Uncertainty and Psychology—in which emergent themes led to significant findings about what the process of exhumations can achieve within the context of Cyprus.

The process of exhumations (defined as the recovery, identification and reunification of the Missing with their loved ones) is a powerful tool in affecting uncertainty that is debilitating and causes paralysis for the relatives of the Missing. All of my study participants claimed that knowledge of death of the relatives loved one is of primary importance. This knowledge is empowering for the relatives of the Missing. The uncertainty of wondering what happened to them and the unanswered questions as to whether they are still alive is debilitating thus in its recognition comes about acknowledgment that they are in fact deceased. Therefore, it can be understood that knowledge of death/life is a basic human need for relatives of the Missing, which empowers them to change their lives.

Unfortunately in some cases, bodies are recovered but the fully articulated remains are not present or available, including artifacts that aid in the identification and acceptance confirming the identity of the family's relative. However, the fact that evidence and knowledge about the retrieval process is still transparent and is provided and explained during the Viewing process regarding the family's loved one challenge the paralyses of closure for them.

Closure in relation to uncertainty is a highly problematic concept particularly in regard to Missing Persons and relatives yet it provides fruitful insight into the various challenges facing this process. The Viewing process was discussed with my participants who revealed (significantly so) that it aids in the transmission of knowledge and therefore, in the recognition of the death and identity of the relatives' loved ones that aided in bringing the issue to closure.

Moreover, during the Viewing process the physical reunification of skeletal remains with relatives ensures that the relatives are further empowered with respect to the uncertainty of identity and recognition of the remains by access to the material reality of their loved one so that the remains and artifacts are memorabilia of that person's identity. Closure in regards to the family's recognition and acceptance of the remains as belonging to "my brother, sister, mother, father, son, daughter, etcetera," is made possible through the knowledge that challenges their uncertainty and provides access to their loved one's remains.

In addition, during the Viewing process, questions about culpability often arise. My study participants discussed the humanitarian nature and mandate of the CMP in which culpability is not known, therefore the uncertainty of culpability (who did it) is not answered and remains unchallenged with respect to bringing about closure for the families. Yet significantly, most of my participants stated that the culpability issue remains with relatives and therefore the right to justice and retribution (in the context of Cyprus) is left out of the equation. Cyprus has not yet reached a political settlement and the CMP needs access to territory in the north and south in order to find Missing Persons as well as information from witnesses, which would be almost impossible to attain if justice and retribution were a part of the CMP mandate. Because of the delicate nature of the Cypriot context and conflict—what I call *advantageous uncertainty* of justice—justice in the form of punishment of offenders might necessarily be left out in place of the more important humanitarian reunification of the Missing with their loved ones. Quelling all uncertainty with regards to closure and Missing Persons (such as culpability and justice) may not be possible or advantageous in post-violent contexts. As one of my study participants stated, there may be another way of fulfilling the right to justice during or after the process of exhumations in Cyprus that is through the formation of a Truth and Reconciliation Commission (TRC) similar to the one in South Africa. This method may aid in bringing about closure and the uncertainty of justice. This certainly leaves food for thought.

Next, a key finding was revealed from the study participants with regards to the cultural practices and religious rights of burial that are significant for Turkish and Greek Cypriots in relation to death. Consequently, when the survivor's uncertainty of death and identity is challenged through the process of exhumations (what one study participant called the *ceremony of identification* that leads to the *release* of the body after the viewing process), the relatives and loved ones of the Missing Person are simultaneously *released.* They are then empowered to fulfill the necessary religious and cultural practices of death and mourning. It is important for the families to have knowledge of the person's death to fulfill these practices for Cypriots from both sides that is why the process of exhumations is so important. Greek and Turkish Cypriot survivors believe that the empowerment to fulfill rights, rituals of death, and mourning means there will now be a burial site and grave for the dead person that are also needed to fulfill their religious practices. Relatives of the Missing can now visit and pay respects to the deceased, which is significantly healing for them. Further, the relatives of the Missing are empowered to choose where their loved one will be buried and most of the time when the Missing are returned to the families they are buried in individual plots and in their villages (when available); and not collectively with other Missing Persons in collective memorials. Thus, the process of exhumations empowers relatives and loved ones of the Missing to fulfill the necessary cultural and religious practices of death, ritual, and mourning through burial. This was previously suspended because of the uncertainty of death and not having access to remains both of which are necessary for the families of the bereaved to bring about closure.

A final key finding revealed by my study participants was the relationship of time to uncertainty. As time passes the certainty of fully recovered articulated remains becomes complicated and arguably harder, as well as the recovery of artifacts (which aid in the process of exhumations.) My study participants all stated that a major challenge is the reunification of partial remains of the Missing with their loved ones. One participant stated that it can create distrust between communities because a significant lapse of time increases the chance that a secondary crime can take place with regards to the relocation of remains and the commingling of body parts.

In addition, the potential for natural environmental changes alongside human made changes (such as soil erosion and the building of roads) can cause increased difficulty for the CMP in locating both remains and artifacts. With this in mind, the sooner the process of exhumations is started in a post-violent conflict society the more likely the recovery, identification, and reunification of fully articulated bodies and artifacts with their families. The dispelling of uncertainty issues around death, identification and closure, for the purposes of mourning, burial and reconciliation are reduced over time if the process of exhumations is not implemented quickly for the return of the Missing to families as soon as possible after a post-violent conflict. In Cyprus the process of exhumations has become a vital method of healing for Greek and Turkish Cypriots. I now turn to the second core finding of this chapter namely Psychology and the importance of time.

When reviewing the data, a significant finding emerged which detrimentally affects relatives of the Missing. In effect, a paralysis occurs as having a Missing Person in the family can significantly stop and stunt the family member's psychological processes of change and healing. Time stands still when the relatives and loved ones of the Missing wait for the return or news of their loved one. The initial trauma of their relative not coming home, and the absence of knowledge regarding her/his fate—whether s/he is dead or alive—can lead to the relatives becoming psychologically paralyzed at that traumatic moment in time. Even though the disappearance occurred over forty years ago and the husband, wife, son or daughter did not come home, people still continue to wait. They are effectively paralyzed, for example, the family brings the son's best suit to dress his body at the Viewing, and the wife who maintains her husband's shoes and their house on a daily basis, awaiting his return to come home, people still continue to wait.

However, the paralysis of time and trauma are fractured because the process of exhumations puts into question the uncertainty of reunification and the knowledge of the person's death. Hence, the process of exhumations provides the family's access to healing and by extension, significantly changes the antagonistic forces held between communities. Thus, I unpacked the key theme of healing and catharsis that led to the concept of *Relief* as a key component of reunification with the Missing Persons. My respondents expressed that it had a significant psychological effect with regard to the relative's empowerment for the processes of grieving and mourning that were previously paralyzed or frozen.

During the Viewing, the empowerment process of providing the family with knowledge, and finally access to the Missing Person, a *relief experience* or catharsis is possible that challenges the bereaved paralyses of time and thus contributes to their psychological healing. The concept of relief as a function of the process of exhumations is very significant. This was evident when the Turkish Cypriot relatives of one of the Missing who were reunited with their loved one brought flowers for both the Greek and Turkish Cypriot scientists. Psychological relief is arguably a significant factor in the inter-ethnic transformation of relationships and reconciliation in post violent conflict societies and it is particularly related to the Missing Persons issue via the necessity for the relatives to move past frozen grieving for healing when dealing with ambiguous loss.

Following psychological relief is the theme of psychological closure. Several words came up in the data in relation to psychological closure, namely *relief*, *healing* as mourning and burial, and *grief* and *pain*. These key findings were reflected in each family's need to say goodbye to their loved ones because it gave them the ability to have a proper burial, and to use the rituals of mourning and death that provides them with a grieving process that was previously paralyzed and frozen that is necessary for their individual and psycho-social healing. However, an additional key finding regarding pain also came up in the interviews.

Several study participants stated that the pain of loss may never leave and as such, complete closure is most likely impossible. Yet through the pain of loss, the study participants discussed *shared suffering* and *common pain*. This concept may be advantageous in creating a common space of suffering for relatives of the Missing for both Turkish Cypriot and Greek Cypriot families. The recognition of suffering suggests the families no longer see one another as antagonistic forces but as human beings who have a Missing Person in their family as well. This key finding ruptures the idea of pain and loss solely as a negative force. The understanding of common pain emerges due to the families shared experience of having a Missing Person that in some cases leads to cooperation between Greek and Turkish Cypriots in finding out and providing information about the disappeared for one another. The possibility of recovery, identification, and reunification through the process of exhumations demonstrates to the families and ethnic communities at large that they both share the hardships, difficulties, and pain of loss. Thus, my study participants stated that a shared future may also be possible because an understanding of shared suffering was possible.

The CMP's strictly humanitarian mandate leaves out culpability, and creates space for commonality due to the fact that the perpetrator of a crime is an unidentifiable, uncertain third party so that the *advantageous uncertainty* of justice may provide space for shared suffering. This key finding is also significant because it can be argued that the particular circumstances found in Cyprus could offer a space for a shared victimization narrative. The victimization narrative and psychological *transgenerational transmission of trauma* are already entrenched on both sides. Both Turkish and Greek Cypriots claim innocence and see themselves as victims of conflict perpetuated by the other side. However, my study participants revealed that they had not seen or experienced an exacerbation of violence when the process of exhumations was underway.

In many post violent conflict societies, victimization narratives are entrenched on both sides. Many scholars discuss the need to deal with this narrative because it can be dangerous in inciting an us and them mentality, potentially creating a repetition of atrocities from the past (Volkan, 1998). Interestingly, my study participants claimed that both Turkish and Greek Cypriot relatives of the Missing are also victims. Thus, instead of getting rid of the victimization narrative perhaps the process of exhumations can offer a shared victimization and understanding of a shared suffering. Another key finding rests in what the majority of my study participants discussed in terms of what the process of exhumations means for the next (and future generations) of Cypriots. The process of exhumations was cited as a tool that teaches future generations what forms of misery and suffering can occur when a person goes Missing. This understanding reduces the chances of a *historical reoccurrence of violence*. My interviewees also stated that families will be able to say that although their loved one went Missing during the Cyprus conflict that afterwards, both Greek and Turkish Cypriots, did something together about it in trying to locate the Missing. Thus, the transgenerational transmission of trauma and stories of loss and suffering will be effected by the process of exhumations.

This understanding took place most significantly during the Viewing in which vertical lines of the Missing (nuclear family members), and horizontal lines (relatives and distant relatives) took part. This deeply affected their understanding of suffering and the conflict when they realized that Greek and Turkish Cypriots worked together to find and return the remains of relatives from both sides.

Finally, the process of exhumations can, in one way or another, be perceived as sort of an indirect apology from both sides which may relieve some underlying community guilt. This significant statement offers insights into the importance of apology and forgiveness that is further discussed in the next chapter. The individual and family processes of receiving the remains of their loved one's effect on a larger scope the societies and communities of Turkish and Greek Cypriots as well.

In conclusion, this chapter examined both the individual and family level of the process of exhumations and its effects on the core concepts of Uncertainty and Psychology. In the next chapter I carefully examine what the data revealed about the participants' perceptions and experiences with the CMP organization, and how the process of exhumations is changing bicommunal relationships.

Chapter Five

Bicommunal Relations

JOURNAL ENTRY

Date: August 1st, 2014
It's been a couple of weeks since I began volunteering with the CMP in Cyprus. I've been treated very well by the scientists here. In the days I've spent observing the process of exhumations, they've been nothing but kind, welcoming, and patient. A general break-down of my day went something like this. I would spend a certain amount of time with a specific scientist on a certain phase of the process where I would learn about it (It could be anything from recovery and archaeological findings, or anthropological analysis of remains to the reunification and Viewing phase). Yet this never occurred in any particular order because they were all extremely busy, working with heavy case loads.

As I observed the process unfold in each phase and had a chance to observe the work accomplished, I was amazed at how efficiently they organized data and information sharing. The information was meticulously typed into computer programs, accompanied by diagrams. The data on each phase was ultimately presented to the families of the Missing in a collaborative process when they are unified with them. However, individuals from each phase participated in a final phase before the reunification of the Missing with their relatives called the Reconciliation Process between scientists. In this process, information was presented by each scientist to other scientists with respect to their specialization such as DNA analysis or remains analysis with regards to the decision on the identification of the remains. This afforded scientists the opportunity to raise any issues in order to consolidate the findings. If everything was agreed upon based on the data and information and the identity of the remains, the families and loved ones of the Missing were then notified.

What struck me as fantastic were the collegiality, professionalism, and friendly inter-play that went on in the anthropology laboratory between the scientists. The CMP is a bicommunal organization filled with an equal number of Turkish and Greek Cypriots. Personally I had never seen so many Turkish and Greek Cypriots interacting together at any one time. It was a beautiful co-creation based on mutual interests and superordinate goals. Given what I had experienced on the island it was not only unusual, it was miraculous and inspirational.

Greek and Turkish Cypriot scientists were not just working together; they were sharing stories, playing, helping one another, eating together and most notably sharing in everyday activities inside and (as I was informed) sometimes outside of work. These weren't just scientists working on reuniting the Missing with their loved ones, they were friends. They shared Turkish and Greek Cypriot food. They shared jokes. They shared stories of their lives with each other and about their community.

In the United Nations Protected Area they were not Greek or Turkish Cypriots. They were Cypriots. Period. And so were the bones they unearthed and identified. They all worked together in common purpose. Prior to identification, no scientist tried or cared to determine the identity of a skull as being that of a Greek or a Turk, because beneath it all, it didn't matter. Everyone whether Turk or Greek was composed of the same material—bones.

INTRODUCTION

> I guess at the societal level it does similar things. It removes wounds that stand in the way of . . . cross reconciliation with the other side . . . Specific at the level of our committee it's a very useful process because through it we engage people from both sides —about 80 scientists . . . work on this together on a daily basis. That sets a very good and very rare precedent in Cyprus: how both sides can cooperate and work together—which they don't usually do.
> (CMP Staff Member, interview and personal communication, June 6, 2014)

Chapter five focuses on the nature of *Bicommunal relations* in Cyprus with respect to Missing Persons and the process of exhumations. During the interview process, the concept of *Bicommunal relations* led to key themes that highlighted the significance of inter-ethnic relations from the organizational level of the CMP. These relations affect the societal level in terms of the transformation of relationships inter-ethnically which are necessary for inter-ethnic reconciliation (Lederach, 2010). Therefore, this chapter discusses the following six themes: Percentage of Missing; Bicommunal List Formation and Bicommunal Fairness of Reunification; Bicommunal Contact and Time; The Bicommunal CMP Organization and Inter-ethnic Friendship development; and Bicommunal Leadership. The themes outline some of the challenges to reconciliation and the transformation of inter-ethnic relationships through the process of exhumations in a post-violent conflict society, and the advantages of bicommunal relations with a specific focus on the CMP and its positive effects on inter-ethnic societal relations on the island of Cyprus.

PERCENTAGE OF THE MISSING

One major consequence of post-violent conflicts is Missing Persons. The devastating consequence of Missing Persons has lasting effects on relatives of the Missing which in turn affects communities, regions, and nation-states especially when the proportion of Missing Persons is very high in relation to the respective populations. Thus, Ho-Won Jeong's (2005) *Peacebuilding in Post Conflict Societies: Strategy and Process* expresses the challenges faced when a formal peace accord's efforts are to be carried out.

> As efforts are made to carry out the provisions of a formal accord, the society will be marked by intense uncertainty and struggle over the scope and pace of prescribed reforms. Divergent expectations, feelings of insecurity, and a lack of established political procedures and normative standards increase tension (p. 5).

Hence, it is highly important to express some of the reasons, challenges, and normative standards that are necessary to understand how and why the process of exhumations is to be completed with respect to Missing Persons in a post-violent context, and its importance with respect to peacebuilding and reconciliation.

In the analysis of the interviews, several of the study participants discussed the size of Cyprus, its population, and the fact that when a significant percentage of the population goes missing, it is impossible to experience reconciliation without addressing the problem systematically. For example, Paul-Henri Arni notes the following in his narrative:

> In Cyprus, large numbers of people were killed in a very short amount of time often by paramilitaries. After long negotiations between the sides in the CMP, 2,001 names were accepted on the official list of Missing Persons. Soldiers who went missing in action were not included on the list. So, for such a small population of just over 600,000 (in those days), 2,001 persons represent a very large proportion. When you have such a proportion of Missing Persons you have a problem for decades to come. The impact of these disappearances on families and communities is very negative because they cannot turn the page and cannot reconcile. There is no way you can reconcile politically when you

> have such a large number of people who went missing because emotionally it is too much and it touches everyone, from ordinary people to leaders. Therefore the issue of Missing Persons has to be addressed and solved if one wants a solution.

This is not to say that a smaller proportion of Missing Persons would have been any less important, when Missing Persons disappear *en masse* it creates a significant obstacle to peacebuilding and reconciliation between societies because so many people are affected by it. For example, CMP Staff Member had the following to say in his story:

> . . . In Cyprus arguably it is necessary . . . certainly it is very conducive because of the high percentage of Missing and the fact that so many families are affected . . . [it] is bound to be an obstacle to attempt to reunify the island and . . . (short of reunification) simply reconcile societies . . . it's clearly an important instrument (the process of exhumations) to achieving that . . .

CMP Turkish Cypriot Scientist 3 concurs by expressing how many families are affected by the disappeared along with their communities. He claims that the process of exhumations is good for peacebuilding and reconciliation. He says that the return and release of remains to the families is in a way, like "handshaking" between the ethnic communities.

> The project does not only provide identification. As I mentioned a bit on previous questions, it is very good for peacebuilding and reconciliation and I think we need this project. You know, Cyprus is such a small country, when we say 2,000 Missing Persons imagine how many families you have and a lot of people have Missing Persons in their family or neighbor or cousin so it is a big issue. Once you identify and release their pain, in a way it is good for peacebuilding and you accept. It is like handshaking in a way (I believe). Of course when we release, they will not forget what happened, but they can open a new page. Maybe I am hoping.

To reiterate, when a large percentage of the population goes missing due to violent conflict, the participants' claim that societies cannot reconcile because they cannot turn the page to a new beginning until it is addressed. But when the Missing Persons issue is addressed through the process of exhumations, it can positively impact peacebuilding and reconciliation processes. I now turn to the beginning of bicommunal relations between Turkish and Greek Cypriots in regards to some challenges that post violent conflict societies face when addressing the issue of Missing Persons.

LIST AGREEMENT AND BICOMMUNAL CHALLENGES

After a violent conflict is over a nation is faced with the devastation and tragedy that emerges as a result. People, societies and the nation-state must deal with its inevitable aftermath. A list of the Missing is necessary in order to conduct investigations of the whereabouts of Missing Persons, their condition and return as some were imprisoned and interned, internally displaced or declared deceased. Yet this act fulfills components of peacebuilding, such as democratic implementation and political stability (Jeong, 2005).

As my study participants stated with respect to Missing Persons (some of whom may be imprisoned and interned, internally displaced or tragically dead), it is up to the families and relatives to report their loved one as Missing. The disarray of post-violent conflict societies leaves in its wake, disjointed governments. Thus, the process must begin with relatives, extended families, and friends. The social and political aftermath of a violent conflict leaves a society lacking any real and systematic method to find Missing Persons. People are at a loss when dealing with the Missing Persons issue. As Paul-Henri Arni states:

> The ICRC helped the MPI a lot on that—to establish lists of Missing Persons not based on governmental lists. The government is the government; they don't serve dinner to an empty chair. It is the family who is responsible in the end . . . whose moral authority [it] is to say "my husband came home after the war" or "he didn't come home". Only the family can tell that.

Thus, the list formation starts with the families who notify authorities and in this example INGOs such as the International Committee of the Red Cross (ICRC) who helps families formulate lists of the Missing and for that matter attempt to find them has been a contested issue in Cyprus (Sant-Cassia, 2005).

Next, is the need of the conflict communities and governments to agree together upon a common list of the Missing. This can be a trying process on Cyprus particularly because of hostilities that remain between the conflict groups namely the Greek and Turkish Cypriot. Also, as stated in the previous chapter, governments, the militaries, and people from either side of the conflict have information regarding the Missing so that their cooperation is necessary in order to find the Missing. In addition, there is the question of territorial access to the north and south of Cyprus due to the lack of any post-conflict political settlement. Permission is needed to conduct research and get access to locations where both Greek and Turkish Cypriots went missing. This is not to say that this problem would be eradicated in other conflicts that have a political settlement (because territorial access can be limited as well), it adds difficulty to the equation because of ethnic hostilities and the perceived threat associated with uncovering the whereabouts of the Missing in Cyprus. As Paul-Henry Arni claims, an agreed upon list is the "cornerstone of any effort on Missing Persons" but in Cyprus as in other places, this can be a trying task:

> One of the serious issues they had (like in Cyprus) . . . was no agreed list on Missing Persons. That's the cornerstone of any effort on Missing Persons. You *have* to agree on a list of Missing Persons. And each side has a political interest—to blow up this list in order to project the other side as the perpetrator and us as the victim. Here (in Cyprus) it took fourteen years—[the]1981 creation of the CMP and [the] 1995 agreement on the lists. It took fourteen years of negotiation—name by name—to agree on the common lists. And in Bosnia, the same.

The formation of lists and commonly agreed upon lists can be a difficult process especially for families who were/have been waiting for the return of their loved ones in Cyprus for over 20 years or more up to the formation of the agreed upon list of 1995.

This is not to say that families and nongovernmental organizations (comprised of families and relatives) did not continue to put pressure on their respective governments in Cyprus and take matters into their own hands. Some of these organizations include the *Cypriot Committee of Parents and relatives of Unknown Prisoners and Missing Persons; The Pan-Cyprian Committee of Relatives of Missing Persons* as well as continual demonstrations by mothers and wives of the Missing by both Turkish and Greek Cypriot relatives. One recent example took place in 1998 when two middle-aged Greek Cypriot women broke into a military cemetery looking for their husbands by digging up the ground with pick axes. This passionate act of desperation hit national newspaper headlines in which they were quoted as saying they just needed to know whether their husbands were dead or alive (Sant-Cassia, 2005, p. 1).

There was a need to form a bicommunal organization to find Missing Persons in Cyprus because of the lack of access to the north of Cyprus that is separated by the Green Line. Both Turkish and Greek Cypriots didn't have legal travel access until 2004 to either side. Plus, there is the need to provide documents and to gather information on the Missing from either side; or the reality that the Cyprus conflict is not settled politically makes a bicommunal organization necessary in Cyprus.

Also, certain criteria had to be implemented when establishing the bicommunal CMP. Any organization going through a process of exhumations must not neglect the importance of establishing *rules on recovery, identification, and reunification.* These rules were designed to be fair and proportional with respect to equality so as to represent equal and fair treatment for families from both sides of the conflict namely Greek and Turkish Cypriot in order to prevent problems of favoritism, and an escalation of victimization narratives and conflict escalation (Sant-Cassia, 2005; Wagner, 2008). As Dr. Marios Cariolou notes:

> The only rules that I have seen put on the program . . . are between the two communities . . . sometimes . . . they would discuss the process of exhumations and they try to balance the exhumation process as to the numbers or percentage of the Missing that would be found in one mass grave as opposed to another mass grave found to the other side. So that at the end, the number of Missing Persons that would be identified would be either proportional to the Missing individuals that are Missing from each community . . . because if they don't do that sometimes one community would complain that, "well you know three hundred Turkish Cypriots have been identified but only twenty Greek Cypriots have been identified." But these rules, (if again rules may not be the right word), these [would] be imposed by the CMP itself—the rules of how to carry out the exhumation process. Maybe there is . . . I don't want to use the word bargain because it is not a nice word . . . but I believe there is some discussion on which mass graves will be handled at a given time.

Thus, the nature of the process of exhumations is very delicate when it is aiding peacebuilding and the societal processes of reconciliation between both ethnic groups in terms of equality in the return of the Missing.

BICOMMUNAL CONTACT AND TIME

When discussing with my study participants the nature of the Cyprus conflict and Missing Persons, a theme emerged about—*time*. In the analysis of the data and the development of the core concept of bicommunal relations an emergent theme of *bicommunal contact* also arose. Several scholars suggest that bicommunal contact works for children and their political perceptions and world views in integrated schools in Belfast (Byrne, 1997) while the importance of linkages via the public (associational) and private realm (everyday forms of engagement) with respect to assessing the origins of conflict (intra-ethnic civil societies engagement and inter-ethnic) are critical (Varshney, 2001) and can have a positive impact on inter-ethnic relationship development and the preventative escalation of violence. Thus, many of my study participants discussed the nature of time and bicommunal contact as important factors that maintain the Cyprus conflict. As Sevgül Uludağ noted in the following way:

> You see the main problem in Cyprus is that the two communities were kept completely separate for forty years and they heard the worst about each other. So, we need to learn how to work together again and if you create opportunities, why shouldn't we be able to work together? I mean we can work

> together with a German, with French, with an American, with a Canadian, and we cannot work with our own? It's the same culture.

Several of my study participants discussed how the lapse of contact *en masse* between Greek and Turkish Cypriots for over forty years could be considered one of the main problems in the Cyprus conflict.

Narratives of fear and hate can promote illogical reasoning that cooperation is impossible. But contact and bicommunal relations can dispel this problematic image of the other. Thus, a conflict transformation and peacebuilding process includes the movement from latent conflict to confrontation to negotiation in achieving the peaceful relationships of a secure community (Lederach, 1995; Jeong, 2000). In order to move toward the de-escalation of

conflict we must change psychological dimensions of unequal relations to the need of being with one another etcetera; inevitably structural transformations must also occur for long term resolution (Jeong, 2000; Lederach, 2010). The resolution of the Cyprus conflict is associated with matters of inter-ethnic reconciliation in which a key ingredient is the necessary development of inter-ethnic relations and relationship formation between Greek and Turkish Cypriots to take place. John Paul Lederach (2010) claims that relationship development is a must for reconciliation and sustainable peace to happen between the conflict parties, yet in order for this process to occur people need to have the opportunity for an encounter in the first place.

CMP Turkish Cypriot Scientist 1 offers an example of how little contact there was between both communities before the opening of the Green Line in 2004. After the opening of the line he worked in the Greek Cypriot South with Greek Cypriots for the first time. They empowered him through their sharing of knowledge and experience about who these Greek Cypriots were. As he notes below:

> Before I worked for the CMP, I worked in South Cyprus as a worker with Greek Cypriots. And I saw that when you do something together, like working or having fun, people are not only saying "good morning" and "have a nice day" after work. You see that people are speaking about the Cyprus Problem and daily life . . . at the break times. I will give you an example: when I was working with them, an accident happened . . . a group of wood fell from the building and when I turned my back I didn't see the master, which was the Greek Cypriot. I said, "Where are you Master?" I was afraid that something happened to him. Before the day that I started to work with Greek Cypriots I didn't meet with any. And I was like, "who are they? And what kind of people [are they]?" That day I noticed that I worried about him. So whenever there is contact, people start to accept the other one if there is no other opposite pressure from somewhere else. Another example, when I was speaking with a Greek Cypriot builder who was much older than me, he was speaking with me about the Cyprus Problem. But when the other Greek Cypriots came he stopped speaking. He pretended like we were not speaking. I saw that if there

> was not any other worry or pressure . . . people are having good connections . . . they start to do it at least.

In consequence, when a lot of time has lapsed and contact has not been possible between conflicted parties, uncertainty of who the party is and the narratives of fear and hate may prevent reconciliation.

However, this is not to say that a cooling off period isn't needed between communities in order to prevent a re-escalation of violence in post-violent context societies. However, as Turkish Cypriot Scientist 1 noted particular conditions allowed for the shared space and for people to converse—even about the conflict. The condition was dependent upon whether there was any worry or pressure behind it and that is when "people can have good connections" he said. With that in mind, I now turn to what my study participants had to say about the bicommunal nature of the CMP and its effects on bicommunal ethnic relations. Perhaps this is one entity that could be considered as a space for making good connections.

BICOMMUNAL CMP ORGANIZATION AND INTER-ETHNIC FRIENDSHIP DEVELOPMENT

John Paul Lederach's (2010) *Building Peace: Sustainable Reconciliation in Divided Societies* set out through his praxis experience the reconciliation initiatives to understand what comprises a sustainable peace. His conclusions emphasize that "peacebuilding must be rooted in and responsive to the experiential and subjective realities shaping people's perspectives and needs [and therefore] toward a frame of reference that focuses on the restoration and rebuilding of relationships" (p. 24). Thus, reconciliation must include those who went through the conflicts who were formulated by their experiences and who now want to focus on building relationships. He suggests that the recipe for what comprises reconciliation must have a focus that builds relationships and in this case the humanitarian return of the disappeared remains unresolved yet it is a locus which provides avenues for encounters. He claims, "People need opportunity and space to express to and with one another the trauma of loss and their grief at that loss, and the anger that accompanies and the memory of injustices experienced" (Lederach, 2010, p. 26).

Further, Lederach (2010) states that with the focus and locus four pillars of reconciliation will emerge, namely Truth, which is acknowledgement of past wrongs; Mercy, which is acceptance, support, healing, and forgiveness; Justice, which is right relationships and making things right; and Peace that encompasses well-being, security, respect, and unity (p.30). As we will see through the analysis of the data the process of exhumations particularly within the CMP organization fulfills Lederach's recipe for the inter-ethnic building of relationships aided by the four pillars of reconciliation.

The Committee on Missing Persons in Cyprus (CMP) is comprised of scientists from various fields with expertise in recovery, identification, and reunification of the Missing with their loved ones. There are photographers, forensic archaeologists, forensic anthropologists, investigative researchers and political representatives. Two teams were developed—one for the north and one for the south of Cyprus—made up of Turkish and Greek Cypriots, with directors for each field and team leaders. In addition, there are international personnel and committee members that aid in the process of exhumations who are appointed by the United Nations who help with cooperation and logistics. The United Nations was invited and asked to aid in the process by both respective governments.

While volunteering, observing, and working alongside the CMP scientists, I experienced first-hand how all the work was done cooperatively between Greek and Turkish Cypriots. As I write this chapter, I recall one particular day where I was sifting through dirt and shoveling for hours in the hot Cyprus sun. Having identified a suspected gravesite, we were about to start the process of recovery of remains. But prior to the day's work, Greek and Turkish Cypriot scientists made and drank coffee and shared and ate food together. What's more, they shared everyday stories with one another. As I ate and shared stories of my own, we joked, we laughed, and I experienced a real sense of caring between them. It was infectious. In the entire time I spent with them, I never once saw or sensed any hostility among the CMP members.

When discussing with participants the bicommunal nature of the CMP, it is impossible not to take this into consideration. The CMP members expressed their own perceptions and the affect that working together has on them and on the society. One major impact mentioned by several of my research participants is that it shows both societies, Greek and Turkish Cypriot, the possibility of working well together. As Sevgül Uludağ stated, “Yes, it is good because it shows how we can work together in the future.” CMP Staff Member also suggested that it demonstrates on a societal level how both sides can cooperate and work well together. The organizational level is fairly large, and comprised of both Turkish and Greek Cypriots.

> I guess at the societal level it does similar things. It removes wounds that stand in the way . . . in cases of cross reconciliation with the other side. Cyprus, specific at the level of our committee, [is] a very useful process because through it we engage people from both sides—about 80 scientists who work on this together on a daily basis. That sets a very good and very rare precedent in Cyprus—how both sides can cooperate and work together—which they don’t usually do.

Further, he explained how it is the only institutionalized bicommunal organization in Cyprus that works on a daily basis. CMP Staff Member suggested that making decisions bicommunally (and problemsolving five days a week for nine hours a day) is a significant achievement in post violent conflict societies. This is what he had to say:

> Well it's essentially the only bicommunal institution that . . . is fully institutionalized and works on a daily basis . . . To my knowledge no other institution in Cyprus does anything like it. There is a Committee on Cultural Heritage but these are more people who have regular jobs who meet regularly to make decisions together. We employ people essentially who work 9 hours a day at 5 days a week in mixed teams, [taking] decisions together . . . we have Turkish scientists analyzing Greek remains and the other way around. So for Cyprus it's unique. And hopefully something that will be emulated elsewhere in the future.

CMP Staff Member's opinion is that the CMP encourages positive relations between both ethnic communities due to its bicommunal nature within the organization while it promotes peacebuilding and confidence-building between the two sides. "[It is] generally positive. Certainly in terms of the people who conduct it. That is itself an exercise in peacebuilding and confidence building among the two sides because of the fact that eighty Cypriots from both sides do it together." Hence, as many interactive problemsolving scholars suggest the groups initially involved in the conflict must be involved in the analysis and resolution of it (Fisher and Ury, 2011). They need to be involved in its design (resolution and reconciliation) and be active agents in its implementation for the need to sustain dialogue (Saunders, 2003; Lowry and Littlejohn, 2006; Nemeroff, 2008; Zartman, 2008) so that they can avoid liberal Western top-down approaches to peacebuilding models and focus on local everyday peacemaking models that aid in the care of relationships (Walker, 2004; Mac Ginty, 2008). Arguably, in one way or another, due to the active engagement and everyday problemsolving of both Greek and Turkish Cypriots with respect to the process of exhumations via the CMP, positive interpersonal relationships, caring, via interactive problemsolving is aiding in inter-ethnic reconciliation in Cyprus.

In addition, the study participants expressed their own ideas about how the CMP scientific work affected their own thoughts on difference. For example, CMP Greek Cypriot Scientist 2 claims that because the knowledge of the ethnicity of the Missing Person is unknown, he or she is treated just as a person and with respect. So that Greek and Turkish Cypriots all look the same inside and that the work they do is for everyone, Greek and Turkish Cypriots alike. This is what he had to say on this issue:

> Yes, the bicommunal element is necessary because we all work for everyone. There are Missing Persons from both communities. While we are working, we don't know whether the person is Greek Cypriot or Turkish Cypriot and it

> doesn't even matter. It is a person. We all look the same inside. Of course it is necessary and I think it is the only way it could be . . . Within the organization everyone works together. No one is forced to work together. But from what I have seen, out in the field and in here, we all work together very amicably and [are] helpful with each other. My personal opinion [is] I don't see any difference between anyone. There is no difference, we are working for one cause and that's the bottom line. Totally and honestly.

Turkish and Greek Cypriots are composed of the same things inside, and externally they share a similar problem looking for Missing Persons, which is an acknowledgement of Truth and Mercy via compassion that are central to reconciliation (Lederach, 2010). The very nature of the CMP as a bicommunal organization and most importantly its scientific work produces a dynamic understanding of the similarity of people. As CMP Turkish Cypriot Scientist 1 avers, the Missing Persons issue is a bicommunal problem, with bicommunal access needs (in terms of territory). He argues that the CMP provides a significant example to both societies about the possibilities of working together:

> I think it is much better to be done bicommunally because it is not just a problem of just one community—it is a bicommunal problem. Therefore I think we should do it bicommunally. Also, we have to work on both sides. Therefore I think it is not possible to work alone. Imagine Greek Cypriots going to [the] north and digging on their own and Turkish Cypriots going to the south. I think it has to be bicommunal, and bicommunal is better by the way of the peace process because people can see that Greek Cypriots and Turkish Cypriots can still work together and they can create something which is very, very important. So I think it has a very good impact on people and [it] is promising.

This necessity of working on both sides of the Green Line creates interdependency for both Greek and Turkish Cypriots for the recovery of remains. Logistically, this interdependency must exist between different territories under different government control and is entirely necessary in order to get things done. The nature and necessity of both groups working together in the bicommunal organization fosters interpersonal and inter-ethnic relations as well. John Paul Lederach (2010) states that interdependence from relationships via reconciliation forms so that a vision of a shared future becomes possible. Thus, from the organizational level of the CMP and its bicommunal nature, CMP Turkish Cypriot Scientist 1 states that CMP Turkish and Greek Cypriots are exhibiting caring for each other and protection for one another when working together in dangerous conditions. This caring and protection also aids in the building of communication between people. He gives examples from working in the field together below:

> At the CMP I see the same thing. When we are working, of course no one wants to see anyone suffering because of an injury. I will give you an example. Now I am working at the anthropological laboratory but before I was working in the field as an archaeologist. When you are working, you are working on cliffs in the mountains, in dangerous areas, in wells—anything can happen, anytime. We have snakes in Cyprus, scorpions, spiders that give pain when they bite. I will give an example from this point of view. When we are working with machines we are sometimes over-excited and we are jumping over machines when it is working and it can cause trouble. Or, when we are working on cliffs or in a well, people are very careful. Always I was careful. Sometimes you don't see anything but they see that something will fall on you and they catch you and put you somewhere else and it helps me and I am taken care of. It doesn't matter if it is a Greek Cypriot or Turkish Cypriot. We see that people are protecting each other when we are working and it is something very nice I think. It is building communication and working together is very important.

The CMP bicommunal organization has developed inter-ethnic relationships through the nature of its work based on caring, protection, and communication. The everyday interaction between Cypriots on an institutional and organizational level has, as some of my research participant's state, led to friendships inside and outside of work, which can be seen as a form of justice by righting relationships (Lederach, 2010). CMP Turkish Cypriot Scientist 1 provides one example of relations outside of work:

> At CMP, I saw this at my wedding. I invited Greek Cypriots and they came. They invited me and I went to a church. And when one of my friend's father passed away, I went to his funeral. If it's not communication then what is it? When you work together you start to make communication and I believe it is very useful to make communal works fun. Communal and social organizations were not uncommon during the Annan Plan time period. Day by day it is becoming less but at least some people met. Greek Cypriots and Turkish Cypriots are spending time together travelling together in Cyprus and outside of Cyprus and they are doing work in Cyprus. This is not only because of the CMP or other bicommunal practices but because by chance they met and they [became] friends.

When I pried further about developing friendships with Turkish Cypriots, CMP Greek Cypriot Scientist 2 vehemently stated "Yeah. Of course [yes]." Consequently, as CMP Turkish Cypriot Scientist 3 states, "this project has been for several years and it is working very good and we've made a lot of friends,"—not only within the bicommunal work teams but also on a societal level, offering inter-ethnic spaces of socialization and communication that once existed before the violent conflict. CMP Greek Cypriot Scientist 2 also expresses below how in one way or another the CMP's scientific work is bringing Greek and Turkish Cypriots together to not only communicate within the CMP but also on a societal level that once existed which aids in the dispelling of negative differences:

> I know that in the field there have been cases where the archaeologists are digging and the family members or onlookers are coming to see what's going on and they are from both communities and they strike up conversations and stuff like that. Yes, it brings people together and people do start speaking and people do see each other after many, many years. Because before they used to live together and they used to know each other. My generation and a bit further back from my generation have never seen a Turkish Cypriot before because of borders and everything. Then you see that there is no difference. The problem is not down here where the people are. It is somewhere else.

Thus, indirectly the bicommunal process of exhumations is having the effect of bringing people together from both communities because contact is necessary to create inter-communication between all the members. This may eventually have the effect of fostering relationships once again between Greek and Turkish Cypriots, which is primary for inter-ethnic reconciliation (See Lederach, 2010).

However, the bicommunal nature of the CMP isn't just creating interpersonal connections between Cypriot workers and fostering friendships within and outside of work, interpersonal relations are also rippling outward through the phases and process of exhumations. Iosif Kovra's work entitled (2012) "De-linkage processes and grassroots movements in transitional justice" points out that "Enforced disappearances and reconciliation has a negative correlation in post conflict settings in the dominant academic discourse" (p. 95). However, he argues that when it is done through *de-linking* humanitarian processes from high politics and transitional justice formulations that deal with solving impunity and criminal law, community building grassroots movements and healing emerges as a result. Hence, an individual that helps the CMP and Cypriots in general fostering inter-ethnic relationships and healing is Sevgül Uludağ . She is a Turkish Cypriot journalist from the north and also a participant in this study. Sevgül is gathering information on the whereabouts of Missing Persons by bringing together Greek and Turkish Cypriots. CMP Staff Member states the following during our discussion on inter-ethnic relations and friendships:

> CMP Staff Member: Among our scientists . . . there's other people involved in it, there's journalists who help us find witnesses. I have been personally present when witnesses and relatives of Missing Persons were brought together and this can be a highly emotional healing type of occasion. So it certainly [has] a great impact.
>
> Kris: And . . . inter-ethnically, between Turkish Cypriots and Greek Cypriots?

> CMP Staff Member: Yeah that is what I mean. You know, there was one event where a Turkish Cypriot's family gave a pair of glasses to the widow of a Greek Cypriot soldier who disappeared; and it was his glasses that they took when he was taken away and killed. And for the first time they told her what happened to her husband and she was immensely grateful because she had no idea what had happened. So yeah . . . this happens.

Not to mention that even the investigative phase of the process of exhumations leads to bicommunal connections, improved communication and interpersonal opportunities between witnesses and family members. These are all occasions for people to heal from the encounter that is necessary for reconciliation and the development of inter-ethnic relationships to happen (Lederach, 2010).

However, one dimension of the process of exhumations that is not bicommunal in nature is the Viewing process. Indirectly, the process of recovery, identification, and reunification was jointly worked on by both Greek and Turkish Cypriots, yet the presentation of information and reunification of the remains with relatives is left to the respective ethnic group members of the Missing. This leaves one food for thought with respect to the reconciliation process and how the process of exhumations should be conducted. It might be best to conduct the Viewing process mono-ethnically in post-violent conflict societies due to its traumatic and emotional nature. This does not mean that relatives and loved ones are not aware that Greek and Turkish Cypriots worked together on finding and returning their loved one through the scientific phases of recovery and identification and are not thankful. For example, CMP Turkish Cypriot Scientist 1 stated the following in his account:

> I am a Turkish Cypriot and I don't know what's happening at the Greek Cypriot viewings. More or less it is the same procedure but we don't know what the families reactions are if they don't send a thank you to us and only tell the scientists that were at the viewing. From my experience they are saying thank you for this issue and it doesn't matter whether you're a Turkish Cypriot or Greek Cypriot. One or two times a Turkish Cypriot family came with flowers and they said to us, "this is not only for the Turkish Cypriot scientists, it is for both scientists—Turkish Cypriot and Greek Cypriot scientists. Can you tell that we are saying thank you to you? And can you tell them thank you?"

In consequence, the bicommunal nature of the CMP offers indirectly, a way for inter-ethnic reconciliatory aspects by aiding in opportunities that foster bicommunal relations, and directly by reuniting relatives with the Missing based on its humanitarian mandate.

BICOMMUNAL LEADERSHIP

When I was volunteering with the CMP in the summer of 2014, I was very fortunate because the President of the Republic of Cyprus, Nicos Anastasiades and the President of the Turkish Republic of Northern Cyprus, Dervis Eroglu visited the CMP Anthropological laboratory together for the first time. This symbolic act of visiting the only bicommunal institutional organization in Cyprus was a rare precedent. According to the participants, the CMP officially invited the Presidents to come at the same time, effectively showing their bicommunal support to the bicommunal project. As Paul-Henri Arni notes the significance of their visit as follows:

> It was useful. It was the first time—on the 24th of July 2014—that we had the two leaders visiting the lab together. The two leaders accepted to come together to our lab and to face for the first time the victims of what they call the Cyprus Problem—the victims of 1963 and 1974 on the laboratory tables. They were quite impressed to see with their own eyes because it is the only place in Cyprus where you can see the victims of the disappearances. So the fact they came is a very good first sign. We invited them because we need their support for two things: we need their support for them to call their own communities for additional information and we need their support to fund the CMP because we would like them more and more to contribute financially to the efforts of the CMP.
>
> Thus, the leaders were filmed and photographed together. They made separate statements in Greek and in Turkish that were intended for their respective television stations on the importance of the CMP project and for witnesses to come forward to provide information on grave sites of Missing Persons to the CMP. Unfortunately, settlement talks were suspended before the joint appeal could be broadcast. A new appeal was recorded in December 2015 and broadcast on all TV stations across Cyprus in February 2016.

Thus, the Presidents were filmed and photographed together which included separate statements on respective television stations on the importance of the CMP project and for witnesses to come forward to provide evidence to the CMP of the whereabouts of Missing Persons. This bicommunal act and show of support was seen by hundreds of thousands of people all over Cyprus. However, Paul-Henri Arni contends the reasons for this act were to fulfill the humanitarian mandate of finding the Missing Persons. Consequently, it reached a wide audience for the first time. Both Presidents efforts to show-up at a bicommunal organization that is supported by a bicommunal act could arguably be considered a symbolic reconciliatory act.

Further, the CMP scientists do not directly interact with tens of thousands of Cypriots on the island; however their organization is influencing reconciliatory actions/displays of top leadership officials that have high visibility and a large degree of influence (Lederach, 2010, p. 39). Moreover, the humble

CMP workers because of the positions they hold in the CMP are respected by both communities, and they didn't declare themselves as leaders or direct influencers in the peacebuilding processes. They are able to reach top leadership officials and affect people and societies while conducting the process of exhumations so that they are, in effect, bicommunal "middle-tier" leaders in their own right (Lederach, 2010).

John Paul Lederach's work, *Building Peace: Sustainable Reconciliation In Divided Societies* (Lederach 2010) states that humanitarian leaders and respected intellectuals/academics have rare access to both grassroots people and top leadership political actors, which he calls—Middle Range Leadership (pp. 39–42). Effectively, the CMP can be considered to be a bicommunal Middle Range Leadership organization with its mandate to fulfill a humanitarian objective in which leadership is highly important for peacebuilding and reconciliation (Lederach, 2010; Rice, 2011).

It should be acknowledged that the objective goal of the CMP is not political. It is to fulfill its humanitarian mandate of finding Missing Persons and reuniting them with their loved ones. However, several of my research participants acknowledged that the Presidents' visit and their collective support of the CMP were good for popular optics and also important on a psychological level for families. For example, CMP Turkish Cypriot Scientist 1 noted the following:

> CMP Turkish Cypriot Scientist 1: As you mentioned, the leaders were here not long before. It was very good. Because when people will watch it on television and read newspapers and when they will see our President was here together with the other President, maybe it will encourage witnesses to give information to locate new sites. On the other hand, I think psychologically it . . . shows how important CMP is for them . . . It is good and families will also see they were here and they are working for this project.

Similarly, CMP Greek Cypriot Scientist 2 observed that the Presidents' visit was important for public morale:

> CMP Greek Cypriot Scientist 2: . . . The visiting Presidents are showing that they came together and they both support the work here that is done and it's a good thing to show that the elected officials of both communities are backing this. This is important for general perception.

Therefore, the study participants all agree how important leadership is when presented to the general public and the relatives of the Missing in both the TRNC and RoC with respect to the process of exhumations and how it can lead to particular peacebuilding outcomes. If leadership in regards to finding the Missing in the context of Cyprus is perceptually understood as bicommunal; then a bicommunal message will be understood namely, that

Missing Persons is a bicommunal issue with a bicommunal solution. Hence the CMP and other bicommunal organizations are promoting the possibility of inter-ethnic problemsolving, cooperation in work activities and in building new relationships by setting an example.

In the next chapter, I delve deeper into what the participants expressed as helpful with respect to dealing with the process of exhumations and how powerful storytelling can be—whether it promotes inter-ethnic reconciliation or not. In addition, I further discuss other features of bicommunal leadership and how story can aid in the process of exhumations (or perhaps stunt it) and in building inter-ethnic reconciliation.

CONCLUSION AND SUMMARY OF KEY FINDINGS

In conclusion, chapter five outlined the idea *Bicommunal Relations* in which emergent themes led to significant findings about what the process of exhumations does as well as the bicommunal nature of the CMP specific to the Cyprus context.

The process of exhumations defined as the recovery, identification and reunification of the Missing with loved ones is a powerful tool in Cyprus that can promote positive bicommunal relations. When analyzing the data and the key theme of Bicommunal Relations, several interesting findings emerged that are significant factors to consider for a post-violent conflict country with the issue of Missing Persons.

The first key finding with respect to peacebuilding and reconciliation is to consider whether the number of Missing Persons is high compared to its population. If the Missing Persons ratio is too high then the participants claim that it affects too many relatives, family members, and both communities, to be dealt with unsystematically. Further, by extension of the interrelated networks, the participants claim that societies will not be able to heal when a high percentage of the population is Missing. The question arises as to what percentage of a population that goes Missing because of violent conflict is large enough to be systematically addressed by respective governments, NGOs, INGOs, and Intergovernmental Organizations such as the United Nations for peacebuilding purposes?

With regard to Cyprus, all of my study participants agreed that the population that went Missing was too high in which out of the roughly 600,000 citizens at the time (from 1960 to 1974) 2,001 went Missing (a large amount of these were non-combatants). This is a fairly large proportion of the population to go Missing considering that 78 percent of the 600,000 were Greek Cypriot, and 18 percent were Turkish Cypriot (Sant-Cassia, 2005). The Missing affected too many people from both communities and, the Missing issue must be addressed to forge deep reconciliation in order to achieve a sustainable peace. Reconciliation between Greek and Turkish Cypriots is directly and indirectly affected by the CMP bicommunal organization in the recovery, identification, and reunification of the Missing with loved ones. One participant noted that for families, searching for Missing Persons from each community it becomes a sort of handshaking or building trust between both communities.

When analyzing the data, the next key finding that emerged was that the process of exhumations must start with a list of the Missing. Any country recently recovering from violent conflict must compile a list of the Missing, which is essential to addressing the issue. The list was initially the responsibility of relatives and loved ones of the Missing that had to notify the authorities such as both governments, NGOs, and INGOs, etc. With respect to Cyprus, the importance of finding the Missing was so high that families empowered themselves by organizing their own NGOs and they made up their own Missing lists. However, the NGOs in Cyprus were not bicommunal which reduced the opportunity to aid, gather, and share witness information as well as gain access to different territories (because they are ethno-politically separated and hostile). Further, the creation of a "common list" shows a "common interest" by both respective communities/governments in aiding in the recovery of Missing Persons and begins the reconciliation process through confidence building.

The fact that both ethnic communities and respective governments compile a common list can be seen as highly important in post conflict societies because access to government documents and information on the Missing will aid in finding Missing Persons, particularly with respect to post conflict societies that do not have a political settlement yet such as Cyprus. However, creating a list can also be a slippery slope to division if it is used by the respective governments and communities to enhance victimization and perpetrator narratives.

Several of the participants discussed the nature of the Cyprus conflict as a problem of lack of contact between both communities. Until the opening of the Green Line in 2004, inter-ethnic contact was suspended separating Turkish and Greek Cypriots for over 30 years. Several of my research participants (Greek and Turkish Cypriots) discussed how the separation disempowered their understanding of the other ethnic group and increased their opportunity for the maintenance and dispersion of victimization and perpetrator narratives of hate. However, my study participants agreed that experiencing contact and interactions with the other changed their perceptions and images. It promoted a humanization process, better communication, and an empowerment of knowledge of the other, creating good connections as one participant put it through his experience of working in the south outside of the CMP.

The study participants mentioned that when an opportunity for contact does emerge through various avenues it is dependent on certain conditions.

The key finding was that if there was no external pressure from an in-group mentality, good connections and enhanced communication could emerge between Greek and Turkish Cypriots. Thus, inter-group contact or superordinate goals can aid in good communication and connections when opportunities are made available that are bicommunal.

It can be argued that the bicommunal CMP organization and inter-ethnic friendship development offers an excellent example of creating good conditions for good connections and communicative opportunities within CMP that trickle outside to the wider society. CMP is the only institutionalized bicommunal organization in which eighty Turkish and Greek Cypriots work together five days a week for nine hours a day as it sets a precedent of inter-ethnic cooperation, peacebuilding, and reconciliation. Further, Turkish and Greek Cypriot scientists need to problemsolve everyday as a result of the scientists' work (the process of exhumations). This working peace system offers an educational example to society that communities can work well together and as such it becomes a confidence building tool for others to witness.

One very interesting key finding was with respect to skeletal remains. My study participants stated they saw no difference between Greek and Turkish Cypriots in the sense "that we're all made of the same stuff underneath" so that working with bones led to a *simulated similarity*. This understanding triggered by the idea of working blindly with respect to the ethnicity of the Missing Person's bones can be said to aid in a common and shared understanding of a common/shared problem, for example, Missing Persons and a shared solution of reunification of the Missing with their loved ones. Cyprus does not have a political settlement yet it has a context of interdependence with respect to the process of exhumations. The shared problems between both ethnic communities require things such as access to territories and governmental agencies and witness information, which foster a necessary interdependence between the respective communities of Greek and Turkish Cypriots.

The interdependence and working relationship between CMP workers has led to improved inter-ethnic interpersonal relationships and friendships. This powerful transformation of relations within a large organization made up of roughly eighty scientists also affects their own families and relatives in a ripple out effect. It should not be underestimated as to what far-reaching effects might be achieved with respect to inter-ethnic reconciliation on an island with a population of just over a million.

The CMP is fostering *friendships* between Turkish and Greek Cypriots, and some of the participants expressed that because the working conditions can be dangerous this led to caring, protection and good communication between the workers as improved bicommunal relations and friendships developed between CMP staff. And those friendships were not limited to working hours. For example, one of the Turkish Cypriot study participant's gave me examples of being invited to a Greek Orthodox Church, sharing in the marriage ceremony with Greek Cypriot work friends, and being supportive at his Greek Cypriot friend's father's funeral.

The bicommunal nature of the CMP has also led to the transformation of inter-ethnic relations between CMP workers within and outside of work. Another key finding is that this transformation of inter-ethnic relations is having, in some cases, a spillover effect on their respective societies. The bicommunal work has manifested spaces of interaction and communication between Cypriots—both Turkish and Greek due to the nature of gathering witness information and working together on archaeological sites. Thus, the bicommunal nature of the CMP and its work—the process of exhumations—has led to the emergence of bicommunal spaces in society that Greek and Turkish Cypriots can see, interact, and communicate with each other. In some cases, this has led to reconciliatory moments between Greek and Turkish Cypriots as in the case of the return of the Greek Cypriot soldier's glasses to his widow by a Turkish Cypriot family.

Yet while the bicommunal process of exhumations is having a positive bicommunal effect on inter-ethnic relations, during the final stage of the Viewing process where relatives are informed of the process and then reunified with loved ones, the bicommunal nature of the CMP must be momentarily suspended. Although both Turkish and Greek Cypriots aided in the recovery, identification and reunification of the Missing Person, the transmission of knowledge of the process to relatives is by the scientists from the respective ethnic group of the Missing. This does not mean that the relatives of the Missing Persons do not know that both Greek and Turkish Cypriots worked and aided in reunifying them with their loved one (as in the example of the family giving flowers to both parties) but it leaves food for thought as to the delicate nature of a bicommunal process of exhumations, and how it can/should be handled within the context of Cyprus or other post-violent conflict societies.

Finally, the last key finding revealed in the data was how the CMP also effected the actions of top leadership officials. Effectively, the CMP can be considered to be a bicommunal Middle Range Leadership organization because it is trying to fulfill its humanitarian mandate in the reunification of the Missing with their loved ones. Consequently, by inviting both Presidents to the CMP to show their support of this bicommunal organization's work (through the media for purposes of gathering witness information and in the hopes of receiving further financial aid), the CMP is presenting an image and affecting the general population's perceptions of its bicommunal solidarity and inter-ethnic reconciliation process.

By working bicommunally, not only are CMP scientists affecting onlookers and relatives of the Missing alike, they are also aiding in the process of uniting families on both sides by participating outside of work in each other's activities such as marriage ceremonies and funerals. These inter-ethnic friendships are constantly aiding in the transformation of relationships while also setting an educational example for both ethnic communities of cooperation and friendship.

Yet how far is the reach of the bicommunal message of the bicommunal organization and its effects on both societies in terms of inter-ethnic reconciliation? My research participants had several things to say about this process that relates to storytelling. I next focus on the process of storytelling in relation to the process of exhumations and its powerful effects on reconciliation.

Chapter Six

Storytelling—Even the Dead Have a Voice

The Bones Are Telling a Story

JOURNAL ENTRY

Date: August 12th, 2014
I had already been at the CMP for several weeks. I knew that my time with the CMP would soon come to an end. While volunteering with the scientists I had observed and aided in some of the processes of exhumations. At the anthropological laboratory I observed the analysis of bones to determine age, sex and stature of remains. I watched as the scientists meticulously laid out the bodies on white tablecloths, forensically analyzing parts like pieces of a puzzle. In the field, I participated and observed in the archaeological phase; attempting to recover remains from a possible gravesite of Missing Persons. And finally, I experienced several Viewings when the final family reunification process occurred when the identified person and their remains were given back to the family and relatives.

I spent most of one day observing a designated professional photographer whose job it was to document the material remains, the artifacts, and articulated body parts. Photographers document the process of exhumations from the field to the lab through pictures. That day I was in the lab with a photographer who was taking pictures of skeletal remains when we came across a watch. I asked about the watch and she said it was found at a grave site. The watch was near a table that belonged to an articulated body. I took a closer look at the watch and realized that it had stopped. Then I thought to myself this watch could have stopped at the moment this person was killed. It was cracked and the hands on the clock were fixed at a specific time—likely the time of his or her death. Time at that moment had stopped still. So did his or her life. I thought to myself who is this person? Who did s/he love? What did s/he do? Where are his or her loved ones? It challenged the concept of linear time for me because the watch, in one way or another—perhaps forty years later, was telling us something; about a person, who had lived, loved and died and who had managed time. And yet in another way, the watch was like a message sent from that person. And I realized time is not linear. Even after death our stories live on.

That's when it hit me. The bones are telling a story. When artifacts are found with the body, they are telling a story. The suspected grave sites are telling a story. The scientists that are recording the data and returning the remains are telling a story. During the Viewing the families (literally in some instances) are telling stories of their loved ones. The information gathered from eye witness testimony are connecting stories of the past, present, and future, which are reunifying loved ones with their Missing. It is what Marshall McLuhan had said fifty years ago, "The medium is the message."

Here the medium is comprised of the artifacts, the remains and the bones of the Missing are affecting, creating, and perpetuating an environment of bicommunal communication and exchange and in so doing affecting the social organization of Cyprus society. The bones are inadvertently speaking beyond the grave and telling a story. Perhaps they are telling a shared story, of a shared future and past, through a shared process of exhumations.

INTRODUCTION

> I have been doing this for the last ten years, so . . . (she chuckles and so do I). Yes, because when you tell the story you humanize the process. When you tell the story it stops being a number, a figure, and a statistic. It starts hitting home and you give them the identity they had—the Missing. It is not a bunch of soldiers, it is not a bunch of people who went Missing we don't know. Its humans, real humans, who have stories of their own because maybe death is the end of human life but it doesn't stop the relationship. The relationship with the living continues when you are Missing. You have to tell that story in order to be able to humanize the process and normalize the process among the people. And I have been doing that for the last fourteen years. It is clear you see what happened for instance when they read a story of a certain Greek Cypriot that went missing and what sort of suffering the family went through. My readers on each side didn't necessarily call me to tell me something about that particular Missing. But they knew other relatives of the Missing, other stories, and they called me to share what they know. So it encouraged them to speak because their hearts were touched. We managed to touch the heart of the people. That was the turning point.
> (Sevgül Uludağ, interview and personal communication, July 1, 2014)

Chapter six focuses on the process of *Storytelling* in Cyprus with respect to Missing Persons and the process of exhumations. During the interview process this core concept was unpacked, that led to the emergence of key themes that highlight the significance and importance of storytelling for the process of exhumations.

Storytelling can be seen as the keystone in the center of an arch that holds together the process of exhumations. Its importance cannot be underestimated in understanding and fulfilling what the process of exhumations does or rather can do in regard to inter-ethnic reconciliation and in building sustainable peace. This chapter also expresses what the participants had to say about storytelling and the process of exhumations. Consequently, it also highlights the study participants' thoughts about how story is used in/for the recovery, identification, and reunification of the Missing with relatives and the healing processes that can occur if story is constructively done. I will present their ideas around Dr. Jessica Senehi's framework of "constructive storytelling" in comparison to "destructive storytelling" to articulate their thoughts on the power of story within the process of exhumations (Senehi, 2011).

This chapter outlines the following five themes: What is Storytelling; The Bones as Story; Storytelling and Information; Constructive Storytelling and Destructive Storytelling; Storytelling and Historical Non-reoccurrence of Violence. In this chapter, five themes are unpacked about what storytelling is in conjunction to the process of exhumations according to my study participants. Storytelling is understood as a process that is spoken or told to someone else (Smith, 1981 cited in Senehi, 2011, p. 202) and an oral relation of a story considered as a social interaction (Ryan, 1995 cited in Senehi, 2011, p. 202). Finally, it offers some of the challenges that the process of exhumations goes through with respect to storytelling that can aid in "transforming conflicts constructively" (Senehi, 2011, p. 203) in post-violent conflict societies with regards to the issue of Missing Persons.

WHAT IS STORYTELLING?

Storytelling is a very complex and complicated process, particularly with respect to a post-violent conflict society such as Cyprus, which is going through the process of exhumations, (recovery, identification, and reunification of the Missing with their loved ones). Thus, my research participants responded to question nine (See Appendix A): *Can the process of exhumation ever be separated from ethnic hatred, ethno-nationalism, and storytelling?* And question ten: *Is there a role for storytelling in the process of exhumations? If so, how is storytelling conducted and represented during and after the process of exhumations?* They questioned what storytelling was about and in so doing deconstructed it with respect to the process of exhumations. With that in mind, I now turn to what several participants had to say about storytelling in order to give it meaning within our Cyprus context.

The participant designated as the Professor stated that listening to stories plays a vital role in the process of exhumations, but that storytelling during the process of exhumations followed by storytelling afterwards, are two different zones. In one way the process of exhumations is one story and storytelling after the process could be considered as another different story. He argues that what combines the two storytelling zones is that they are about a "discourse of trauma." As he states:

> Yeah definitely, it is a very good question. Storytelling is of paramount importance. We listen to stories about it and it plays a vital role I would say. And if so, how is storytelling represented and conducted during and after this process of exhumations? . . . We are talking about two different situations or zones to say so. Do you know process is [one] story and after the process could be another story? But for sure storytelling is something that creates a shot at a discourse of trauma. This is the discourse of trauma—the storytelling—during and after the process.

Further, the participant Professor goes on to complicate the process of storytelling by expressing how burial ceremonies, memorials constructed, cinema and plays, vocabulary and lexicon used or not (verbal communication), dress and appearance and body posturing (non-verbal communication) are all forms of storytelling that ultimately affect memory. Thus, he states that all of these elements of storytelling, are factors that "constitute a phenomenon of trauma" and operate as an expression of a "meta-trauma discourse and situation" as story.

> Yeah, they have memorials. They have cinema, and also the way people dress up during this. The storytelling is not just the words. It is not just the lexicon, the vocabulary, the words that they use, it is also the way they appear at the memorial; wearing black, or delivering special speeches during the memorial bringing to our minds and/or to our memory about the person who was buried and how this happened. It is a multi-faced multilayered type of discourse. This discourse has a number of layers and dimensions. It is about the language also. You know what I mean? So people may say nothing. People sometimes are speechless during a memorial and they cannot even describe or tell about the Missing Person . . . but their body says a lot. So when we talk about the storytelling we have to take into account the body language, the dressing code—all the types of things that constitute a phenomenon of trauma, the experience of trauma. Let me put it this way: as we talk that came to mind—it is a meta-trauma situation—you can characterize it as a meta-trauma discourse and situation. Yeah, that's it.

According to the University Professor, storytelling is a highly complex, multifaceted meta-trauma discourse and situation that takes place within and after the process of exhumations.

In comparison, Sevgül Uludağ expresses that storytelling in relation to the process of exhumations is a humanization process. The relatives and loved ones live in uncertainty as to what happened to their Missing Person so the relationship of storytelling to the dead and the living continues. This is what she had to say:

> Yes, because when you tell the story you humanize the process. When you tell the story it stops being a number, a figure, and a statistic. It starts hitting home and you give them the identity they had—the Missing. It is not a bunch of soldiers, it is not a bunch of people who went Missing we don't know. Its humans, real humans, who have stories of their own because maybe death is the end of human life but it doesn't stop the relationship. The relationship with the living continues when you are Missing. You have to tell that story in order to be able to humanize the process and normalize the process among the people. And I have been doing that for the last fourteen years. It is clear you see what happened for instance when they read a story of a certain Greek Cypriot that went Missing and what sort of suffering the family went through. My readers on each side didn't necessarily call me to tell me something about that particular Missing. But they knew other relatives of the Missing, other stories, and they called me to share what they know. So it encouraged them to speak because their hearts were touched. We managed to touch the heart of the people. That was the turning point.

According to Sevgül Uludağ, storytelling doesn't have to take place orally between two living person's, it can be a symbiotic process beyond life and death as well something that transpires between the relatives and the Missing Person. When stories are told they humanize the person and the process of exhumations because sharing stories touches the hearts of Cypriots. Therefore, storytelling in this context is also about the humanization of Missing Persons.

From the participants' perspective, storytelling can be seen as organic knowledge, transmitted in various forms through verbal and non-verbal communication, and symbols, etcetera, which produce meaning for social life (Senehi, 2011). As Jessica Senehi (2011) states, storytelling plays a role "in the production of meaning—and access to that process" (p. 203). Perhaps in the context of Cyprus the process of exhumations and storytelling, (the production of meaning) is the humanization of the Missing Persons issue. These methods access a meta-trauma discourse and process that could be a slippery slope to intensifying conflict *or* it could produce a bridge of healing and reconciliation in post-violent conflict societies with the issue of Missing Persons.

THE BONES AS STORY

It became clear in the interviews how integrated storytelling was in the recovery of Missing persons. For example, CMP Turkish Cypriot Scientist 3 states that "Yeah . . . telling stories . . . every aspect of this project is telling stories and there are many stories." One profound and interesting feature of storytelling that one of my study participant's discussed is the fact that the bones themselves are telling a story raising the question whether storytelling must be a process that is conducted by the living? Consequently, is storytelling something that is measurable? Does storytelling reside outside of science? The material reality is that it does not lie outside of science and even when people die their stories are recorded in their bones so that they speak beyond the grave. CMP Greek Cypriot Scientist 2 outlined the following with me:

> CMP Greek Cypriot Scientist 2: The bones always tell a story.
>
> Kris: Could you maybe talk about that a bit.
>
> CMP Greek Cypriot Scientist 2: Yeah of course. Bones could tell you many, many things. They could tell you a story of for example *ante mortem records*—which means records before death [which] could indicate [medical records]; or the mother of a son remembers her son when he was playing one day who broke his right arm when he was seventeen, sixteen, fifteen, and then when you get a body and you see a broken *Ulmer Radius* at that point or the way the mother described it; the bones are telling you scientifically what the mother has told you what she experienced and what she saw. Even like other things that we can see or they remember an old person and they are humped over and we see the vertebra. We know that the person had *kyphosis* or you know some sort of disease of the vertebra, which in life the person would have been humped over. I mean everything can be explained, (rather not everything not a hundred percent because you do not have the flesh), but bones can tell you anything that effected the bones during life [which] will reflect in the analysis. I mean bones can tell you how old the person was, they can tell you if they are a man or women, they can tell you how tall the person was, they can tell you what diseases the person passed through and what affected them. If trauma affects the bones they can tell you exactly what happened; the bullet went through here and exited here in this direction and caused this damage. I mean it tells you everything. Everything you need to know to complete this process.

Henceforth, the bones in one way or another are speaking out. The bones record experiences and environmental effects. I was told while volunteering that you can also make a good guess at what the person did for a living (if they were a farmer or office worker) and what the person's diet consisted of based on the bones and *ante mortem* data. Therefore, the bones can be said to record our personal histories and leave traces of who we are. Further, with new "technologies of power" such as DNA testing coupled with blood sampling from relatives, the bones can aid in offering up the person's "social identity" (Wagner, 2008) meaning the person's family name.

The social identity and recognition of the Missing Person is a dialogical process between the living and the dead. The Missing Person can be understood to be telling the story of her/his life through her/his bones, which complements the storytelling of the relatives. This, combined with the scientific analysis of the CMP helps to reveal a person's social identity. Missing Persons are like actors having agency who inadvertently help their families identify them by storytelling through their bones. They communicate with living relatives through their stories, which aid in the scientific identification process, and an understanding of who they are namely, a lover, father, daughter, husband, and wife who lived and died, but are not forgotten.

STORYTELLING AND INFORMATION

My research participants all stated that eye witness information or secondary information regarding the whereabouts of Missing Persons is one of the greatest challenges they face. Several factors exacerbate this challenge because of the time lapse of the violent conflicts in the 1960s and in 1974 in which first hand eye witnesses who have the information are now dying of old age. CMP Turkish Cypriot Scientist 1 noted this issue as follows:

> We don't have enough information about where the Missing Persons [are] buried? This is the biggest problem of this project. With time, eye witnesses are dying. How, if there are second hand witnesses, how correct is the information they have? We cannot be sure because it is heard from someone else probably. Sometimes it is not true; most of the time we are digging for nothing. I mean we are digging and we don't find anything. At least this point is off the list you can say. But, where are they? I think this is the biggest problem.

Thus, some of the information is coming from second hand witnesses, meaning people who were told the stories of the event where the disappeared were last seen or they may have heard of possible gravesites. Therefore, CMP Staff Member observes that:

> The first one is to have the right information. Right now we have a success rate of less than twenty percent when we excavate. We have to dig about ten times . . . to succeed twice. You know, for every eight unsuccessful excavations we have two currently that succeeds.

Due to the nature of post violent conflicts and Missing Persons, people can be hesitant to share information about what they have heard regarding the possible whereabouts of the Missing for many reasons. For example, CMP Staff Member argues that in Cyprus, "both people (ethnic communities) here hesitate to provide information because they think it is looked upon negatively in the community." However, the importance of storytelling cannot be underestimated in the recovery, identification, and reunification of the Missing with their loved ones. The majority of Missing Persons found are due to the sharing of stories about the whereabouts of possible gravesites. It must be stated that the CMP's mandate is the humanitarian return of Missing Persons in Cyprus to their loved ones. Paul-Henri Arni avers that CMP's mission is to simply find and identify the Missing, and reunite them with their families:

> No it's not linked to storytelling. People go missing and therefore their story by definition is not known. To tell the story of a Missing Person is not our job. We have a clear mandate, which is to recover human remains, identify them and return them to their families. That's all.

However, the process of exhumations depends heavily on witnesses stories about the whereabouts of gravesites. Of course many of the stories that have information regarding the whereabouts of the Missing are from both ethnic communities. Therefore, the process of exhumations which is dependent upon storytelling to find the remains of the Missing is an inter-ethnic exchange of communication.

The CMP investigators search for stories of the whereabouts of gravesites in order to return the Missing to their relatives. Moreover, the power of storytelling in the process of exhumations has led to grassroots leaders such as Sevgül Uludağ to also collect and publish stories. For example, CMP Staff Member had this to say about Sevgül Uludağ's work:

> She is central to the issue of Missing Persons in Cyprus. She's a Turkish Cypriot journalist who ten years ago started to work on the Missing Person's issue. She's written us an article about Missing Persons every day. She has a thousand contacts on both sides of the island. She finds a good percentage of the people that we end up exhuming and she does the storytelling. So every day she publishes a column in a Greek newspaper in the South and a Turkish newspaper in the North. Every day she writes an article about the Missing Persons. She provides the stories. She literally does the storytelling. And through the storytelling she obtains information. She tells the story of somebody who disappeared and then writes her phone number under the article and says if you know anything about this call me and people call. So in that sense there's a huge role for storytelling. But we don't do it. We're not involved in it, we can't do it. But she has the liberty to do it.

I was fortunate enough to meet with Sevgül Uludağ and she agreed to be interviewed by me. She is a very charismatic, passionate, strong willed and kind person who speaks from her heart. She even insisted on paying for my coffee during the interview. Sevgül aids in the process of exhumations by providing a space where inter-ethnic dialogue and storytelling can happen anonymously or not. She incites people's hearts to call in and tell their stories of the disappeared. Within the Cypriot stories—Greek or Turkish—information regarding the whereabouts of Missing Persons is revealed. This is what she had to say on the issue:

> We sort of pushed them to share and encouraged them to share. Even if the Greek Cypriots . . . knew about a certain burial site where let's say, three Turkish Cypriots were buried, they kept silent. When my readers came out and told me and we showed them, they had to "dig it" and vice versa. Even if Turkish Cypriots knew about a certain place where ten Greek Cypriots were buried and they kept silent and they didn't want to say, when my readers came and showed it, they had to "dig it." You know we forced them too and we encouraged them because as I told you I publish everything that my readers tell me. It is not my task to find the graves; it is the task of the community which is made up of Turkish Cypriots, Greek Cypriots and the United Nations. I am not an investigator, I am not a policeman; I don't have assistance, I don't have a photographer; nobody pays for my petrol; nobody pays for my phone. We do it voluntarily with my readers and we try to clear the field because unless we clear the field we cannot move to the future. We need to know exactly what happened to these people. They didn't die because of a personal reason; they died because of the conflict.

When Ms. Uludağ publishes these stories in newspapers (every story can be found on her online website at http://www.sevgulludag.blogspot.co.uk/) she promotes what Senehi (2011) calls a safe environment, openness, a shared experience, a co-creation of story with readers/listeners, which emphasizes empowerment (pp. 209–210). Sevgül opens up a *virtual inter-ethnic dialogue* of storytelling to transform the conflict constructively on the issue of Greek and Turkish Cypriot Missing Persons. All of the stories are written as they were told to her and not only does storytelling aid in finding Missing Persons it offers a space or again what Lederach (2010) calls a "locus" for an "encounter" for Cypriots to express themselves and their stories about the conflict and the process of exhumations that forms relationships and promotes inter-ethnic reconciliation. Thus she publishes all information she receives about the disappeared, where they were last seen, the family's funeral after the Missing was reunified with them, etcetera.

Transparent and "transcultural storytelling" (Senehi, 2009) empowers Cypriots with knowledge and understanding, which as Sevgül said "touches their hearts" and that's why they call in. But, as Sevgül also states, storytelling can be a slippery slope because it depends on how one uses it:

> It depends how you handle it. I have a series running and I think we should try to put it in the Guinness Book of World Records. I started in May 2006 and its everyday about the Missing and the untold stories of Cyprus and it continues until now. It is the 2,399th or 2,400th issue today or something like this. I think

> on the earth it is the only series about human pain that has been running so long—more than eight years now. [I have] this series and also my articles in Politis, which is once a week because of translation. And if I could, I would do it in Greek as well every day. I try to show, "look what we did to each other!" It depends how you handle it. If you want, some groups use it for—"look at what Greeks did to us" or "look at what Turks did to us." But, you can show and say "look at what we did to each other, look at this funeral." When I go to a funeral, I write the story of the funeral. I write what they said, I write how they felt. I write who was this man, it is not a number, and he has a human face. He had children for example, a wife. What did they suffer and how did they wait and find him? To create an understanding that we are all beacons and we are all perpetrators. We cannot differentiate from a Greek Cypriot boy whose father went Missing or a Turkish Cypriot's. It's the same pain.

Storytelling is of paramount importance for the recovery of Missing Persons in terms of getting information on their whereabouts. Storytelling is also important with respect to the identification process due to a relative's testimony of a Missing Person's status before death such as any diseases the person may have had, or *ante mortem* trauma the person experienced that only relatives know about. Finally, Sevgül Uludağ contended that stories can be constructive or destructive based on how the stories are told and used in post-violent conflict societies with respect to Missing Persons.

CONSTRUCTIVE STORYTELLING

The participants of the study discussed the role of storytelling with respect to the process of exhumations. When analyzing the interviews, what stood out for me in regards to reconciliation between both ethnic communities was the fact that it all depends on how the process of exhumations is told, and whether the story is told enough. If the story of the process of exhumations and the bicommunal nature of the CMP and the return of the Missing was consistently presented to the public, then an *information affect* or a message of inter-ethnic cooperation, inter-ethnic reconciliation, and perhaps psychosocial healing and rehabilitation might occur because there is a sharing in power, acknowledgement, and how the story is being constructed (Senehi, 2011). However, the majority of my research participants stated that the public in the North (Turkish Cypriots) and in the South (Greek Cypriots) may not be well informed about the role and activities of the CMP, its operations, and how it is organized bicommunally. For example, Greek Cypriot Scientist 2 had the following to say on the issue:

> Kris: As another sub-question: do you believe that it sends a message to the communities in the North and in the South because [the CMP] is a bicommunal and friendship-building organization?

> Greek Cypriot Scientist 2: Of course. But, if you go ask any random person in the street what we do here, nine people out of ten won't know the exact answer to give you. Even some people won't know that we actually exist. So to tell you that it is helping peacebuilding because it is showing a bicommunal aspect I think that if people don't know that we are working together how are they going to know and feel that there is a bicommunal team working together? . . . To be an example people have to know about it and most people don't know about it, so no. But, generally if it was well known I believe it would be, yes.

Other participants also stated that the message being portrayed by the media, (including newspapers in the North and the South) present only one side of the story when identification, reunification and burial occur when it comes to a member of their respective ethnic group. Thus, it is arguable that a promotion of the destructive forms of story are occurring, because by withholding knowledge of the return of the remains of a member from the other ethnic community and the inter-ethnic process that aided in such a humanitarian act, the maintenance of the moralizing victim and victimizer narratives may become further entrenched (Senehi, 2011, pp. 205–7). Therefore, the information affect may maintain dominant narratives of victimization for either side. CMP Turkish Cypriot Scientist 1 noted it as follows:

> The Committee (CMP) is giving a chance to the public to see it. But I don't know if there are a lot of people following what the Committee is doing or if they are only following their part; such as, if they are hearing only Turkish Cypriots are identified and they don't hear about Greek Cypriots also identified and they are buried. And if they don't read it in the Turkish Cypriot newspaper, maybe it will not be useful. The same goes for the Greek Cypriot side, if they don't hear about the Turkish Cypriots identified and buried, they will not know that there are still Turkish Cypriots Missing and so it will be like they are the only victim again.

CMP Turkish Cypriot Scientist 3 observes that people are learning how the CMP operates to a degree, but there should be more media attention focused on what the CMP is doing. Both the Turkish and Greek Cypriot media should share stories with each other about what is happening on the other side namely, stories on the Missing, reunification, and rituals of burial so as to educate the public about their shared past and the tragedy of their shared problem, namely the Missing Persons of Cyprus.

> I believe people are also learning a great deal, but they could learn more about the other side. I think the CMP should be more involved with the media. I believe that people in the Greek Cypriot communities—ordinary people—may not know about the extent of Turkish Cypriot Missing Persons; and maybe Turkish Cypriots may not know how many Greek Cypriots are Missing. I

> believe this would be a good way to teach people in both communities about what the CMP is doing and what happened in the past.

The majority of my research participants claim that there is a greater need of media exposure on the CMP and the process of exhumations to promote reconciliation. Further, they state that for a constructive effect to take place, the media in the North and the South need to share stories from both sides' about their Missing Persons as well as the identification and burial processes. With more media exposure they believe that the CMP, as a bicommunal organization, will serve as a greater example of bicommunal cooperation and both societies will gain an understanding that Missing Persons is a shared problem. This understanding could eventually aid in inter-ethnic reconciliation.

Yet, it is *how* the issue of Missing Persons is presented to the public that my study participants' claim is most important. If media exposure on the return of the Missing is only about Greek Cypriots or Turkish Cypriots, then perhaps instead ethnocentric victimization narratives will be perpetuated and the message of a shared problem will not be heard. CMP Turkish Cypriot Scientist 1 discusses this issue in the following story:

> One day I stopped at the gas station in South Cyprus in Nicosia. A Greek Cypriot helped me to buy petrol when there was no employee around with a credit card from the machine. He said to me, "Where are you from?" I said, "I am a Turkish Cypriot." He said, "Ah your English is better than most of them—you are good educated." He said, "What are you doing here now?" I said, "I am working for the Committee on Missing Persons in Cyprus." He said, "Ah you are looking for the Greek Cypriots Missing in Cyprus." I said, "No, I am looking for Turkish Cypriot and Greek Cypriot Missing." He said, "I didn't know that there are Turkish Cypriot's Missing." And this guy was over fifty years old. He was not a young person. So in this logic (from this experience), some Cypriots are thinking that they are only the victim, it looks like. When we say Turkish Cypriot, there are Turkish Cypriot's Missing. They don't say "I don't believe it" but their faces are surprised. From the way of Greek Cypriot, they are a victim because they cannot go to their house and their land. They have the right to say that they are victims. There are already dead people and they are victims also. There are dead Turkish Cypriots and they are victims. There are Missing Greek and Turkish Cypriot's and they are victims. My father cannot go to his village and he is a victim of the conflict. But, who created this conflict?—Us—and now both sides are victims in my point of view.

Thus, my research participants share the same view i.e., that media exposure is necessary to get the message across and to educate the Cypriot people about what the CMP does and how it operates bicommunally. It is important to send a message that both Turkish and Greek Cypriots are victims so that a sharing in the story of loss will emerge. Moreover, due to the sensitive nature of the process of exhumations and the return of the Missing to loved ones in Cyprus, the importance of how the story of the process is told should not be underestimated because it can also be understood as a political mine field that may exacerbate conflict and encourage narratives of ethnocentric victimization.

Hence, my study the participants expressed their views about how storytelling can be constructively done with respect to the process of exhumations and inter-ethnic reconciliation. Many of my research participants stated that a shared story of apology from the political leaders about what happened would aid in the process of exhumations and reconciliation, which can be perceived by Cypriots as a necessary aspect of restorative justice via restitution without retribution (See Zehr, 2002). For example, Sevgül Uludağ had the following to say on the issue:

> Nobody came out from the official leaders at the political level—nobody apologized. None of the sides that were involved: England, Turkey, Greece, Cyprus's both communities. Leaderships never apologized for what happened in Cyprus. But this conflict did not rise out of the earth by itself; it was manipulated and it was perpetuated and it was cooked and seeds were planted. A lot of sides carry responsibility but nobody wants to claim responsibility. It's easier to show yourself as a victim and continue to use the issue, this humanitarian issue of the Missing and the people who were killed in the war for your own political ends. We don't like this attitude and we think that it damages both communities' mentality. One good thing that has not been done is that the two leaders together never went to the funeral of the Missing. The two leaders never came out and said we are very sorry for what happened in Cyprus in 1963 and 1974. We don't want this to happen and please speak up and tell us what you know. There has been no mutual apology or mutual acknowledgement.

Sevgül claims that a mutual apology and mutual acknowledgement of the dead from high political offices with respect to the consequences of the violent conflict i.e., Missing Persons would aid as a form of constructive storytelling. Further, as Zehr claims (2002) that restitution is a basic need of restorative justice where upon the offender takes some sort of responsibility for the crime committed, which offers vindication and is also part of Lederach's (2010) formulation of justice as a pillar of reconciliation. Through restitution and apology, mercy via forgiveness, which is another pillar of Lederach's reconciliation for sustainable peace process, has a better chance of coming into fruition. This is not to say that apologies from other levels of society are not important as well. As CMP Greek Cypriot Scientist 2 states regarding admission of guilt and aspects of forgiveness, ". . . I don't see anyone saying I'm sorry. And I think that's the main point. Admission of guilt makes people move on and if it happens good, but I don't think it will ever happen." According to Turkish Cypriot Scientist 1, apology and acknowledgement in the storytelling process would aid in an inter-ethnic understanding of the past and the forging of a lasting peace:

> . . . If you don't say sorry to each other and I don't let my son know about the truth about Cyprus and [the] Greek Cypriot doesn't let his son [know] (or if he doesn't learn the truth about Cyprus), even with a contract we will say we made peace but later on we will have problems. Because I didn't say sorry and what does it means saying sorry? [It means] I see and I know what we did and I will not do it again.

The power of apology and the forms in which it is presented at multiple levels of society from the household to high political offices and burial ceremonies are important avenues of constructive storytelling from the participants' perspectives with respect to the process of exhumations, because it impacts the restorative justice and reconciliation processes. However, my study participants expressed a concern that an apology must be done by both sides from the family level of social organization and particularly as a bicommunal action at the political level of high offices. This act would send a message of shared victimization and shared culpability in a powerfully shared story, which is a part of "constructive storytelling" (Senehi, 2011).

It isn't that tragic stories shouldn't be told or expressed. However, the concern is that stories that express the friendship and love between Greek and Turkish Cypriots prior to the 1974 division are not being given enough representation through the media, political organizations, and by families themselves. There are many untold stories that send a message of inter-ethnic reconciliation and conflict transformation thanks to the process of exhumations, which has provided an avenue for this type of healing particularly at burials after family reunification, has taken place. Sevgül Uludağ had the following to say on this issue:

> I think it again depends on how you handle it. I was at a funeral last week in June at a Cypriot village. It was a funeral of a Greek Cypriot who went Missing in 1964. It was fifty years—half a century—the relatives waited for any news about it. Imagine that. The son made a speech and this speech is available on my blog. He said, "My father was killed because of chauvinism and because of the rivalry. And he was innocent. He had lost his way coming to Nicosia and he was kidnapped by some Turkish Cypriots and he died under torture. They didn't waste any bullets on him. There are no bullet marks, which is obvious from his skeleton." Despite all this he gave a message of peace—the relative. He also said, "You are also a hero of reconciliation because here in this church now, we have Turkish Cypriots who came to say goodbye to you" (his father). A lot of Turkish Cypriots also came to that funeral. Together they/we buried him. It depends on how you handle this trauma. It depends on the family, the politicians, or the associations when they

> attend. I have been to many funerals in the north of Turkish Cyprus when the leader of this association—called the Martyr's association (supposedly for the Missing)—takes the microphone and says, "You see what the bloody Greeks and Greek Cypriots did to us? We can never live together with them and our only guarantee is the Turkish army" and things like that, which perpetuates hate and gives the message of hate instead of peace. I have been to some funerals of some Turkish Cypriots where they say we want peace and reconciliation on this island and this is the only way out. So, it depends on the family because the relatives choose how to bury them, who to invite, and what sort of message to give.

To reiterate, as Sevgül Uludağ and many others have expressed to me, it all depends on how the storytelling is being done with respect to Missing Persons in the process of exhumations. If storytelling is expressed in an ethnocentric manner through the narratives of victimization and hate then the role of story may be seen as destructive in terms of the transformation of relations between Turkish and Greek Cypriots toward peace. As many of my research participants stated, narratives of victimization are already prevalent within both ethnic communities. For example, CMP Staff Member claims that, "Well . . . the victim narrative is entrenched on both sides. There is nothing you have to do to bring that about. It's already there." However, as CMP Turkish Cypriot Scientist 1 also states, there are many stories of inter-ethnic friendship and living together peacefully before and during the violence of the 1960s and 1974 that were shared with him as a child. He tells a recent story that he experienced as follows:

> The stories I heard from where I live now, from my grandparents around that time, they were angry with the Greek Cypriots and they said they were bad because they want to kill us. From my other grandparents [who] lived in a mixed village, [and] they were living with Greek Cypriots, I heard very nice stories. Stories such as how friendly they were, how they helped when my grandmother gave birth. I saw after the gates opened we went to my grandmother's village and I saw an old lady walking towards us very fast and you can't imagine her walking that fast. She came and asked, ". . . you are the family of my grandmother?" and I said "yes" and she cried ten minutes non-stop. There are these kinds of stories. There is one story from one side of my family and there is one story from another side of my family. This is the bad one—Greek Cypriots are bad and they tried to kill us—this statement was made by my grandmother whose grandmother was Greek Cypriot.

The role of storytelling can take on many forms. Stories of inter-ethnic friendship and relations can counteract dominant narratives of ethnocentric victimization if they are shared and heard broadly. Moreover, it all depends on whether the stories are given a voice or an opportunity of expression that could aid in transforming the Cyprus conflict constructively.

Another major facet of storytelling and the role that it plays within the process of exhumations is its powerful effect on time, memory, history and remembering. For example, Senehi (2011) states that, "Time, memory, and history are significant in inter-group conflicts because the conflict is often framed as being about past events that have been unjust or that have disrupted relationships" (p. 207). Hence, many of the participants stated that the media in the North and South of Cyprus publicize mass grave sites, which can instill past trauma and destructive memories among people. For example, CMP Staff Member states the following in his story:

> . . . Mediatizing the results—if important mass graves have been opened and people have been returned to their families— . . . certainly helps bring closure to these families and to entire communities. So overall it has . . . a positive impact. It's always an issue . . . [when] opening graves you also tend to open up memories of horrific incidents . . . but overall I think the positive impact outweighs the negative.

He states that closure surrounding the uncertainty of what happened to the loved one will outweigh the reopening of traumatic events and memories because they are already prevalent because the victim narrative is prevalent in both ethnic-communities.

Many of my research participants expressed to me that memory as part of the process of exhumations was a powerful effect of storytelling and of *remembering*. As the Cyprus University Professor stated, *Missing comes . . . as a memory, as part of history. As one piece of history*. Moreover, my study participants expressed the point that remembering *needs* to be done yet that remembering through storytelling (as a result of the process of exhumations) is dependent upon *how* one remembers. And how the person remembers is dependent upon how the process of exhumations is conducted and further how the media, the relatives of the Missing, and the nation-state talk about the issue of Missing Persons and its resolution. As CMP Greek Cypriot Scientist 2 notes, "It needs to be done. I don't disagree with remembering. It's how you remember. That's the whole point."

My research participants began to unpack storytelling and memorialization of the dead and Missing by discussing ceremonies of mourning, and about constructing memorials. They stated that ceremonies and memorialization have an impact on remembering and victimization. They all claimed that if the ceremonies and memorials were outside of politicization and sensationalizing ethnocentric victimization narratives, then they could become more *constructive* forms of story. Paul Arthur (2011) argues that memory is complex with respect to silence, forgetting and remembering past violence and events, in which he argues "Lack of communication can be the property of a society without empathy . . . [however] Remembering may not always produce the truth . . . [where perpetrators] create vital lies . . ." (pp. 372–73).

Further, he states that, "Remembering and forgetting, then, carry their own health warnings. Memory is multifaceted and manipulative. It is traumatic and capable of political appropriation but lack of memory and remembering can lead to oblivion" (p. 375). Memorials of constructed sites (museums, monuments) and found sites (killing fields), and activities (commemoration of specific events), effect memory and remembering that must avoid triumphalism and victim narratives (pp. 377–78).

Thus, memorialization ceremonies and memorials themselves are presented as a message of victimization and for nationalist purposes through nationalist symbols of anthems and flags, so that they become a form of destructive storytelling. For example, Paul-Henry Arni reports on the issue in the following way:

> The only true ceremonies that I know of are two kinds: family ceremonies, where families are left to deal away from cameras and away from national flags and national anthems and speeches and are left to mourn indignity. The second one is a sort of monument that helps former enemies or Missing Persons of any side to be remembered in a dignified manner—but not one side having a ceremony for their own victims and another side for their own victims, but rather together: a monument to the people who went Missing. And that's probably what a country like Spain should be doing with a proper monument and then history books, to teach the young Spanish children that crimes were committed on both sides; that their grandfather was killed, but not because . . . the other side was full of bad people and our side were victims, but it was a bloody civil war where people went Missing on both sides and therefore should be honored as victims through an effort of memorialization that is common. When you memorialize human suffering with events in each community you usually don't prevent—even years or decades later—you don't prevent politicization; because of the presence of dignitaries and because of the presence of flags and speeches which remind these poor people that their loved ones were killed by the enemy. So it's not a contribution to peace, it's a contribution to the perpetuation of a hostile memory towards the other side.

Henceforth, when the memorialization of a conflict and Missing Persons are conducted, the message of these events is best done outside of ethnocentric politicization, nationalism, and through family ceremonies. As some scholars suggest nationalism and coopting politics for in- group and out-group purposes is always a major problem with regard to conflict escalation and the formation of ethnopolitical boundaries (Anderson, 1983; Byrne, 2000, Anastasiou, 2008) and with respect to remembering the past with the capacity to cause inter-ethnic competition (Wagner, 2008). Thus, remembering the past should be done in *common* as a memorial of loss and as a monument to all victims. For example, CMP Greek Cypriot Scientist 2 suggests that the effect of memory and remembering through ceremonies and memorials (including burial rituals of the Missing that have been returned) should be remembered outside of perpetuating forms of nationalism:

> If you are going to remember in a way that feeds nationalism, [it] is wrong. If you're going to remember in the way that these people were lost . . . or were gone and we have to move on because mistakes were made . . . because we have [made] many, many mistakes . . . and they were made from both communities, but not only from both communities but from external reasons . . . many, many things going on? [Yes]. Monuments are good if they are used correctly. But as always, some people will use them differently for their own agendas. This is one of the only things that I consider is sacred and you shouldn't use things like this for forwarding agendas.

CMP Turkish Cypriot Scientist 1 differs in stating that nationalism is part of both communities and that in itself is not a bad thing. However, an extreme form of nationalism such as chauvinistic Greek or Turkish nationalism should be avoided during the process of exhumations and memorialization lest it ends-up as destructive storytelling. Nationalism is a part of a healthy identity and only becomes dangerous when it passes boundaries of pathology in an extreme form of us and them, i.e. us good and them bad (Smith, 1986; Volkan, 1997). Thus, CMP Turkish Cypriot Scientist 1 recognizes that these destructive forms of nationalism are maintained and promoted primarily by families and the education systems of both communities:

> Many years ago I went to Limassol for a festival and I saw a portrait on the wall of a Greek Cypriot nationalist hero of the conflict . . . For [the] owner of the place, do you really think it will make a difference if he has a Missing and we gave him his relative's skeleton and he will change?—No. If he is a nationalist, he will most probably be a nationalist again. It doesn't make a difference. If we can stop extreme nationalism and I am not saying nationalism is bad, but extreme nationalism, Greek nationalism or Turkish nationalism—I am not talking about Cypriot nationalism. It depends on the education system and the family which, affect[s] this and not the CMP; what they taught me at school and what my family told me. I don't think the CMP can help much about decreasing or increasing nationalism.

Consequently, the majority of my research participants expressed to me that the process of exhumations and remembering the past are intimately tied together through ceremonies and burials from memorialization to the family to societal levels. However, when the story is told and memory is ignited, extreme forms of nationalism such as nationalist speeches and symbols are best left out of the picture; and instead the focus should be a common memorialization of loss. When the topic of nationalism arose, several of my study's participants began to discuss the nature of memory, history, and education with respect to the process of exhumations and Missing Persons that are connected to Senehi's (2011) model of constructive storytelling. These were viewed as some of the most powerful tools for future generations in terms of inter-ethnic reconciliation and the promotion of a common or shared narrative of victimization and suffering.

STORYTELLING AND HISTORICAL NON-REOCCURRENCE OF VIOLENCE

The nature of story as an expression of meaning is very powerful. How story is told and understood during and after the process of exhumations with respect to Missing Persons may potentially escalate conflict and entrench narratives of ethnocentric victimization. Thus, several of my study participants expressed to me the importance of educating the youth about Missing Persons. They stated that educating people about the conflict and the devastating effects of Missing Persons on loved ones must be transparent and expressed in a bicommunal manner and as a bicommunal issue (i.e., shared suffering).

As Senehi (2011) suggests storytelling is connected to time, memory, and history, "Stories encode and transmit everyday understandings of conflict and what to do about it" (p. 205). Stories then become tools of socialization processes that affect emotions such as the mind and hearts of youth (Senehi, 2011), which can empower youth to become peacemakers (Senehi and Byrne, 2006). In particular, it can aid in what Volkan (1997) expresses as the "transgenerational transmission of trauma" and with respect to historical transference of "chosen trauma" or "chosen glory" in which nation-states formulate the celebration of triumphal narratives of victory or loss and focus on their group's victimization. Some grassroots organizations are trying to empower their youth through new narratives using storytelling that aids in avoiding the transmission of ethnocentric victimization and glorification because of the recovery, identification, and reunification of the Missing in Cyprus. Sevgül Uludağ shares information about her bicommunal organization called Together We Can as follows:

> Yes, ours is the only group that works together. They have some other associations but they don't cooperate because they follow more or less the official policy of victimization; "you see what the Turks did to us?" Or "you see what the Greeks did to us?" But we have an alternative stance on these issues. We have done many activities, we have visited schools, and we spoke to youngsters. Whenever I go to a school I always bring with me a Greek Cypriot and Turkish Cypriot relative of the Missing and they speak to the kids together. They try to show that there is no one side to blame; we are both victims and we are both perpetrators, if you know what I mean. We need to stop the victimization process because it does a lot of damage and it doesn't help reconciliation.

In addition, CMP Turkish Cypriot Scientist 3 avers that Cyprus's history needs to be rewritten. A rewriting of history must discuss the shared problem of Missing Persons in order to avoid ethnocentric victimization narratives and nationalism.

> I feel like our history of Cyprus should be written again. This is not a scientific perspective and I am speaking about how I think. And it is not about my role here. But I am a member of a community and I am speaking about that. So . . . as we know we have Missing people since the 1960's but I think that both sides don't know each other's narratives and I feel like the nationalism is still there in Cyprus—I mean maybe in both communities—and people don't know what happened. Let's say in one community so many people, (adults), don't know what happened to the other community. One side always, (I mean each) . . . consider themselves as victims. But the truth is kind of behind . . . So I think this must be changed. The politicians and the media must show positive aspects of our jobs.

It must be restated here that the CMP's mandate is the humanitarian return of the Missing to their loved ones, and it is not to record or rewrite history. Yet it should be acknowledged that perhaps they *are* making history. Thus, Michalinos Zembylas's analyzes both groups' reactions to exhumations in which the Mothers of victims share in the experience of mourning, which creates a bridge of relatedness through shared vulnerability and suffering (Zembylas, 2011, p. 771) that is possible because of the process of exhumations. Further, in order to ensure the historical non-reoccurrence of violence Michalinos Zembylas states that education that reduces dualistic thinking of we are good and they are bad and we are victims and they are victimizers is necessary to change the politicization of trauma via a critical emotional praxis in education that provides space for awareness of inhabitation, meaning, the reproduction of the same world view (Zembylas, 2008).

The history of Missing Persons in Cyprus and the process of exhumations may be aiding in the construction of a new story particularly with respect to the power of sharing the stories, which can be seen as a form of psychosocial rehabilitation when storytelling is constructive (Senehi, 2011). It provides a shared understanding of victimization, of shared loss, pain, and suffering and of a common memorialization of the past for to forge a sustainable peace. Paul-Henri Arni suggests below:

> Every conflict produces antagonistic narratives and demonizes the other side. What are needed in today's world are neither heroes nor devils, but to reach an understanding once the political settlement is taken care of and once victims are taken care of—including the families of Missing Persons. And then the third stage of reconciliation is to reach a common narrative. The only way to reach a common narrative that won't be explosive is to let independent histo-

> rians work. France and Germany managed to find a common narrative after three terrible wars fought against each other. It is possible.

Perhaps the final stage of the process of exhumations will be its effects on the history and storytelling of the Missing Persons issue in Cyprus and how in resolving it constructively, the process of exhumations was instrumental in nurturing reconciliation and helped to produce a lasting peace aiding as some suggest in the formation of an agreed upon political settlement (Kovras, 2012). But it is just one piece of the puzzle. As Paul-Henry Arni states, "The process of exhumations and the return of Missing Persons are important, but are not enough either. You need the third aspect in order to prevent historical recurrence like in the Balkans, when we talked about the five wars in the 120 years; in order to prevent that vicious circle of recurrence you need to address also history, history books, and memorialization."

CONCLUSION AND SUMMARY OF KEY FINDINGS

In conclusion, the discussion of *Storytelling* in chapter six focused on five emergent themes that led to significant findings about how the process of exhumations operated in a dynamic relationship with storytelling. This chapter expressed how the process of exhumations is itself a process of storytelling and how the return of Missing Persons to their families aids in creating ceremonies of mourning and memorialization that are aspects of story that can be *destructive* or *constructive* with respect to inter-ethnic reconciliation.

The first emergent theme explored the question of *what is Storytelling.* My research participants unpacked what storytelling was in relation to the process of exhumations. Several significant factors were revealed. For example, one participant related to me that all storytelling with regard to Missing Persons and the process of exhumations in Cyprus deals with the phenomenon of trauma. Further, he expressed the forms in which storytelling was represented (and performed) either by verbal or nonverbal acts of communication that ultimately affected individuals and/or families traumatic memory. These forms included memorials, cinema, burial ceremonies, information and much more.

Another significant finding was that storytelling was an expression of the humanization process. Through storytelling, the Missing are humanized and so is the process of exhumations. Further, storytelling is in a dynamic relationship with the dead because the relatives of the Missing are left with the uncertainty of what happened to them. This uncertainty unveiled how storytelling began to unfold as an organic knowledge system that transmits various information to the relatives that produces meaning for the social life of each person. Perhaps the production of meaning can be best understood as the humanization of the Missing Persons issue in Cyprus by accessing a meta-trauma discourse, thereby, aiding in matters of inter-ethnic reconciliation if the storytelling as a key component of the process of exhumations was conducted in a constructive manner.

A very significant finding with respect to storytelling and how it is conducted revealed that the Missing Persons themselves are communicating their own story to the world. The bones of the Missing have a recorded history or a trace history that begins with their lives as well as the environmental factors that have affected their bones. The bones can tell the scientist the person's age, sex, stature, trauma from *ante mortem* data (before death), *peri mortem* data (at time of death), and *post mortem* data (after death). In addition, the person's relatives assist greatly in the identification process when they share stories of how the person lived and the physical traumas and diseases s/he may have experienced. And finally, the person's social identity is revealed when all of this information with DNA testing is brought together.

To reiterate, the process of exhumations is a dynamic story of communication between the dead and the living. Consequently, the process of exhumations maybe said to reveal an agency that Missing Persons possess (even after death). Perhaps one can argue that the Missing empower the process of exhumations and vice versa. They are communicating beyond the grave saying "This is who I am; a lover, a wife, mother, daughter who once lived but I'm not forgotten." In effect, who tells the story and what forms it takes is a very complex and dynamic process. It could be seen as an inter-play of science and storytelling (by both the living and the dead).

One significant challenge faced by the process of exhumations and the CMP is in regards to information about the place of the Missing. Accurate information can be very difficult to come by. In addition to geographical changes and the difficulties associated with time, valid information is often dependent upon the other ethnic group who possesses stories and eye witness information regarding the sites of the Missing. This factor creates a necessary inter-ethnic exchange of communication. Several of my research participants stated that storytelling is the most important factor in finding the whereabouts of the Missing. Yet ethnic communities frown upon sharing the stories with others, which makes it difficult for forensic anthropologists to access information regarding the location of the Missing.

Grassroots leaders such as Sevgül Uludağ—one of the most important people in the recovery of Missing Persons in Cyprus—have provided a critical and safe space for inter-ethnic exchange and storytelling. Sevgül Uludağ began a *virtual dialogue* on her website (and through newspaper publications in the North and South of Cyprus) for the purpose of sharing stories about the exhumation process in the hopes of healing wounds with respect to the conflict. The stories themselves don't necessarily have to do with information regarding the possible whereabouts of a Missing Person but the published stories can be about any facet of the process of exhumations (or on Cyprus's past and the conflict, and funerals for the Missing and mourning, etc.). Yet within the stories lie buried information and a humanization process that (as she stated) "touches the hearts" of all Cypriots, which also leads to people sharing their stories and often information that ultimately aids in the recovery, identification, and reunification of the Missing with loved ones. Her website and publications represent shared pain, friendships, closure, and empowers all Cypriots to share their stories. In so doing, they humanize the other because Cypriots—whether Greek or Turkish—experience the same shared suffering.

Storytelling holds a significant position in the process of exhumations not only for the recovery, identification, and reunification of the Missing with their relatives but also in terms of inter-ethnic reconciliatory matters. Yet another finding suggested that it wasn't just *any* story that was important but it was *how* the storytelling was carried out that mattered. If storytelling was conducted in a constructive manner—in which a message of shared suffering, pain, and the past took place then a message of inter-ethnic reconciliation and healing might occur. If stories of ethnocentric victimization were conveyed in which one ethnic group was the victim and the other was portrayed as the perpetrator, then storytelling could be a highly volatile and destructive force with respect to the process of exhumations.

In the data, the participants' perceptions of what could be considered constructive storytelling and the transformation of inter-ethnic relationships was revealed to me. They stated that an *information affect* through the media in Cyprus was sorely lacking with regard to understanding how the CMP was organized bicommunally and what it actually does. The participants also expressed to me that the respective media from both the Turkish Republic of Northern Cyprus and the Republic of Cyprus were primarily in the habit of representing their side of the Missing Persons issue only.

If a mass grave is found or a Missing Person from one particular ethnic group is returned, then the media will represent, publish and express their stories, but not so with respect to the other side's recovery, identification, or reunification with their Missing relative. Thus, if the story of the process of exhumations and the bicommunal nature of the CMP and the return of the Missing was consistently presented to the public with regards to *all* Cypriots (*Greek and Turkish*) then an *information effect* or a message of a shared problem that is aided by inter-ethnic cooperation and reconciliation could perhaps encourage the psycho-social healing of all Cypriots. If the story of the process of exhumations is represented as an ethnocentric problem and the nature of the CMP as a bicommunal organization is not understood or revealed, then narratives of ethnocentric victimization may remain dominant and those stories then becomes destructive.

The participants also expressed other views about the use of storytelling and the process of exhumations in terms of how storytelling can aid in inter-ethnic reconciliation. Many of my study participants expressed to me the power of apology as an ingredient of storytelling. The data revealed that the nature and power of apology was a significant factor in the process of forgiveness that was comprised of acknowledgment of past wrongs by both ethnic communities that could possibly aid in terms of people's psycho-social healing. Thus, my study participants expressed to me that an apology should be conducted bicommunally from both respective Presidents in the form of verbal communication and joint speeches in the acknowledgment of past wrongs, as well as in the form of non-verbal communication by showing up together to the funeral and burial process of any returned Missing Person, regardless of her or his ethnicity.

Another key finding with respect to the role of apology as a powerful effect of inter-ethnic reconciliation and storytelling is that my participants expressed to me it was necessary at the societal and family levels of organization. Hence, the apologies made by multiple Cypriot actors at multiple levels will empower the next generation through stories of shared pain and mistakes made by both sides that would serve as a lesson to create new and valuable knowledge to build a lasting peace in Cyprus.

Another finding was that stories of inter-ethnic friendship before, during, and after 1974 need to be shared as well. For example, as in the case of the Turkish Cypriot scientist who told me the story of reuniting with his grandparents' Greek Cypriot friend after 30 years when the Green Line opened up. These constructive stories of past inter-ethnic living and friendship may also aid in empowering all Cypriots. If these stories are given a voice and a life of their own then destructive narratives of the impossibility of cooperation and peace between both ethnic groups could be dismantled; it all depends on what stories are expressed, and how they are expressed.

The next key finding is that the process of exhumations has the powerful effect of affecting memory and memory is intimately connected to how story is expressed, which gives meaning to inter-ethnic relations. As stated by all of my study participants, the dominant narrative of an ethnocentric victimization is prevalent on both sides. However, what became apparent through the analysis of the data is that memory with respect to the process of exhumations and storytelling is about the process of *remembering*. A key finding is that remembering is a characteristic of the process of exhumations that has to be done. Yet that remembering through storytelling as an effect of the process of exhumations is dependent upon how one remembers the past. How one remembers is dependent upon how the process of exhumations is conducted and how the media, the relatives of the Missing, and the nation-state express and resolve the issue of Missing Persons.

My research participants also unpacked forms of remembering through ceremonies of mourning, memorialization, and constructed memorials for the Missing. Key findings revealed that when remembering is done outside of politicization and sensationalizing activities that are ethnocentric and promote group victimization, it is a form of constructive storytelling. And when nationalism and in some cases, extreme forms of Greek and Turkish nationalism, are coupled together with memorialization, then remembering through rituals of burial, state memorials, etcetera, can also be forms of destructive storytelling. The most constructive forms of remembering are represented through common memorials that promote a shared story and experience, and a common narrative of Missing Persons as an effect of violent conflict.

In addition, my study participants revealed to me several significant findings that relate to the basic statement that history repeats itself. A key finding was that the history of Cyprus and its conflict needs to be rewritten. In addition, the education systems in the Turkish Cypriot North and Greek Cypriot South sustain ethnocentric narratives of victimization and extreme forms of nationalism. Bicommunal organizations are informing the Cypriot youth (Turkish and Greek) on the effects of the violent conflict in Cyprus and the Missing Persons through the process of bicommunal storytelling from the relatives of the Missing. Thus, the story of Missing Persons must be told and written as a shared narrative of Cypriot history, in the hopes of preventing the historical reoccurrence of violence in Cyprus and to inform the youth that Missing Persons is a shared issue (inter-ethnically) with a shared solution.

Finally, the history of the Cyprus conflict and the history of the process of exhumations and Missing Persons will need to be written and told publicly as a necessary condition of reconciliation between both ethnic groups. In so doing, a shared narrative of pain and suffering through the issue of Missing Persons for *both* sides will be revealed. The process of exhumations written as a Cypriot history is significantly powerful because it will reveal a bicommunal process of cooperation, friendship building, and psycho-social healing that could ultimately result in promoting a lasting peace in Cyprus. It is my sincere hope that this work and the arguments within it have served to accomplish this understanding.

This chapter dealt with the core concept of *Storytelling* with respect to its dynamic relationship to the process of exhumations. The chapter unpacked the concept of storytelling and the particular effects it can have on matters of inter-ethnic reconciliation through either destructive or constructive storytelling. Next, I turn to the conclusion of the manuscript with a reflection on the overall key findings found in chapters four, five, and six. In addition, I express the direction of future research with respect to the process of exhumations in post violent conflict societies and Cyprus.

Chapter Seven

A Common Future

INTRODUCTION

> Giving back his or her identity to a Missing Person has a direct impact on individual healing, family healing, but also collective healing. If not addressed, this issue can become toxic and very damaging for individuals and for communities. This is why it is of paramount importance after a conflict that has produced large numbers of Missing Persons, to deal with this issue. If you don't, there are chances that the unresolved tragedy of Missing Persons will contribute to create the conditions of a new conflict.
> (Paul-Henri Arni, interview and personal communication, August 8, 2014)

This research started out with the intention of understanding one simply stated yet complex question (See Appendix A), namely just what does the process of exhumations really do in terms of peacebuilding and reconciliation on the island of Cyprus? Therefore, in this final chapter I present as clearly and precisely as possible what the research unearthed through two distinct sections, which are interrelated with a brief section on further research. The first section is about why the process of exhumations is critical as a central component of peacebuilding and inter-ethnic reconciliation in the post-violent context of Cyprus. The second section is on the challenges faced by people, families, organizations, communities, and nation-states and the important factors that need to be addressed when conducting the process of exhumations in the context of Cyprus and beyond.

Within both sections I offer templates (See Appendices B and C) to help guide the reader in understanding the key findings of the research. The templates are labeled in accordance with the aforementioned sections: 1) Empowerment and Uncertainty (Appendix B) and 2) Challenges of the Process of Exhumations (Appendix C). Hence, my objective is to argue that my data analysis on the process of exhumations clearly shows that it is absolutely necessary with respect to the Cyprus conflict and its context in order for a lasting and sustainable peace to be built. Moreover, the process of exhumations has had unforeseen effects in aiding the development of a political settlement as others have indeed suggested (Kovras, 2012). Yet, nonetheless the process of exhumations aids in the survivors' fulfillment of their non-negotiable basic human needs that must be addressed, resolved, and dealt with for the development of a sustainable peace to take shape in Cyprus for generations to come.

EMPOWERMENT AND UNCERTAINTY

The process of exhumations which is the recovery, identification, and reunification of the Missing with their loved ones has to do with the empowerment of the Missing Person, the relatives of the Missing, and the Greek and Turkish Cypriot societies and their inter-ethnic relationships by extension. As one can see by the diagram titled Empowerment and Uncertainty (See Appendix B) one path leads to the inevitable empowerment in general of the Turkish and Greek Cypriot societies enhancing peacebuilding in the form of restorative justice and inter-ethnic reconciliation through relationship development, individual and societal psycho-social healing and rehabilitation that offers a sustainable peace and a common future for all. The other path leads to the continuation and maintenance of uncertainty with respect to the ambiguity of knowledge of the Missing that paralyzes living relatives within a frozen space of grief and perennial mourning. This results in possibly transmitting the trauma to future generations with the conclusion of an uncertain peace and the continuation of a sustained conflict in Cyprus. Thus, I now break down the model briefly as an analytical tool to express my reflection on the key findings.

The diagram (See Appendix B) from left to right starts with the process of exhumations. The development of inter-ethnic relationships and as the research showed—friendships—are coming to life due to the complex nature of the process of exhumations and how it is being conducted in Cyprus, through the leadership of the CMP, the relatives of the Missing, and civil society organizations that are created by grassroots leaders such as Sevgül Uludağ's Together We Can.

Research on reconciliation and peacebuilding illustrates that relationship development is paramount in nurturing a sustainable model of peacebuilding (Zehr, 2002; Jeong, 2005; Lederach, 2010). Henceforth, it is the unique bicommunal nature of the CMP that aids in the development of relationships inter-ethnically between Turkish and Greek Cypriots throughout the process of exhumations. The CMP provides the opportunities for what Jean Paul

Lederach (2010) calls an "encounter" that offers a "focus" and a "locus" of relational aspects of the Cyprus conflict. Therefore, as expressed throughout chapter five Bicommunal Relations, interactions between Greek and Turkish Cypriot's at the CMP develops cross communal relationships especially when the workers are out in the field during the recovery of remains and during burial and memorialization services that all serve as a model for inter-ethnic relationships for all Cypriots to see and experience. Further, the process of exhumations is possible because of the development of DNA technology through "technologies of power" (Wagner, 2011) and with the intersection of "constructive storytelling" (Senehi, 2011). The empowering stories of the Missing Persons through their bones and their lived lives, including the stories and memory of the relatives of the Missing, and the sharing of these stories also offer a locus for inter-ethnic relationship development and a focus for finding the Missing.

As one can observe from the diagrammatic template Empowerment and Uncertainty (See Appendix B), the Basic Human Psycho-social Needs (Burton, 1990) are aligned from north to south with Storytelling/Science and below it, Ambiguity and Absence. The Basic Human Psycho-Social needs that provide the route to the bicommunal process of exhumations that leads to sustainable peace are burial, mourning and grieving, relief, communication, remembering, and access to closure, knowledge of death, truth, and restitution.

As the data revealed in chapter four titled Uncertainty and Psychology there is a basic human need for the family to know what has happened to a loved one that is Missing as well as the knowledge of the disappeared person's death or life in order to dispel uncertainty. The knowledge of the person's death through the identification and reunification of the remains with relatives offers an opportunity and empowers the family when the personification and reunification that the relatives' basic human psycho-social needs of mourning and closure via *relief* are satisfied. The relatives' basic human needs were previously paralyzed with the uncertainty of the fate of a Missing loved one that results in an un-relieved trauma that has caused them paralysis of healing. This finding is also attested to by studies of unresolved trauma of the development of post-traumatic stress disorder and perennial mourning (Herman, 1997; Volkan 1998, 2012).

The development/maintenance of relationships can be very difficult for people who are going through ambiguous loss and frozen grief with respect to Missing Persons (Boss, 1999, 2002). When the survivors' aren't able to pass through what anthropologist's suggest as the stage of liminality or limbo (Sant-Cassia, 2005) it reduces their ability to heal and for the conflict at the societal level to move toward healing and the co-creation of a common future. Thus, the risk of the "transgenerational transmission of trauma" (Volkan, 1997) to the next generations can be arguably high with the increased risk of a future of uncertain peace and sustained conflict in Cyprus regardless of any political settlement. The majority of violent inter-ethnic and intra-state conflicts over the past several decades indicate the instability of negotiated settlements thatlasted only from 3–5 years for over half or two-thirds of them (Hartzell, Hoddie, and Rothchild, 2001 cited in Borer, Darby, and McEvoy-Levy, 2006; Licklider, 1995 cited in Borer, Darby, and McEvoy-Levy, 2006; Olson and Pearson, 2010). Thus, new directions for peacebuilding with a focus on sustained reconciliation are a must as political settlements alone can be a slippery slope to a repetition of past violence and conflict without inter-ethnic reconciliation development and restorative justice.

However, when looking through the empowerment scope of the model provided (See Appendix B) one must notice that the relatives of the Missing gain access to the remains of their loved ones that aid in the closure and grieving processes. The relatives and communities at large are empowered to share in a process of mourning that is decided on by the relatives of the Missing in which they are empowered to fulfill their basic human psycho-social needs of ritualized burial, commemoration, remembrance, and access to a gravesite so that they can maintain respectful relations with their dead (Sant Cassia, 2005; Eppel, 2006).

Moreover, one component of uncertainty that is left unresolved that reveals itself in the diagram provided (See Appendix B) is the uncertain knowledge of the perpetrator's and their punishment. However, as I argued in chapter four's Uncertainty and Psychology Cyprus lacks a political settlement, yet the people's access to the land in both the TRNC and RoC to search for the remains of the Missing is possible due to *advantageous uncertainty* that is arguably aiding in positive and constructive inter-ethnic relations in Cyprus. For example, the participants exclaim that stories are told and people are sharing what they know about the whereabouts of the Missing because of amnesty and the uncertainty of culpability with a focus on the humanitarian mandate of the return of the Missing. In other words, it would be much more difficult to recover the Missing if culpability was at play as people would therefore remain silent. Hence, the focus ofthe CMP is on recovery, identification, and reunification of the Missing with their loved ones that is aiding in the development of a needed and shared relationship and interdependence of both groups which is a large part of reconciliation (Lederach, 2010) and the development of inter-ethnic civil society organizations to aid in this process (Kovras, 2012).

The process of exhumations in Cyprus is arguably taking on a model of restorative justice in which information about why the offence happened was due to the conflict and not to the specific parties, namely, the Greek and Turkish Cypriot's. Truth telling of the crime or one's knowledge of it is expressed through storytelling by perpetrators, victims, and witnesses that offer healing and relationship development opportunities to audiences in many avenues. The empowerment and agency formation of the victims is occurring through case processes of Missing Persons and the restitution of the CMP bicommunal team, which is aided by the storytelling of those involved and their involvement can be seen as a form of trust building (Senehi, 2011; Zehr, 2002). Further, the process of *advantageous uncertainty* also avoids the pitfalls of extreme forms of nationalism that are destructive to the process of exhumations as expressed by the participants with regards to conflict escalation (See Volkan, 1998; Byrne, 2000 Anastasiou, 2008) through publicized competing victimization narratives similar to the case of Bosnia and the ICTY (Wagner, 2008).

Consequently, the process of exhumations in the specific context of Cyprus is providing a locus of empowerment with a focus on the reunification of the Missing with their loved ones. If the process is done in a manner of constructive storytelling in which as Senehi (2011) states, "narratives may enhance peace when they involve a dialogue characterized by shared power" (p. 203) then the CMP workers who share in the recovery, identification, and reunification of the Missing with their loved ones is evidence of this point.

Journalists who tell stories of loss and who provide testimonials of the whereabouts of the Missing and who aid in the inter-ethnic storytelling with relatives of the Missing at schools through organizations such as, Together We Can are also helpful and arguably necessary. Hence, when storytelling engenders mutual recognition of each group's suffering and victimization and when the stories promote consciousness raising and serve to resist domination, or teach conflict resolution strategies then they are constructive and can build peace (Senehi, 2011, p. 203). The locus of righting relationships by offering an encounter involves the four pillars of reconciliation with the first being the Truth in the acknowledgement (Lederach, 2010; Senehi, 2011) of Missing Persons by the act of finding and returning them to their loved ones. Mercy is the acceptance that there is an issue that needs to be resolved, namely, uncertainty while Justice is the righting of relationships and providing equality in the return of both Greek and Turkish Cypriot remains, and Peace is the promotion of well-being and harmony for the families as expressed by what this process can and does do for them. Thus, sustainable peace cannot be fully achieved in Cyprus without this non-negotiable process of exhumations. Consequently, I provide a brief diagrammatic template (See Appendix C) on the greatest challenges and questions that arise when conducting the process of exhumations in Cyprus that may aid other societies transitioning out of violence in the present and future.

CHALLENGES OF THE PROCESS OF EXHUMATIONS

The greatest challenges presented by my research participants operating within a post-violent context on the effect of Missing Persons that have to go through the process of exhumations are as follows (See Appendix C): 1) Determine the List, its Agreement, and Equality of Return; 2) The Percentage of Missing is large enough; 3) Time; 4) Partial Remains; 5) Bicommunal Organization and Context? 6) Retribution or Restitution? 7) Storytelling and Information effect; and 8) Historical Non-Reoccurrence.

The first objective is determining who is on the list of the Missing by collecting all of the evidence gathered, which is first and foremost the responsibility of the relatives to inform the national and international (ICRC) authorities about their Missing. In some cases families take it into their own hands to form organizations as in the case of Cyprus and Bosnia in order to organize intra-ethnically who is Missing (Sant-Cassia, 2005; Wagner, 2008). Second is the slippery slope of the fairness of return issue, which can cause or indeed escalate many problems if it is not handled well such as escalating ethnocentric victimization narratives, coopting politicization, and competitive memorialization (Sant-Casssia, 2005; Wagner, 2008). After the recognition of fairness of return comes the need to agree who is on the list that can take a long time especially if the percentage of the Missing is large enough that it is necessary for people to organize themselves into a fully institutionalized organization such as the CMP in Cyprus, or the ICMP in Bosnia or the Missing Persons Institute (MPI). Further, in order to form such an organization local people need to consider what constitutes the percentage of Missing Persons in the first place with respect to the geography, population size, and the relation of Missing civilians to Missing military, and that carries with it the slippery slope of actually escalating inter-communal conflict.

A next great challenge mentioned by my research participants is that the longer the time taken to find the Missing Persons in a post violent conflict society the greater the harm to the families of the Missing and the society because of the physical and psychological paralysis as a result of landscapes change or the locations of bodies maybe disrupted by secondary crimes of the mismanagement of time for the recovery of remains. Moreover, the loss and thedecomposition of remains also occurs, and the relocation and commingling of remains from different gravesites (called secondary graves) in order to cover the crimes do in fact happen (this did happen in Bosnia) (Wagner, 2008). In addition, the maintenance of the trauma caused by uncertainty and absence of the Missing that paralyzes the fulfillment of the survivors' basic psycho-social human needs of closure and healing increases the chances of the transgenerational transmission of trauma are all affected by time mismanagement (Herman 1997; Volkan, 1997; Boss, 1999, 2002). Further, the time lapse in contact between the conflicting Greek and Turkish

Cypriot groups, which as some of my participants stated can either aid in forming of relationships when the encounter is possible and has the right chemistry (which bicommunal organizations and CMP aid in). On the other hand, it could entrench and maintain victimization narratives due to the uncertainty of just who are these people and whose stories have been transmitted by chosen traumas, the nation-state, and through people's unresolved trauma and grief.

The partial remains of the disappeared are the next major challenge faced by those conducting the process of exhumations because over time it is harder to recover fully articulated bodies and artifacts that aid in the recognition of remains and bring about closure for the family. In this sense the question arises—how much of the remains is enough for the relatives to recognize that this is in fact their relative without a re-traumatization occurring? My study participants realized at least that the uncertainty of the person's death is revealed to the relatives of the Missing when very little remains are returned to them by the CMP. However, this is a major challenge that must be dealt with in respect to the proper authorities conducting the process of exhumations and working with relatives of the Missing.

The context collaboration and the formation of the bicommunal organization that is conducting the process of exhumations are also important in inter-ethnic conflicts. The development of inter-ethnic relationships and friendships in the CMP because the process of exhumations is done in the manner of bicommunal teams made up of Greek and Turkish Cypriots with United Nations capacity building leadership is a necessary component of reconciliation and in building sustainable and lasting peace in post-violent conflict societies (Zehr, 2002; Lederach, 2010). Moreover, the NGOs and grassroots movements are also taking on the bicommunal model in promoting a shared understanding of victimization and suffering in terms of creating a shared process of healing.

Next, context is highly important in understanding a society's culture (Eppel, 2006) for the purposes of fulfilling people's psycho-social basic human needs that are non-negotiable in the prevention of future conflict as many human needs scholars suggest (Galtung, 1979; Burton, 1990; Max-Neef, 1992; Nussbaum, 1996; Cavanaugh, 2000; Sen, 2001; Redekop, 2002). Thus, the identification and return of their relative's remains was necessary for Cypriot people to exercise their cultural and social and religious rights with regards to the Missing and their need to bring about closure and for healing to occur.

The challenge of addressing the harm done through retribution or restitution can weigh heavy on the relatives right to justice (Zehr, 2002; Wagner, 2008). The Cyprus conflict is still not politically resolved while the interdependence needed for the recovery of remains exists so that *advantageous uncertainty* as an intrinsic part of a restorative model of justice be undertaken, perhaps, with the idea of creating a future Cyprus Truth and Reconciliation Commission as part of a restorative justice and truth telling process (Zehr, 2002). There are other forms of rights such as the family's humanitarian right to know what has happened to a loved one and to have accessto their remains that may outweigh the need for justice and punishment. In one way or another, the respective leaders of the TRNC and RoC should offer an apology as a form of bicommunal justice and restitution. In addition, the CMP's actions on the return of the Missing and the involvement of witnesses and the perpetrator's testimony, etc., are also an apologetic action that may be enough for forgiveness and closure to take place.

However, the main challenge of the process of exhumations is to understand what the necessary ramifications and prescriptions are to be to aid in the control of the victimization narratives and extreme forms of ethnonationalism that can cause rather than prevent conflict during the process of exhumations and be part of a destructive storytelling (Senehi, 2011). Thus, storytelling and the information effect fare two of the three major challenges expressed in this work by my study participants. Storytelling permeates all realms of the process of exhumations, and if those stories are in a form of extreme ethnonationalism than destructive storytelling is taking place (Senehi, 2011) in the promotion of the already victimization narrative that exists for both Greek and Turkish Cypriots. As other scholars have claimed "chauvinistic nationalism" is in itself inherently violent (Anastasiou, 2008) or it is not so bad if it lies within the normal boundaries of identification with a group; but if those boundaries expand then they can become very dangerous (Smith, 1986; Volkan, 1997).

When stories are shared about the nature of inter-ethnic friendships and community living prior to the conflicts of the 1960s and 1974 in Cyprus then constructive storytelling can be a positive influence in building peace between both communities (Senehi, 2011). Hence, my study participants suggested that the Cyprus governments in the North (TRNC) and the South (RoC) need to express stories that reflect the bicommunal make-up of the CMP and the equal return of the Missing Greek and Turkish Cypriots to both sides so that a joint understanding of a shared problem exists and a shared solution is taking shape. The Information Effect is necessary to get the message across in Cyprus that Missing Persons is a Turkish and Greek Cypriot issue that has a Greek and Turkish bicommunal resolution.

Therefore, the return of the Missing Turkish and Greek Cypriots' remains to their families are not all at the reunification component of the Viewing process yet, the project is bicommunal and therefore both Turkish and Greek Cypriots are aiding in the process of exhumations and constructive storytelling is expressed by the CMP workers; in a manner that ensures that the nature of the issue as a shared problem with a shared solution aids in the power dynamics of the story told (Senehi, 2011).

The last challenge that was expressed by my study participants was that the next generation of Greek and Turkish Cypriots are affected by the "transgenerational transmission of trauma" from relatives stories of pain and loss and through the educational knowledge and history that are chosen by the state (Volkan, 1997). In order to aid in the prevention of an entrenched victimization narrative and trauma, a *shared narrative* must be presented as an expression of a shared history, and as of great importance in building a sustainable peace. In essence, Michalinos Zembylas (2008) states that integrated education that reduces dualistic thinking of we are good and they are bad and we are victims and they are victimizers is necessary to change the politicization of trauma via a critical emotional praxis in education that provides space for awareness of inhabitation or the reproduction of the same world view.

The eight major challenges of the process of exhumations (See Appendix C) were expressed by my research participants to give some positive direction to the Cyprus conflict to focus on and address such as the information effect and the politicization of the work of the CMP in terms of inter-ethnic reconciliation in Cyprus. Further, it is not an exhaustive list of the challenges facedon Cyprus but it centers on the challengesthat arise during this complex and multifaceted process. Thus, the hope is that these eight components of the process of exhumations may aid the relatives of the Missing, organizations, societies, nation-states, and inter-state organizations in understanding just what does the process of exhumations do to build a sustainable peace on the island of Cyprus.

CONCLUSION AND FUTURE RESEARCH

This is not the first or the last word on post-violent conflict societies with regards to Missing Persons and the process of exhumations. For example, in 2011 it was documented that more than 50,000 cases of Missing Persons in 83 countries were processed by the UNWGEID (UN 2011: 6, cited in Kovras, 2012). It is a travesty and an injustice when a family's loved one is involuntarily disappeared that has dire consequences for relatives, loved ones, and societies at large. These tragedies have resulted in the psychological paralyses of those suffering and waiting for news of what happened to their husband, daughter, and brother, mother or father, for over forty years in Cyprus. They continuously live in a state of limbo and are stuck in liminality during the process of mourning with respect to performing the religious and cultural rights of death and burial.

Many relatives and loved ones of the Missing are stuck in a state of frozen grief and ambiguity (See Boss, 2002) in which they lack the access to some form of closure and relief from a continual state of uncertainty. This is not to say that many are not searching for answers and aiding in the restoration and reconciliation processes within their families and societies and for that matter between the Greek and Turkish Cypriot communities who work in the common interest of finding their Missing. However, the reality is that the loss and ambiguity created by uncertainty also permeates and consequently fosters an uncertainty with regards to inter-ethnic reconciliation because people's basic human needs, primarily, psycho-social basic human needs are not met.

This research suggests that this study's participants' experiences, perceptions and expertise indicate that the process of exhumations is necessary to forge a sustainable and lasting peace in Cyprus. Further, this unique process of the recovery, identification, and reunification of the Missing with their loved ones is a process of empowerment and healing for the relatives of the disappeared. From the individual standpoint the process empowers the relatives of the Missing to fulfill their basic human needs and commence processes of healing. Consequently, it also provides a locus of inter-ethnic relationship development between Turkish and Greek Cypriots through bicommunal encounters such as in the respective societies of the TRNC and RoC by fulfilling the CMP's humanitarian mission of returning the Missing to their relatives. The reconciliatory model is a restorative justice model where inter-ethnic relationships are formed within and outside of civil society organizations due to the nature of how the process of exhumations is conducted bicommunally in Cyprus without retribution via punishment, and because of its unique context that engenders the much needed interdependence of Cypriots to fulfill such a mission.

Moreover, I also presented this research as a narrative outlining the many experiences that I went through because the process of exhumations itself would not exist without its most important factor namely—Storytelling. Stories from the bones, relatives of the Missing, victims, perpetrators, journalists, the online media, and civil society organizations share the message inter-ethnically that Missing Persons is a bicommunal issue with a bicommunal solution. However, the stories chosen to be told can also be a slippery slope when messages of group victimization and extreme ethnonationalist agendas take root instead of constructive forms of story that share power and aid in people's empowerment to co-create a sustainable future.

The process of exhumations which is the recovery, identification, and reunification of the Missing with their loved ones is a story of Cypriots' empowerment in Cyprus. Arguably, without it the chances of a historical reoccurrence of ethnic violence in Cyprus and the escalation of conflict is possible, and the chances of creating a sustainable peace would be uncertain even if a political settlement is reached. I provided my interviewees perceptions and understanding of the most significant challenges with regards to the relatives of the Missing, and those going through and conducting this process in order to provide direction for future research with respect to comparing the situation in Cyprus, to other post-violent conflict societies. Their interviews also aid in our understanding of the CMP's efforts to conduct such a monumental task as the recovery, identification, and reunification of the Missing with their loved ones in a constructive manner as well as avoiding destructive factors. They also offer us a generalized understanding of what people who are living the experience of having a Missing Person in their family are actually going through.

Finally, further research in the form of qualitative analysis of family member's experiences of going through the process of exhumations in Cyprus and the power of storytelling as a core component of reconciliation and healing would be useful (Senehi, 2000, 2002, 2006). In addition, research with respect to how the Greek and Turkish Cypriot youth both feel about the recovery, identification, and reunification of the Missing as an intrinsic part of inter-ethnic reconciliation and sustainable peace is paramount in understanding just what this process is doing for future generations with respect to peacebuilding and transgenerational trauma. For example, a new emphasis of work in the field of Peace and Conflict Studies has focused on the challenges of youth in peacebuilding efforts after peace-accords with regard to the violence they have faced or conducted, and their reintegration into post-peace accord societies (Borer, 2006; Byrne and Senehi, 2012). Little is understood of the role of youth in inter-ethnic integration within Cyprus with regard to the process of exhumations and the Missing Persons issue.

However, other research regarding the inter-ethnic integration of schools and its effects on the perceptions of youth and peacemaking in other comparable contexts (Byrne, 1997a; Byrne 1997b; Bekerman, 2011) could definitely aid with respect to understanding the role of Cyprus's Missing Persons and youth perceptions of the conflict and in building peace. The education process is reproducing narratives to socialize youth (Onen et al, 2010; Zembylas, 2007, 2008, 2011). And finally, an in-depth analysis of Cypriots sociocultural and religious practices of the mourning of the dead and Missing with respect to their return would definitely prove to be important and fascinating research regarding the similarities and differences of the Greek Orthodox and Sunni Islamic rituals of death and bereavement. It would aid in our understanding of how important it is for relatives and communities of the Missing to have access to these rights to mourn the dead as scholars have suggested (Sant-Cassia, 2005; Eppel, 2006; Wagner, 2008).

The list presented above of future directions for research is not exhaustive. However, because this manuscript provides opening templates of the complexities of the process of exhumations as a strategy of peacebuilding and reconciliation in Cyprus; future research is suggested on all aspects of the diagrams offered (See Appendices B and C). Thus, the hope is that my research inspires peacebuilders to examine my findings, challenge and develop them, to understand how the process of exhumations can aid in inter-ethnic reconciliation and toward forging a sustainable peace among divided communities.

Appendix A
Research Questions

Q1: What does the process of exhumations which I define as, the recovery of Missing Persons, identification, and reunification of the Missing with loved one's do?

Q2: Do you think the process of exhumations which again I define as the recovery of Missing Persons, identification, and reunification of the Missing with loved ones is necessary for reconciliation and peace-building?

Q3: What are the problems that arise when the process of exhumations are done?

Q4: How does the process of exhumations impact the relations between ethnic communities?

Q5: Does the process of exhumations facilitate the process of healing for individuals and society? Or does it increase communal trauma?

Q6: Does the process of exhumations relieve community guilt, or does it allow for the victim narrative to be dominant for victim or perpetrator?

Q7: Does international influence through visiting dignitaries to events to remember past atrocities and their provision and direction of economic aid for exhumations exacerbate or ameliorate inter-ethnic relations or co-existence?

Q8: Does the process of exhumations just provide the identification of victims or does it also provide community healing, reconciliation, and bring closure as an aspect of peacebuilding.

Q9: Can the process of exhumations ever be separated from ethnic hatred, ethno- nationalism, and storytelling?

Q10: Is there a role for storytelling in the process of exhumations? If so, how is storytelling conducted and represented during and after the process of exhumations?

Appendix B

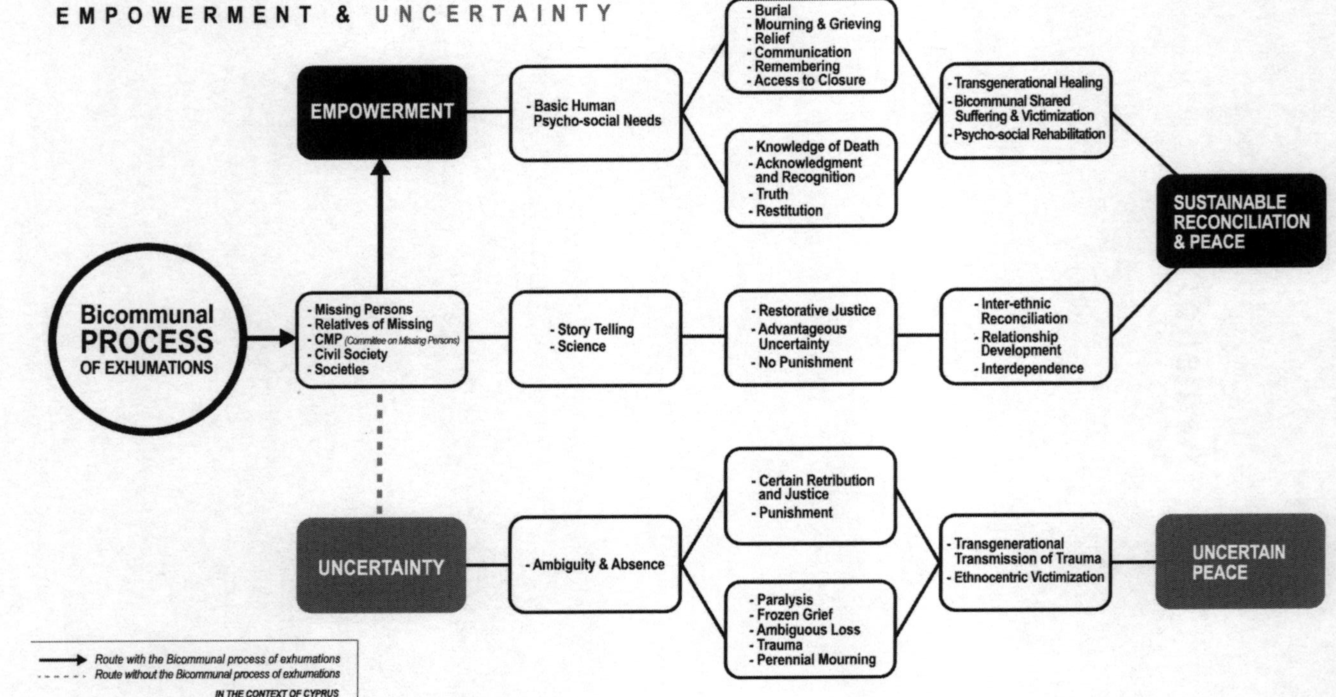
EMPOWERMENT & UNCERTAINTY
Bicommunal PROCESS OF EXHUMATIONS
- Missing Persons
- Relatives of Missing
- CMP (Committee on Missing Persons)
- Civil Society
- Societies
EMPOWERMENT
- Basic Human Psycho-social Needs
- Burial
- Mourning & Grieving
- Relief
- Communication
- Remembering
- Access to Closure
- Knowledge of Death
- Acknowledgment and Recognition
- Truth
- Restitution
- Transgenerational Healing
- Bicommunal Shared Suffering & Victimization
- Psycho-social Rehabilitation
- Story Telling
- Science
- Restorative Justice
- Advantageous Uncertainty
- No Punishment
- Inter-ethnic Reconciliation
- Relationship Development
- Interdependence
SUSTAINABLE RECONCILIATION & PEACE
UNCERTAINTY
- Ambiguity & Absence
- Certain Retribution and Justice
- Punishment
- Paralysis
- Frozen Grief
- Ambiguous Loss
- Trauma
- Perennial Mourning
- Transgenerational Transmission of Trauma
- Ethnocentric Victimization
UNCERTAIN PEACE
Route with the Bicommunal process of exhumations
Route without the Bicommunal process of exhumations
IN THE CONTEXT OF CYPRUS

Appendix C

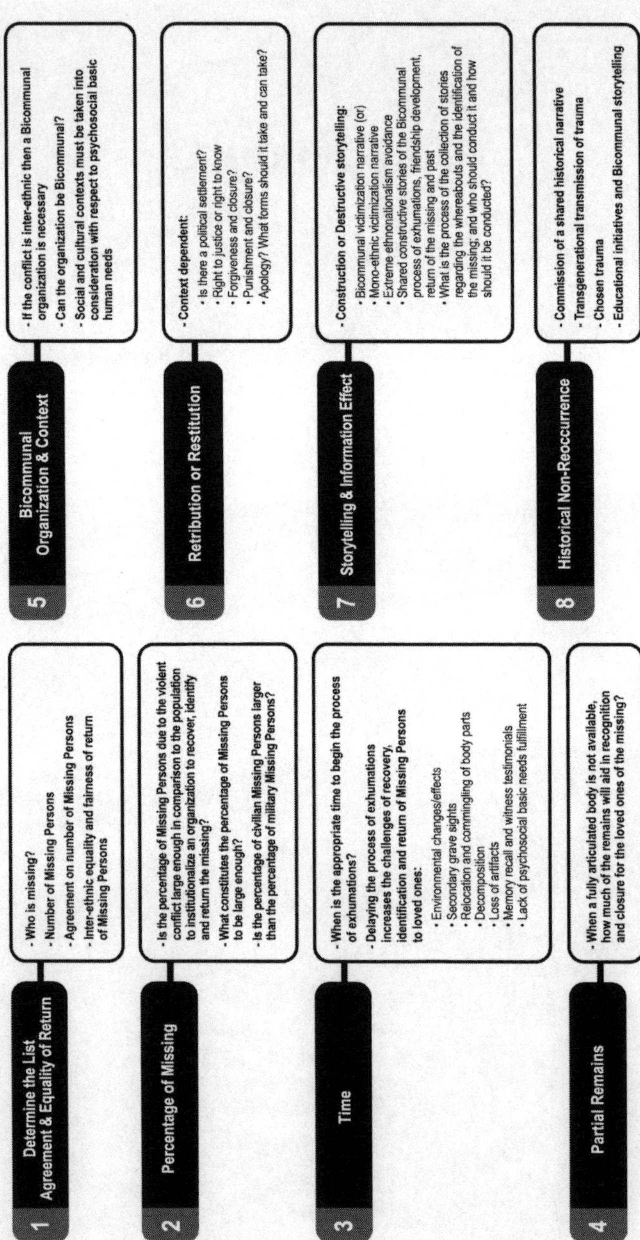
CHALLENGES OF THE PROCESS OF EXHUMATIONS
1 Determine the List Agreement & Equality of Return
- Who is missing?
- Number of Missing Persons
- Agreement on number of Missing Persons
- Inter-ethnic equality and fairness of return of Missing Persons
2 Percentage of Missing
- Is the percentage of Missing Persons due to the violent conflict large enough in comparison to the population to institutionalize an organization to recover, identify and return the missing?
- What constitutes the percentage of Missing Persons to be large enough?
- Is the percentage of civilian Missing Persons larger than the percentage of military Missing Persons?
3 Time
- When is the appropriate time to begin the process of exhumations?
- Delaying the process of exhumations increases the challenges of recovery, identification and return of Missing Persons to loved ones:
• Environmental changes/effects
• Secondary grave sights
• Relocation and commingling of body parts
• Decomposition
• Loss of artifacts
• Memory recall and witness testimonials
• Lack of psychosocial basic needs fulfillment
4 Partial Remains
- When a fully articulated body is not available, how much of the remains will aid in recognition and closure for the loved ones of the missing?
5 Bicommunal Organization & Context
- If the conflict is inter-ethnic then a Bicommunal organization is necessary
- Can the organization be Bicommunal?
- Social and cultural contexts must be taken into consideration with respect to psychosocial basic human needs
6 Retribution or Restitution
- Context dependent:
• Is there a political settlement?
• Right to justice or right to know
• Forgiveness and closure?
• Punishment and closure?
• Apology? What forms should it take and can take?
7 Storytelling & Information Effect
- Construction or Destructive storytelling:
• Bicommunal victimization narrative (or)
• Mono-ethnic victimization narrative
• Extreme ethnonationalism avoidance
• Shared constructive stories of the Bicommunal process of exhumations, friendship development, return of the missing and past
• What is the process of the collection of stories regarding the whereabouts and the identification of the missing; and who should conduct it and how should it be conducted?
8 Historical Non-Reoccurrence
- Commission of a shared historical narrative
- Transgenerational transmission of trauma
- Chosen trauma
- Educational initiatives and Bicommunal storytelling

Appendix D

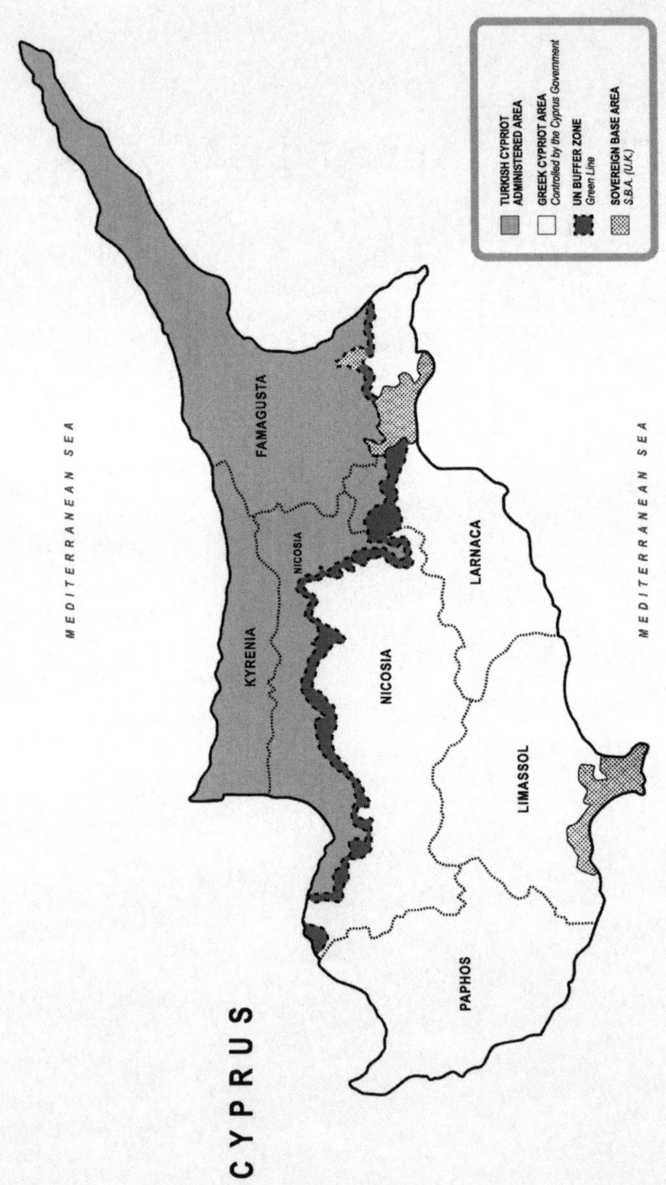
CYPRUS
MEDITERRANEAN SEA
MEDITERRANEAN SEA
KYRENIA
FAMAGUSTA
NICOSIA
NICOSIA
LARNACA
LIMASSOL
PAPHOS
TURKISH CYPRIOT ADMINISTERED AREA
GREEK CYPRIOT AREA
Controlled by the Cyprus Government
UN BUFFER ZONE
Green Line
SOVEREIGN BASE AREA
S.B.A. (U.K.)

References

Anastasiou, Harry. (2008). *The broken olive branch: nationalism, ethnic conflict, and the quest for peace in Cyprus. Volume One, The impasse of ethnonationalism* (1st ed.). Syracuse, N.Y.: Syracuse University Press.

———. (2008). *The broken olive branch: nationalism, ethnic conflict, and the quest for peace in Cyprus. Volume Two, Nationalism versus Europeanization* (1st ed.). Syracuse, N.Y.: Syracuse University Press.

———. 2009. "Conflict Transformation in Greek-Turkish Relations: Between Belligerent Nationalism and Conciliatory Europeanization." *Peace Studies Journal* (September) 2(1): 15–40.

———. (2011). "Encountering nationalism: The contribution of peace studies and conflict resolution." In *Handbook of Conflict Analysis and Resolution*, ed. Dennis J.D Sandole, Sean Byrne, Ingrid-Sandole-Staroste and Jessica Senehi, 32–45. London: Routledge.

Anderson, Benedict. (1983). *Imagined Communities: Reflections on the Origin and Spread of Nationalism.* London: Verso.

Arthur, Paul. (2009). "Memory, retrieval, and truth recovery." In *Handbook of Conflict Analysis and Resolution*, ed. Dennis J.D Sandole, Sean Byrne, Ingrid-Sandole-Staroste and Jessica Senehi, 369–83. London: Routledge.

Attilides, Michael. (1979). *Cyprus Nationalism and International Politics.* New York: St.Martins Press.

Bekerman, Zvi. (2011). "The Ethnography of Peace Education: Some lessons learned from Palestinian-Jewish integrated education in Israel." In *Handbook of Conflict Analysis and Resolution* Dennis J.D Sandole, Sean Byrne, Ingrid- Sandole-Staroste and Jessica Senehi 144–57. London and New York: Routledge.

Onen, Mehves B., Jetha-Dagseven, S., Karashan, H., Latif, D. (2010). *Rewriting History Textbooks: History Education: A Tool for Polarisation or Reconciliation.* Nicosia, Cyprus: Tipograf Arts.

Belnap, Barri. (2012). "Turns of a phrase: traumatic learning through generations." In *Lost In Transmission: Studies of Trauma Across Generations*, ed. Gerard M. Fromm, 115–31. London: Karnac.

Brad K. Blitz. (2006). *War and Change in the Balkans: Nationalism, Conflict and Cooperation.* Cambridge: Cambridge University Press.

Bogdan, R.C & Biklen, S.K. (2003). *Qualitative Research for Education: An introduction to Theories and Methods* (4th ed.). New York: Pearson Education group.

Borer, Tristan A., Darby, J., McEvoy-Levy, Siobhan. (2006). *Peacebuilding After Peace Accords: The Challenges of Violence, Truth, and Youth.* Notre Dame: University of Notre Dame Press.

Boss, Pauline. (1999). *Ambiguous loss: learning to live with unresolved grief.* USA: Harvard University Press.

———. (2002). "Ambiguous loss in families of the Missing." In *The Lancet, Medicine and Conflict,* (December) 360 (1): 39–40.

———. (2006). *Loss, Trauma, and Resilience: Therapeutic Work with Ambiguous Loss*. New York: W. W. Norton & Company.

Bowlby, J. (1973). *Attachment and Loss: Separation, Anxiety and Anger*. Volume II. London: Hogarth Press.

Bomberger, Kathryne. (2015, July 21). *Why we are excavating the dead of Srebrenica.* Retrieved from http://www.ic-mp.org/news/why-we-are-excavating-the-dead-of-srebrenica-2/

Bryant, Rebecca. (2001). "An Aesthetics of Self: Moral Remaking and Cypriot Education." *Comparative Studies in Society and History*, 43 (3): 583–614.

———. (2006). "On the Condition of Postcoloniality in Cyprus." In *Divided Cyprus: Modernity, History, And An Island In Conflict*, ed. Y. Papadakis and N. Peristianis, and G. Weltz, 47-66. Indiana: Indiana University Press.

———. (2010). *The Past in Pieces: Belonging In The New Cyprus*. Pennsylvania: University of Pennsylvania Press.

Buglass, E. (2010). "Grief and Bereavement Theories." In *Nursing Standard,* 24 (41): 44–47.

Burton, John. (1990). *Conflict: Human Needs Theory.* New York: St. Martin's Press.

———. (1990). *Conflict Resolution and Provention*. New York: Fernwood.

Boutros Boutros-Ghali. (1992, June). "An Agenda For Peace: Preventative Diplomacy, Peacemaking, and Peacekeeping." *United Nations*.

Byrne, Sean. (1997). *Growing Up in a Divided Society: The Influence of Conflict on Belfast School Children.* London: Associated University Press.

———. (1997). "Belfast schoolchildren's images of political conflict and social change: Signs of hope in integrated education." *Mind and Human Interaction,* 8(3): 172–85.

———. (2000). "Power politics as usual in Cyprus and Northern Ireland: Divided islands and the roles of external ethno-guarantors." *Nationalism and Ethnic politics*, 6 (1): 1–23.

Byrne, S., and Carter, Neil. (1996). "Social Cubism: Six Social Forces of Ethno-Territorial Politics in Northern Ireland and Quebec." Retrieved from http://www.gmu.edu/programs/icar/pcs/bryce.htm

Byrne, Sean, and Senehi, Jessica. (2012). *Violence: Analysis, intervention, and prevention.* Athens: Ohio University Press.

Byrne, Sean and Senehi, Jessica. (2012). "Ethnopolitical Conflict: causes, intervention, and prevention." In *Violence: analysis, intervention, and prevention,* ed. Sean Byrne and Jessica Senehi, 138–66. Ohio: Ohio University Press.

Cassia, S. Paul. (2005). *Bodies of Evidence: Burial, Memory and the Recovery of Missing Persons in Cyprus*. Oxford: Berghahn.

———. (2006). "Guarding Each Other's Dead, Mourning One's Own: The Problem of Missing Persons and Missing Pasts in Cyprus." *South European Society and Politics,* 11(1): 111–28.

———. (2006). "Recognition and Emotion, Exhumations of Missing Persons in Cyprus." In *Divided Cyprus: Modernity, History and an Island in Conflict*, ed. Papadakis, Yiannis., Peristianis, Nicos and Welz , Gisela, 194–213. Bloomington: Indiana University Press.

Cavanaugh, A. Kathleen. (2000). "Understanding Protracted Social Conflicts: A Basic Needs Approach." In *Reconcilable Differences: Turning Points In Ethnopolitical Conflict*, ed. Sean Byrne and Cynthia L. Irvin, 65–79. Connecticut: Kumarian Press.

Carmen Lowry and Stephen Littlejohn. (2006). "Dialogue and the Discourse of Peace Building in Maluku, Indonesia." *Conflict Resolution Quarterly*, 23(4): 409–26.

Creswell, John W. (2012). *Qualitative Research Design: Choosing Among Five Approaches,* (1st ed). USA: Sage Publications.

Crisis Group Euro-Report. (2006). "The Cyprus Stalemate: What Next?" Retrieved from https://docs.google.com/viewer?a=v&q=cache:r24AID0jt90J:www.crisisgroup.org/~/media/Files/europe/171_the_cyprus_stalemate_what_next.pdf+when+is+the+next+cypriot+referendum&hl=en&gl=ca&pid=bl&srcid=ADGEESgkazQcyAUHMxLpeBIxdaEopVU1hpvUzAJWcCs05uvdkaej4GBQdBFbBViIS7jpU86qq9nwa2KlE4qtf5KAJKq7_nDBRK9E9AMaG9a6

xNQ_dOtTGY9ecDBcHzL1mjlSVpOqF3&sig=AHIEtbQ2WTx1xt3fXTJYDiojeYpb jnPVFg

Committee On Missing Persons In Cyprus. (2015, August 31). "Committee on Missing Persons Fact Sheet." Retrieved from http://www.cmp-cyprus.org/progress-report/all-the-cmp- fact-sheets/

———. (2015). Retrieved from http://www.cmp-cyprus.org/

———. (2015). "What we do." Retrieved from http://www.cmp-cyprus.org/what-we-do/ phase-iv-identification-and-return-of-re/

———. (2015). "What we do." Retrieved from http://www.cmp-cyprus.org/what-we-do/

BBC News. (2015). "Cyprus Profile." BBC News Europe. Retrieved from http:// www.bbc.com/news/world-europe-17217956

Denktash, R. Rauf. (1988). *The Cyprus Triangle*. London: K. Rustem & Brother.

Dodd, Clement. *The History And Politics Of The Cyprus Problem*. (2010). London: Palgrave and Macmillan.

Drexler, F. Elizabeth. (2010). "The failure of international justice in East Timor and Indonesia." In *Transitional Justice: Global Mechanisms and Local Realities After Genocide and Mass Violence*, ed. A. Hinton, 49-67. New Brunswick, NJ: Rutgers University Press.

Druckman, Daniel. (2005). *Doing Research: Methods of Inquiry for Conflict Analysis*. California: Sage.

Eppel, Shari. (2006). "Healing the Dead: Exhumation and Reburial as Truth-Telling and Peace-Building Activities in Rural Zimbabwe." In *Telling the Truths: Truth Telling and Peace Building in Post-Conflict Societies*, ed. T.A. Borer, 259–88. Notre Dame: University of Notre Dame Press.

Fisher and Ury. (2011). *Getting to Yes: Negotiating Agreement Without Giving In*. London: Penguin Books.

Fromm, Gerard M., ed. (2012). *Lost In Transmission: Studies of Trauma Across Generations*. London: Karnac.

Fromm, Gerard M. (2012). "Treatment resistance and the transmission of trauma." In *Lost In Transmission: Studies of Trauma Across Generations*, ed. Gerard M. Fromm, 99–115. London: Karnac.

Freud, S. (1961). "Mourning and Melancholia." In *The Complete Psychological Works*, ed. Strachy J. London: Hogarth Press.

Galtung, Johan. (1979). "The New Economic International Order and the Basic Human Needs Approach." *Alternatives*, 4(4): 455–76.

Guelke, Adrian. (1989). *Northern Ireland: The International Perspective*. New York: St. Martin's Press.

Gurr, T. Robert. (1993). *Minorities at Risk: A Global View of Ethnopolitical Conflicts*. Washington, D.C.: United States Institute of Peace Press.

Haglund, William D. (2000). "Recent Mass Graves: An Introduction." In *Advances in Forensic Taphonomy: Method, Theory, and Archaeological Perspectives*, ed. Haglund and Marcella, 244–59. USA: CRC Press.

Hartzell, Caroline, Mathew Hoddie, and Donald Rothchild. (2001). "Stabilizing the Peace after Civil War: An Investigation of Some Key Variables." *International Organization*, 55 (01): 183–208.

Hermann, Judith. (1997). *Trauma and Recovery: The aftermath of violence – from domestic abuse to political terror*. New York, USA: Basic Books.

ICMP. (2014, May). "ICMP Origins." Retrieved from http://www.icmp.int/about-us/history

ICRC Missing Persons. (2010, October 29). "Missing Persons and International Humanitarian Law Overview." Retrieved from https://www.icrc.org/eng/war-and-law/protected- persons/ Missing-persons/overview-Missing-persons.htm

ICRC. (2002). "International Review of the Red Cross 848-Missing Persons." Retrieved from *https://www.icrc.org/eng/resources/international-review/review-848-Missing- persons/index .jsp*

Ingrao, C., Emmert, T.A., eds. (2009). *Confronting The Yugoslav Controversies: A Scholar's Initiative.* West Lafayette, Indiana: Purdue University Press.

Jeong, Ho-Won. 2000. *Peace and Conflict Studies: An Introduction*. Burlington, VT: Ashgate.

———. (2005). *Peacebuilding in Postconflict Societies: Strategy and Process*. London: Lynne Rienner Publishers.

Ker-Lindsay, James. (2011). *The Cyprus Problem: What Everyone Needs To Know*. Oxford: Oxford University Press.

Kovras, Iosif. (2012). "De-linkage Processes and Grassroots Movements in Transitional Justice." *Cooperation and Conflict*, 47(1): 88–105.

Kriesberg, Louis. (1991). "Review" (Review of the book *Conflict Resolution and Provention*, by John Burton). *Contemporary Sociology,* 20(1): 573–74.

Kubler-Ross. (1969). *On Death and Dying*. New York: Macmillan.

Kuhn, S. Thomas. (1996). *The Structure of Scientific Revolutions*. Chicago, IL: University of Chicago Press.

Kyrris P., Costas. (1985). *History of Cyprus*. Nicosia: Nicocles Pulishing House.

Lederach, P. John. (1995). *Preparing For Peace: Conflict Transformations Across Cultures*. New York: Syracuse University Press.

———. (2010) *Building Peace: Sustainable Reconciliation in Divided Societies*. Washington, D.C: United States Institute of Peace Press.

Licklider, Roy. (1995). "The Consequences of Negotiated Settlements in Civil Wars, 1945-1993." *American Political Science Review*, 89(3): 681–690.

Lindeman E. (1944). "Symptomatology and Management of Acute Grief." *American Journal of Psychiatry,* 101(3): 141–49.

Loewenberg, Peter. (2012). "Clinical and historical perspectives on the intergenerational transmission of trauma." In *Lost In Transmission: Studies of Trauma Across Generations*, ed. Gerard M. Fromm, 55–71. London: Karnac.

MacDonald, David. (2009). "Living Together or Hating Each Other?" In *Confronting The Yugoslav Controversies: A Scholar's* Initiative, ed. Ingrao C., Emmert T.A, 390–425. West Lafayette, Indiana: Purdue University Press.

Mac Ginty, Roger. (2008). "Indigenous Peace-Making Versus The Liberal Peace." *Cooperation and Conflict,* 43(139): 139–63.

Markides C., Kyriacos. (1997). *The Rise and Fall of the Cyprus Republic*. London: Yale University Press.

Max-Neef, Manfred. (1992). "Development and human needs." In *Real-life economics: Understanding wealth creation,* ed. Paul Elkins and Manfreed Max-Neef, 197–213. New York: Routledge Press.

Moustakas, Clark. (1994). *Phenomenological Research Methods.* USA: Sage Publications.

Nemeroff, Teddy. (2008). "Generating the Power for development through sustained dialogue." *Action Research*, 6(2): 213–32.

Nussbaum, Martha. (1996). "Compassion: The Basic Social Emotion." *Social Philosophy and Policy*, 13(1): 27–58.

Parkes, CM. (1996). *Bereavement: Studies of Grief in Adult Life.* London: Penguin Books.

Walker, O. Polloy. (2004). "Decolonizing Conflict Resolution: Addressing the Ontological Violence of Westernization." *American Indian Quarterly*, Vol. 28, NOS. 3 &4: 527–49.

Redekop, N. Vern. (2002). *From Violence to Blessing: How an understanding of deep-rooted conflict can open paths to reconciliation.* Ottawa, Ontario: Novalis.

Renshaw, Layla. (2011). *Exhuming Loss: Memory, Materiality, and Mass Graves of the Spanish Civil War*. Walnut Creek, California: Left Coast Press.

Rice, Bryan. (2011). "Restorative processes of peace and healing within the governing structures of the *Rotinonshonni* "Longhouse People"." In *Handbook of Conflict Analysis and Resolution*, ed. Dennis J.D Sandole, Sean Byrne, Ingrid-Sandole-Staroste and Jessica Senehi, 409–420. London and New York: Routledge.

Ryan, P. (1995). *Storytelling in Ireland: A Re-awakening*. Londonderry: The Verbal Arts Center.

Saunders, H. Harold. (2003). "Sustained Dialog In Managing Intractable Conflict." *Negotiation Journal*, 19(1):185–95.

Schirch, Lisa. (2005). *Ritual and Symbol in Peacebuilding*. Bloomfield, CT: Kumarian Press.

Schopflin, George. (1995). Nationhood, Communism and State Legitimation. *Nations and Nationalism,* 1 (1), 81–91.

———. (2006). "Yugoslavia: state construction and state failure." In *War and Change in the Balkans: Nationalism, Conflict and* Cooperation, ed. Brad K. Blitz, 13–29 Cambridge: Cambridge University Press.

Sen, Amartya. (2001). *Development as Freedom*. New York: Alfred A. Knopf Press.

Senehi, Jessica. (2000). "Constructive storytelling in inter-communal conflicts: building community, building peace." In *Reconcilable Differences: Turning Points in Ethnopolitical Conflicts*, ed. S. Byrne and C. Irvin. Westhartford, CT: Kumarian Press.

———. (2002). "Constructive Storytelling: a peace process." *Peace and Conflict Studies*, 9(2): 41–63.

———. (2011). "Building Peace: Storytelling to transform conflicts constructively." In *Handbook of Conflict Analysis and Resolution*, ed. Dennis J.D Sandole, Sean Byrne, Ingrid-Sandole-Staroste and Jessica Senehi, 201–15. London and New York: Routledge.

Senehi, Jessica and Byrne, Sean. (2006). "From Violence toward peace: the role of storytelling youth healing and empowerment after social conflict." In *Troublemakers or Peacemakers? Youth and Post-Conflict Peace Building*, ed. McEvoy-Levy, 235–58 Notre Dame, IN: University of Notre Dame Press.

Smith, D. Anthony. (1986). *The Ethnic Origins of Nations*. Cambridge: Blackwell Publishing.

Smith, B.H. (1981). "Narrative Version, narrative theories." In *On Narrative*, ed. W.J.T. Mitchelle. Chicago: University of Chicago Press.

Stavrianos, L.S. (2000). *The Balkans since 1453*. New York: New York University Press.

Stein, Howard F. (2012). "A mosaic of transmissions after trauma." In *Lost In Transmission: Studies of Trauma Across Generations*, ed. Gerard M. Fromm, 99–115. London: Karnac.

Sito-Sucic. (2013) "Bosnia digging up mass grave 20 years by Serb silence." *Reuters Press*. Retreived from http://uk.reuters.com/article/2013/10/22/uk-bosnia-grave-idUKBRE99L0X I20131022

Tamazian, Roubina. (2015, June 2). "The agony and the uncertainty: Missing loved ones and ambiguous loss." ICRC. Retrieved from https://www.icrc.org/en/document/agony-and-uncertainty-Missing-loved-ones-and-ambiguous-loss

United Nations, Human Rights: OHCHR. (2009, July). "Enforced or Involuntary Disappearances Fact Sheet No.6/Rev.3." Retrieved from http://www.ohchr.org/Documents/Publications/FactSheet6Rev3.pdf

United Nations Human Rights: OHCHR. (1996-2013). Working Group on Enforced or Involuntary Disappearances. Retrieved from http://www.ohchr.org/EN/ISSUES/DISAPPEARANCES/Pages/DisappearancesIndex.asx

United Nations Human Rights: OHCHR. (1996–2015). "International Convention for the Protection of all Persons from Enforced Disappearances." Retrieved from http://www.ohchr.org/EN/ProfessionalInterest/Pages/IntConventionEnforcedDisappearan ce.aspx

United Nations Human Rights: OHCHR. (2009, July). "Enforced or Involuntary Disappearances." Fact Sheet No.6/Rev.3. Retrieved from http://www.ohchr.org/Documents/Publications/FactSheet6Rev3.pdf

United Nations International Criminal Tribunal for the Former Yugoslavia. (2013). Retrieved from http://www.icty.org/

United Nations International Criminal Tribunal for the Former Yugoslavia. (2013). "History." Retrieved from http://www.icty.org/sid/95

United Nations. (1991). "United Nations Manuel on the Effective Prevention and Investigation of Extra-legal, Arbitrary and Summary Executions." University of Minnesota, Human Rights Library. Retrieved from http://www1.umn.edu/humanrts/instree/executioninvestigation-91.html

United Nations Human Rights: OHCHR. (1996–2015). "Working Group on Enforced or Involuntary Disappearances Mandate." UN. Retrieved from http://www.ohchr.org/EN/Issues/Disappearances/Pages/DisappearancesIndex.aspx

Varshney, Ashutosh. (2001). "Ethnic Conflict and Civil Society: India and Beyond." In *World Politics,* 53(3): 362–98.

Volkan, Vamik. (2012). "The intertwining of the internal and external wars." In *Lost In Transmission: Studies of Trauma Across Generations*, ed. Gerard M. Fromm, 75–99. London: Karnac.

———. (2004). *Large Groups and Their Leaders in Times of Crisis and Terror.* Charlottesville, Virginia: Virginia University Press.

———. (1998). *Bloodlines: From Ethnic Pride to Ethnic Terrorism.* Colorado: Westview Press.

———. (1979). *War and Adaptation: A Psychoanalytic History of Two Ethnic Groups in Conflict.* Charlottesville, Virginia: Virginia University Press.

Wachtel, A., Bennett, C. (2009). "The Dissolution of Yugoslavia." In *Confronting the Yugoslav Controversies: A Scholars' Initiative*, ed. Charles Ingrao and Thomas A. Emmert, 12–48. West Lafayette, Indiana: Purdue University Press.

Wagner, Sarah E. (2010). "Identifying Srebrenica's Missing: The 'shaky balance' of universalism and particularism." In *Transitional Justice: Global Mechanisms and Local Realities After Genocide and Mass Violence*, ed. A. Hinton, 25–49. New Brunswick, NJ: Rutgers University Press.

———. (2010). "Tabulating loss, entombing memory: The Srebrenica-Potocari Memorial Centre." In *Memory, Mourning, Landscape*, ed. E. Anderson, A. Maddrell, K. McLoughlin, and A. Vincent. Amsterdam: Rodopi.

———. (2011). *To Know Where He Lies: DNA Technology And The Search For Srebrenica's Missing*. Berkley: University of California Press.

Wagner, S., and Quintyn, C. (2009). "Dismantling a national icon: Genetic testing and the Tomb of the Unknowns." *Anthropology News,* 50 (5).

Warden, J. (1991). *Grief Counseling and Grief Therapy: A Handbook for Mental Health Practitioner* (2nd ed). London: Routledge.

Weinstein, M. Harvey. (2011). "Editorial Note: The Myth of Closure, the Illusion of Reconciliation: Final Thoughts on Five Years as Co-Editor-in-Chief." *Journal of International Transitional Justice*, 5(1): 1–10.

Woodward, Susan L. (1995). *Balkan Tragedy: Chaos and Dissolution After The Cold War.* Washington D.C.: The Brookings Institution.

Yashin-Navaro,Yael. (2006). "De-ethnicizing the Ethnography of Cyprus." In *Divided Cyprus: Modernity, History, And An Island In Conflict*, ed. Y. Papadakis and N. Peristianis, and G. Weltz, 84–99. Indiana: Indian University Press.

Zagar, Mitja. (2000). "Yugoslavia, What Went Wrong? Constitutional Development and Collapse of a Multiethnic State." In *Reconcilable Differences: Turning Points in Ethnopolitical Conflict*, ed. Sean Byrne and Cynthia L. Irvin. USA, Connecticut: Kumarian Press

Zartman, Jonathan. (2008). "Negotiation, Exclusion and Durable Peace: Dialogue and Peace Building in Tajikistan." *International Negotiation*, 13(1): 55–72.

Zehr, Howard. (2002). *The Little Book of Restorative Justice.* USA: Good Books.

Zembylas, Michalinos. (2007). "The Politics of Trauma, Empathy, Reconciliation and Peace Education." *Journal of Peace Education,* 4(2): 207–24.

———. (2008). *The Politics of Trauma in Education*. New York: Palgrave Macmillan.

———. (2011). "Personal Narratives of Loss and the Exhumation of Missing Persons in the Aftermath of War: In Search of Public and School Pedagogies of Mourning." *International Journal of Qualitative Studies in* Education, 24(7): 767–84.

Index

About the Author

Kristian T.P. Fics has a joint Master's degree in Peace and Conflict Studies from the Arthur V. Mauro Center for Peace and Justice at the University of Manitoba and the University of Winnipeg, as well as a Pre-Master's in History and an Arts Degree in Psychology and Anthropology. He volunteered with the Committee on Missing Persons in Cyprus in the summer of 2014. His research centers on issues of inter-ethnic reconciliation, restorative justice, and peacebuilding, in post-violent conflict societies with respect to the return of Missing Persons to their families that aids in healing and sustainable peace. Kristian currently resides in Fort Lauderdale, Florida, and is enrolled in the PhD program in Marriage and Family Therapy at Nova Southeastern University where he is continuing research and clinical work on the psychosocial effects on relatives of Missing Persons.